S0-CPD-183

States of Disorder, Ecosystems of Governance

States of Disorder, Ecosystems of Governance

Complexity Theory Applied to UN Statebuilding in the DRC and South Sudan

ADAM DAY

Great Clarendon Street, Oxford, OX2 6DP,
United Kingdom

Oxford University Press is a department of the University of Oxford.
It furthers the University's objective of excellence in research, scholarship,
and education by publishing worldwide. Oxford is a registered trade mark of
Oxford University Press in the UK and in certain other countries

Impression: 1

Published in the United States of America by Oxford University Press
198 Madison Avenue, New York, NY 10016, United States of America

British Library Cataloguing in Publication Data
Data available

Library of Congress Control Number: 2021952714

ISBN 978–0–19–286389–8

DOI: 10.1093/oso/9780192863898.001.0001

Printed and bound by
CPI Group (UK) Ltd, Croydon, CR0 4YY

Preface

As this book was being finalized, the United States (US) withdrawal from Afghanistan precipitated the Taliban's takeover of the country and perhaps the most definitive failure of Western-led statebuilding to date. Twenty years of counterinsurgency combined with a massive attempt to extend state authority into so-called 'ungoverned' spaces were erased in a matter of hours.

The most remarkable aspect of the August offensive by the Taliban was the ease and speed with which the group toppled the Afghan state. Even the most pessimistic projections by the US military had seen the national army holding on to major cities for several months, whereas the Taliban took every city including the capital within a week. Caught off guard, President Biden lamented the Afghan military's 'lack of will' to fight, senior US officials spoke of poor training and corruption amongst the Afghan forces, and pundits everywhere wondered how up to $2 trillion of US support could evaporate so quickly.

This book is not about Afghanistan, but it offers a lens through which we can understand how a system like Afghanistan's can undermine outside efforts so fundamentally. It suggests that complex systems of governance in places with highly informal networks of actors stretching across private, public, and traditional spheres evolve in ways that contradict the assumptions of Western liberal ideology. The US approach to Afghanistan was premised on a belief that the state could be fixed like a broken machine, that worn out or faulty pieces could be rebuilt or replaced, that resources channelled into state institutions would ultimately result in a stable partner. Trillions of dollars and hundreds of thousands of lives later, this assumption has proven a costly mistake. The Afghan system of governance did not evolve as a linear outcome of US statebuilding, but instead adapted to the US intervention as an immune system might respond to a new virus or medicine. Calling the system 'corrupt' or 'failed' or 'broken' belies the reality that the Afghan system has proven far more resilient and adaptive than Westerners assumed, demonstrating a capacity to absorb enormous resources and political energy over a twenty-year period without changing its underlying rules and patterns.

I believe Afghanistan offers us the starkest example of a problem that has plagued the international community for decades. It is a problem best captured by Francis Fukuyama's notion of the 'end of history', a hubristic assumption that Western liberal democracy is the teleological conclusion to human governance. That is simply not the case. As this book shows, there is no such thing as ungoverned spaces—wherever there are humans, complex systems arise in the relations amongst them (indeed, this book suggests that there is nothing particularly special about humans when it comes to creating complex social systems). There certainly is no single model of governance that can be laid over the myriad networks of relationships that constitute our world.

This book proposes that a better way to think of places like Afghanistan, South Sudan, and the Democratic Republic of the Congo (DRC) is to focus on the relationships and the systems they create. It offers a set of tools drawn from ecosystems thinking and complexity theory to understand how change happens in highly interdependent social networks. Employing these tools, we may avoid the kind of catastrophic outcomes that have characterized much of Western-led interventions over the past thirty years, perhaps helping us develop a more constructive approach in the future. Ultimately, I hope it gives us a humbler starting point for thinking about our place in this world, one based on interdependence, symbiosis, and mutually constitutive existence.

Acknowledgements

Any project based on complexity theory should hesitate before making claims about causality. That said, I am confident that this book would not have emerged without the urging and support of several people, some of whom may be unaware of the extent of their influence.

First and foremost, my thanks to Mats Berdal, who convinced me to set out on a doctorate and has been a source of wisdom ever since. His advice to 'just write a book that someone wants to read', remains a (thus far unproven) aspiration of this project. Here, I am deeply grateful to James Mayall and Koen Vlassenroot, both of whom provided detailed and generous comments on earlier drafts of this project.

My main guide through the vicissitudes of complexity theory was Charlie Hunt, a constant source of new ideas, a companion on field research, and my first reader for each chapter (my apologies to his family for the time this took from them).

I could not have undertaken this project without the support of a Leverhulme scholarship at The Centre for Grand Strategy at King's College London. Special thanks to John Bew, Maeve Ryan, and Andrew Earhardt for taking a gamble on me; I hope I have sufficiently interrogated the Western vision of world order. Oisín Tansey, known as the 'methodology guru' of King's College London, helped me avoid several pitfalls along the way and remains the only person who renders process tracing intelligible to me. And thanks to Jessica Carden, without whom I would not have navigated the byzantine bureaucracy of King's.

I am truly indebted to my various bosses at United Nations University who not only allowed me to pursue this project while working full-time, but actively encouraged it: David Malone, Sebastian Einsiedel, James Cockayne, and David Passarelli, thank you.

Complexity theory understands that apparently minor inputs can have outsize impacts, and this book is no exception. Interactions with Oliver Ulich, Rachel Kleinfeld, Cedric de Coning, Cale Salih, Peter Coleman, Zacharia Ding Akol, Teresa Whitfield, Stephen Jackson, Jason Stearns, Lual Deng, Edmond Yakani, Ian Martin, Michele Griffin, Tatiana Carayannis, Dino Mahtani, Kim Schneider, and Ashley Jackson all helped to shape my thinking even if they did not know it at the time. And I might still be standing on a helipad in Bor without the efforts of Naoki Ishikawa.

I interviewed hundreds of people in South Sudan and the Congo for this project, many of whom had experienced incredible suffering during the civil wars in their countries. While most of them cannot be named here, their experiences are the backbone of my work and a continuing inspiration to try to improve UN interventions, not just to criticize them.

This book draws from more than a decade of living and working in and out of conflict zones. I feel extraordinarily lucky to have a partner who enjoys living in the field even more than I do, two daughters willing to haul their lives across continents, attend new schools, and make friends in new places, and a parent ready to fly anywhere to help take care of all of us. Thank you Wendy, Kaia, Satya, and Mum.

Contents

Introduction

'It's a classic failed state', the general explained to me as we looked at a huge map of the Democratic Republic of the Congo (DRC) tacked to his wall in the United Nations (UN) compound. It showed small green bubbles around towns in the East—Goma, Lubumbashi, Kisangani—while most of the rest of the country was a blank topography, bisected by the long curve of the Congo River. 'You see', he said, pointing at one of the green bubbles, 'here we have an island of stability, a pocket where we've helped the Congolese government fight back the armed groups and hold some territory. The rest is pretty much up for grabs out there. Armed groups, bandits, militias, rapes, killings, no state presence at all. Empty.'

His walls were covered with other maps, some showing the rough locations of the seventy armed groups that roamed eastern Congo, others depicting the team sites of the 15,000 UN peacekeepers deployed around the country. Together, the maps told a story: the UN was meant to help expand those green bubbles, enlarging and extending the islands of stability until they transformed from a scattered archipelago into a solid mass of state controlled territory. The general pointed at the map and said, 'To finish the job, we need to *shape* the conflict theatre, *clear* the territory of armed groups, *hold* it against incursions, and then *build* up the Congolese state.'

This mantra—shape, clear, hold, build—was not new to me. By 2016 when I arrived in the Congo as the senior political advisor to the UN peacekeeping mission there, I had served for a decade in the UN, working in peace operations in Darfur, South Sudan, and the Middle East, and helping plan the UN's mission in Libya after the fall of Ghaddafi. In every setting, we encountered a similar challenge: countries ravaged by decades of corrupt governance and recurrent cycles of conflict were expected to transform gradually into stable, liberal democracies by extending state authority from the central capital to the ungoverned peripheries. Yes, elections were important, power-sharing arrangements among the political elite were necessary, human rights mattered, but at the core of every major UN peace operation was a fairly simple end game: state monopoly of governance equals mission accomplished. 'We can leave', the deputy head of one peace operation told me, 'when the state can govern on its own, when it's no longer failing that basic duty.'

The problem, I found, was that we could never leave, at least according to our own criteria. Over the twenty-year history of the UN peace operation in the DRC, the capacity of the central state to govern the eastern region of the country has

States of Disorder, Ecosystems of Governance. Adam Day, Oxford University Press.
 DOI: 10.1093/oso/9780192863898.003.0001

barely increased while the number of armed groups and illicit business interests has flourished. Today, the overwhelming bulk of Congo's natural resources flows out of the country through illegal channels, enriching armed groups, business powerbrokers, and politicians rather than feeding a set of viable state institutions that could serve the Congolese people. Similarly in South Sudan, the UN's largest ever statebuilding effort did little to stabilize the country ahead of the 2013 civil war, pouring resources into a government that was widely seen as more of a patronage network for a single ethnic group than a representation of its citizens. The hundreds of South Sudanese people I have interviewed over the years overwhelmingly agree: UN statebuilding fuelled the tensions that led to the disintegration of the world's newest country. In fact, across the vast majority of UN peace operations deployed today, this model of building up state capacities shows little prospect of achieving its core mandate: a state capable of monopolizing legitimate governance.

Why does statebuilding fail, so often and so comprehensively, to achieve its objectives of stable, liberal modes of governance?

This question arose from my own experiences in UN peace operations, from a growing sense that we were getting something wrong when we talked about countries emerging from conflict. Across very different missions, I noticed an unwritten assumption that change would take place in a linear, gradual manner as state institutions were developed and expanded over territory. We seemed to think that if we could just reduce the scope of rebel activity and build up the police, army, and judiciary, stability was sure to follow. In our budgets, our input was training to the security services, the output was increased capacity, and the outcome was a country that looked more like Denmark than the DRC. 'The problem', a senior UN official in South Sudan told me, 'is that across most of the country there is nothing. No roads, no police stations, no courthouses, no one delivering the water or turning on the electricity. It's a jungle out there, and that's what makes it dangerous and unstable. But we can fix that.'

In fact, this notion of 'building and extending state authority' has remained the unquestioned mantra behind every major peace operation today, one which presumes that state institutions are the sole source of legitimate governance, even while gesturing towards the importance of civil society and the views of the general population. The mandates of the UN missions in Libya, Central African Republic, Mali, the DRC, and South Sudan all contain reference to building and extending state authority, while the same concept is at the heart of the UN's approaches to Afghanistan, Somalia, Colombia, and Iraq as well.

However, this formula for stabilizing conflict settings stands in direct contrast to the experiences I heard from the people of these countries. When I asked Congolese and South Sudanese community leaders where they turned for safety, justice, education, and basic services, almost none of them pointed to the central state. Instead, they described a web of actors responsible for governance, an interrelated network composed of traditional authorities, armed groups, business leaders, politicians, and ordinary citizens. They experienced the right to exercise public authority as something dynamical and contested within a network of power, not merely an unfettered role of the state to govern. In fact, much of the time they described the national authorities as predatory, dangerous actors, another layer of corruption and venality within a broader system of power that resisted transformation into the kind of liberal state envisaged by the UN. 'The police, they just need to be fed, they aren't interested in protecting us', one Goma resident told me. 'But that doesn't mean we don't have ways of protecting ourselves. We have our own systems, our own ways of doing things.'

These systems of power are the subject of this book. It is my central contention that governance—the exercise of the power to provide security and deliver basic services—is best described as a complex, interrelated system that evolves as its underlying relationships change over time. Unlike merely complicated things like clocks or car engines, complex systems cannot be 'fixed' by removing a broken part and replacing it; the issue in eastern Congo is not about removing armed groups and replacing them with a ministry building, nor indeed is it about trying to impose a new system of governance from the top down via national reform. Instead, the complex Congolese governance system displays emergent behaviour; it adapts to new stimuli in accordance with patterns that have evolved over time. In complex systems, change happens from within, on its own terms. When the UN supports a large-scale disarmament and integration programme for armed groups in the DRC, these underlying patterns respond, pulling resources and political energy back towards the (often violent) forms of governance that have stabilized the system for years. Years may go by in which the UN experiences frustrating failure—armed group fracture and reformation, ex-combatants cycling back into battle, the disintegration of newly formed institutions—but international organizations nonetheless carry on with the same programming. UN officials throw up their hands occasionally and complain about the lack of political will among the leadership of the country, but they seldom interrogate the deeper flaw in their own conception of how change actually takes place.

Here, the application of complexity theory offers a set of tools that can explain the failures of UN statebuilding and provide a more rigorous understanding of how change occurs at a systems level. Complex systems do not change in the linear, input-output fashion envisaged in UN mandates and logframes, but instead evolve on the basis of deeply entrenched patterns that stabilize the system, allowing it to adapt to new shocks without breaking down. In the case of governance in conflict-affected areas like South Sudan and the DRC, their respective systems have evolved a powerful gravitational pull (a 'strong attractor' in complexity theory terms) to violent, predatory relationships in which a combination of armed groups, traditional authorities, business interests, and state actors perform crucial stabilizing roles. Attempting to remove those actors and replace them with government ministries not only has failed in its immediate objective of providing the state with a monopoly on governance, but in many cases has led to an increase in violence as the system restabilized itself in accordance with its own underlying patterns and rules.

By tracing how systems of governance evolve over decades of misrule and conflict in the DRC and South Sudan, I develop an explanation for the failure of UN statebuilding: these systems of governance demonstrate strong resilience against the kind of state-centric support offered by the UN. Instead, the governance systems in both countries have evolved patterns that co-opt and distort UN interventions, reinforcing their own tendencies towards non-state forms of rule rather than being transformed into more liberal versions of the state. In many cases, I find evidence that the UN's intervention has contributed to precisely the kind of predatory, violent behaviour it is working against. When the UN poured resources and political energy into security sector reform in South Sudan, this did not result in the hoped-for increases in the governance capacities of the state, but rather fed into a complex network of state and non-state actors competing over the right to govern. The result, I argue, was an acceleration of the dynamics that led to the outbreak of South Sudan's civil war in 2013.

Complexity theory not only offers a holistic explanation for the UN's statebuilding failures, it also suggests a fundamentally different way of approaching conflict-affected settings. Rather than imagine eastern Congo as a vast ungoverned space in need of state institutions, complexity demands that we focus on the ways in which governance is produced within the interrelated network, that we map the underlying patterns stabilizing the system. A complexity lens allows us to see the symbiotic relationships, recurrent feedback loops, and 'strong attractors' that constitute the system, the forces that organize behaviour into predictable patterns over time. By mapping these systems, this book traces the ways in which they respond to, resist, and co-opt the UN's interventions. Moreover, it identifies the localized 'nodes' that organize the system, the points at which a specific set of relationships creates a broader pattern across the system. This may be how the police interacts with an armed group, how a traditional leader relates to a military commander, or indeed more sprawling networked relations across communities and regions. Change occurs as the result of these relationships, how they shift and respond to new stimuli over time. Relationships are the system itself.

The structure of this book responds to its central question: *Why have UN statebuilding operations in fragile and conflict-prone states not delivered their intended results?* Answering this question, the book proceeds in three parts. Part One advances the argument that UN interventions in conflict settings are a fundamentally state-centric governance enterprise, focused on building effective, legitimate state institutions as the primary means to address the risks of widespread violence and instability. In contrast, a wide range of scholarship has shown that governance in these settings is not an authority built and extended via a central institution of the state, but is better thought of as a set of relations among actors and institutions, some of which fall outside of the scope of vision of traditional statebuilding. I argue that these relations can be described as constituting a complex system that adapts in non-linear ways, often reacting strongly against attempts to impose liberal institutions. Instead of thinking as governance as something that is delivered by state institutions, complexity thinking demonstrates how relationships among actors—some of them collaborative, some competitive—result in a governance system. In some cases that relationship may be quite simple, such as an armed group providing security for a community, or a traditional leader collaborating with a military unit to get charcoal, but over time these societies have developed highly interdependent networks of relationships that form a complex system. Ignoring the underlying relationality of governance, and pursuing instead state-centric, linear models, the UN's approaches to stabilizing fragile settings have failed to grasp reality, becoming swept up in the system itself, often unintentionally strengthening some of the predatory, violent tendencies they are trying to transform.

Part Two explores this argument in two case studies: the UN mission in South Sudan from the country's independence in 2011 to its descent into civil war in 2013, and the UN's efforts to build and extend state authority in the DRC from 2010 to 2017. Drawing on in-depth field research, my own direct experience working for the UN in both countries, and a mapping of governance systems, it employs complexity thinking to understand how statebuilding has failed in both cases. Often, the UN is considered an outside actor, a set of external interventions that try to transform a country. The key contribution of this book is to treat the UN within the system itself, considering how its work is subject to the same patterns and strong attractors as other actors. The UN is not like a mechanic tinkering with the engine of a car, it is more like a troop of ants within a colony, trying to influence the colony as a whole. In short, the UN is not apart from the systems of governance, it is part of them.

Part Three compares the two cases to identify common characteristics of the South Sudanese and Congolese systems, using complexity thinking to demonstrate how very different systems of governance can produce similar statebuilding outcomes. On this comparative basis, it discusses the broader implications of these findings for conflict prevention, peacebuilding, and the liberal worldview. I argue that attempts to impose order via externally produced models and linear outcomes is not only unlikely to achieve the anticipated result, but may cause harm to conflict-affected communities and could reinforce patterns of authoritarianism, exclusion, and disenfranchisement. Moreover, I propose that the response by today's critical scholarship is equally troubling. In seeking to combat the liberal institutional worldview and push back on Western models, critics may have battered the pendulum to the point where it now lacks momentum in any direction.[1] Concepts like 'hybrid orders', the 'local turn', and 'resilience' have helpfully underlined the shortcomings of state-centric approaches, but they also draw an endlessly retreating horizon for the international community, one where the notion of self-governance in conflict settings is continually postponed, and the need for international enabling persists *ad infinitum*. Mired in fuzzy notions of hybridity and paralysed by a lack of universal models or clear end states, today's scholars and practitioners appear to have normalized failure and accepted that any notion of peace may be forever distorted and deferred.[2] As David Chandler points out, our overriding focus on the problematics of intervention may have catalysed a collapse in policy response rather than enhancing it.[3] In this post-liberal malaise, is some form of ad hoc muddling through the best that can be expected of international statebuilders?[4] Here I argue that a form of convergence has taken place between those who consider themselves proponents of liberalism and those who purport to critique it: both sides have come to the conclusion that almost nothing can actually be changed via international intervention in conflict settings, though both remain perversely attached to the need for some kind of engagement by the international community.[5]

Complexity theory has the potential to stir a breeze in these doldrums and catalyse action. A complexity-driven approach would be based on five insights laid out in the final chapters of this book:

1. Moments of violent conflict—typically considered opportunities to reshape failed or failing states—may in fact be the worst points at which to try to alter the underlying rules of complex systems. When systems are in flux, strong attractors often exert their most powerful influence, meaning that interventions during conflict may be least likely to alter underlying rules. Instead, longer term socially focused engagement during periods of relative peace, looking to gradually shift relationships when the system is not under immense pressure, may yield better results.
2. The widely revered concept of 'the local' in peacebuilding discourse should be reimagined; rather than think of local realities as something taking place below or apart from a national or elite-driven life (a sort of idealized village

[1] Roland Paris, 'Critiques of Liberal Peace', in Susanna Campbell, David Chandler and Meera Sabaratnam, eds., *A Liberal Peace? The Problems and Practices of Peacebuilding* (London: Zed Books, 2011), 38 (referring to pendulums of peacebuilding analysis).

[2] Pol Bargués-Pedreny, *Deferring Peace in International Statebuilding: Difference, Resilience and Critique* (New York: Routledge, 2018).

[3] David Chandler, 'Intervention and Statebuilding Beyond the Human: From the "Black Box" to the "Great Outdoors"', *Journal of Intervention and Statebuilding* 12, No. 1 (2018): 80–97.

[4] Roland Paris and Timothy Sisk, eds., *The Dilemmas of Statebuilding: Confronting the Contradictions of Postwar Peace Operations* (London: Routledge Press, 2009).

[5] David Chandler, *International Statebuilding: The Rise of Post-Liberal Governance* (Oxford: Routledge, 2010), 45.

in much of the scholarship), locality should be described in relational terms as the point at which actors intersect and form a node in the system. 'Local' in this context does not mean the daily routines of distant villagers, but instead a focus on the relationships that constitute systems, on the quality of exchange that sustains them, and how they might be gradually reconfigured. Intervenors should focus on relationships like those I encountered in eastern Congo, among armed groups, community leaders, and military actors. Rather than look to eliminate the armed groups, engagement should ask 'What is this relationship delivering to the broader system, and how can it be made less violent over time?'

3. Similarly, the notion of 'resilience' has become a normative construct associated with healthy and highly complex societies, despite ample evidence that conflict-prone and so-called 'fragile' contexts display extraordinary complexity and resilience against change. This requires redefining resilience to reflect the capacity for a system to withstand shocks and interventions, regardless of whether such a system is based on violent, 'corrupt' relationships. Indeed it may require some level of comfort with so-called corruption if interveners wish to enable less violent societies over the longer term. Complexity suggests it is important to be willing to work with the grain, understanding that underlying rules take time to shift, while accepting that some levels of 'bad' governance may be necessary in the short term.
4. Often, when confronted with failure, the UN turns to 'lack of political will', arguing that the national leaders were simply unwilling to support the kind of transformational change required. But this merely begs the core question: How much are individual actors able to change systems of governance? What is their agency? Here, complexity theory offers a way to understand agency that goes beyond the empty notion of political will. By mapping the systems of governance in places like South Sudan and the DRC, we can see the 'strong attractors' in each system, the gravitational pulls that resist efforts to transform them. President Kabila might have been acting in self-interest when he continually stalled on security sector reform, but the broader system also demonstrated a strong resilience against a variety of efforts to implement reforms, including by Kabila himself. Likewise, the protagonists in South Sudan's civil war were constrained by the ethno-military network that had sustained governance through decades of prior wars; they had what I call 'strongly influenced agency' in their own system. Complexity provides a sense of the system's landscapes, the deep valleys that tend to capture political energy and resources, and an empirically backed method for describing the ability of actors to implement change.
5. Finally, complexity demands what John Paul Lederach calls a 'moral imagination', a willingness to embrace the mystery of socio-political systems, even those that appear dysfunctional to outsiders, rather than trying to

reduce them to single, simple narratives or fit them into external (often neo-colonial) models. Taking systems on their own terms, approaching settings with humility, listening to the people who constitute what Séverine Autesserre the 'frontlines of peace',[6] and remaining open to forms of governance that may differ enormously from the familiar Western model, these are the core skills of today's peacemaker.

The book concludes where it started, by considering how the failed states and statebuilding discourse plays into our notions of world order and global governance. Here, I argue that a similar form of liberal paralysis is evident beyond conflict zones and now presents on the geopolitical stage, where advocates of nuanced, empirically grounded strategies for the globe's most complex problems often appear listless and adrift in turbulent seas. Seemingly fixed points in the international order—most importantly the concept of sovereignty—are now thought of as unmoored, contingent, and paradoxically in need of vague forms of global governance if they are to perform their ordering function.[7] However, the prospects of traditional forms of global governance and international cooperation appear to be dimming as state and non-state actors alike appear more willing to pursue their own agendas outside longstanding multilateral frameworks.[8]

To combat this, I propose that the adoption of complexity thinking can anchor and re-energize the discourse and praxis of both war studies and international relations, offering a dynamic heuristic that lends itself to action even in the face of seemingly intractable challenges. In very specific ways, complexity offers tools for practitioners to understand how change takes place, the points of real leverage in different systems, and what kinds of interventions might allow for societies to transform themselves from within. To borrow a metaphor used by Rachel Kleinfeld, we should stop thinking of our work as operating along a train track (where progress is achieved in a linear fashion by putting resources into a machine that advances ineluctably towards the goal of liberal governance) and begin understanding that international interventions sail on turbulent seas, where movement is dictated by invisible currents and winds, and navigation is often by starlight.[9] Sailing is a necessarily dynamical act requiring constant reinterpretation of the surrounding conditions, frequent small alterations of the rudder, and a sense of humility that the surrounding seas are largely unaffected by the passing vessel. But by understanding how the system works, by mapping how and when the tides

[6] Séverine Autesserre, *The Frontlines of Peace: An Insider's Guide to Changing the World* (Oxford: Oxford University Press, 2021).

[7] Autesserre, *The Frontlines*; see also, Karl E. Nell, 'A Doctrine of Contingent Sovereignty', *Science Direct* 62, No. 2 (March 2018).

[8] Richard Haas, 'How a World Order Ends and What Comes in Its Wake', *Foreign Affairs* (February 2019).

[9] Rachel Kleinfeld, 'Improving Development Aid Design and Implementation: Plan for Sailboats Not Traintracks', *Carnegie Endowment for International Peace* (2015).

turn and the winds tend to change, a good captain can chart a course forward. The globe cannot be governed, but it can be influenced if the underlying patterns are well-mapped.

A brief note on my own role in this project. My research benefited greatly from my role half-in and half-out of the UN system, and my previous jobs inside peacekeeping.[10] I was fortunate to have lived and researched for significant periods of time in both countries, and have returned many times over the years. In 2008—prior to South Sudan's secession—I was deployed with the UN in Sudan, following which I made several trips to southern Sudan. In 2010, I conducted a month-long research trip around southern Sudan, co-authoring an analysis of the conflict dynamics that was used as the basis for planning UNMISS.[11] I also served as the Senior Political Adviser to MONUSCO (Mission de l'Organisation des Nations Unies pour la stabilization en République démocratique du Congo / United Nations Organization Stabilization Mission in the Democratic Republic of Congo) in the DRC in 2016, living in Kinshasa and working for extended periods in Goma and environs. After leaving peacekeeping, I was able to return to both South Sudan and the DRC to conduct extended research visits, where I interviewed several hundred people in individual and small group settings. In conducting this fieldwork, and in my decade of work supporting peace processes in Libya, the Middle East, and elsewhere, I was often given access to highly confidential documents, along with the even more valuable ability to meet easily with UN staff, government officials, local organizations, and citizens. The frequent use of UN air assets made travel around the remote regions of South Sudan and eastern Congo far easier than for most researchers, a gift multiplied by the readiness of my former colleagues and friends in those locations to help me access civil society and citizens.

My prior roles within the UN are double-edged. I was keenly aware that South Sudanese and Congolese citizens—often the direct beneficiaries of UN employment and/or development projects—might see me as either a potential provider of resources for them or, indeed, as part of the UN mission itself. Many of the people I spoke with had lived through decades of UN operations, missions, and international mediations; they had been interviewed dozens of times by various researchers and officials, often with a very similar set of questions regarding the effect of the UN on their lives. Some of them were visibly fatigued by these discussions. Many were traumatized by a life spent almost entirely in war. Increasingly repressive state apparati—particularly noticeable in Juba in 2018–19 when National Security attempted to vet all of my meetings with academics and civil

[10] For the period of this book, I served as Director of Programmes in the Centre for Policy Research (CPR) in United Nations University. CPR is an independent think tank within the UN system, which offered me the status of UN staff but also the academic freedom to pursue my own lines of inquiry. Between 2007 and 2017, I served as a political officer in various peace operations and at UN Headquarters, including as Senior Political Adviser to MONUSCO during 2016.

[11] South Sudan Conflict Assessment, January 2010 [confidential, on file with author].

society—meant that many of my interviewees had legitimate fears that expressing their views could result in serious repercussions for themselves and their families. Similarly, during my time in the DRC, I met with people who had endured decades of some of the most brutal violence witnessed in modern times, suffering through recurrent displacements, the loss of immediate family members, and community starvation. Rather than a source of protection, the police on the street were seen by many citizens as yet another threat of violence, more likely to harm them than the armed groups that roamed much of eastern Congo. Both the trauma and the restrictions on political space were risks that had to be accounted for in this project.

But the most striking of my experiences in both the DRC and South Sudan was the candor, bravery, and energy of the people I met. Despite generations of conflict, a political elite that showed little regard for its citizens, and few visible prospects that much would change in their lifetimes, the people I met in South Sudan and the DRC were overwhelmingly optimistic about their own ability to improve the future of their country. In December 2018, while visiting a camp the UN had set up to protect civilians displaced by the fighting in South Sudan, I asked a group of about twenty young men where they saw themselves in five years.

'We might still be here', one man said angrily, poking a stick into the dusty earth at his feet. 'Maybe nothing will change, maybe we'll never be able to go home.'

Immediately the others shook their heads in disagreement. 'No', said a boy of about 19 years who had donned a brightly printed silk shirt for the meeting.

> Things are always changing here. Look at us five years ago. We didn't know if we would go back to war with Khartoum, we didn't even have our own country yet. But now we have something that brings us all together. South Sudan is all of us, Dinka, Nuer, Shilluk, Azande, in a big messy fighting family. We are South Sudan, we are what makes things change. We can't expect someone else to come and change this country. Your peacekeepers won't do it. [President] Salva and [former Vice President] Riek won't do it either. We will, from the inside.

His comments may sound naïve, especially coming from his position seated on a plastic chair in a dusty camp for displaced people. But this book is an effort to validate his and countless others' views, that change emerges within systems, through relationships among people.

PART I
IDEOLOGIES AND LOGICS OF STATEBUILDING

1
'A state in anarchy'

Since the end of the Cold War, Western discourse has developed an obsession with failed states. Areas beset with chronic violence, poverty, and corruption are not merely underdeveloped; they are, as Francis Fukuyama writes, 'the single most important problem for world order'.[1] Countries like Somalia, Afghanistan, and Mali are seen as fertile grounds for extremism, flow-through points for global criminal activity, 'weak links' in the collective effort to maintain world order.[2] Ungoverned territory is the 'black hole' from which terrorism, poverty, refugees, and other risks emanate, a menace to the rest of the globe.[3] The Failed State Index has called state failure a 'virus' and a 'contagion', potentially infecting the globe with disorder, while national strategies of major Western powers began to see equally great threats from weak states as from conquering ones.[4]

Western preoccupation with failed states has underpinned a massive industry of statebuilding since the early 1990s, dedicated to stemming the chaos before it disrupts world order.[5] Defined as the 'strengthening or construction of legitimate government institutions in countries emerging from conflict', statebuilding captures not only the technical activities of institutional improvement, but also the gravitational pull of the state for the full range of peacebuilding work of the international community.[6] In Afghanistan, the US has spent more than $100 billion to rebuild state institutions after the 2001 invasion. International support to Somalia runs in the billions per year, though some estimates indicate that up to

[1] Francis Fukuyama, *State-building: Governance and World Order in the 21st Century* (New York: Cornell University Press, 2004), 92.

[2] Patrick Stewart, *Weak Links: Fragile States, Global Threats and International Security* (Oxford: Oxford University Press, 2011).

[3] Robert I. Rotberg, *When States Fail: Causes and Consequences* (Princeton, NJ: Princeton University Press, 2004), 9.

[4] Mary Manjikian, 'Diagnosis, Intervention, and Cure: The Illness Narrative in the Discourse of the Failed State', *Alternatives* 33, No. 3 (2008): 335–357. Note that the US National Security Strategy in 2005 listed 'ungoverned spaces' as a top priority security risk.

[5] See, e.g., Ashraf Ghani and Clare Lockhardt, *Fixing Failed States* (Oxford: Oxford University Press, 2009).

[6] Roland Paris and Timothy Sisk, eds., *The Dilemmas of Statebuilding: Confronting the Contradictions of Postwar Peace Operations* (London: Routledge Press, 2009), 14. See also Organisation for Economic Cooperation and Development, 'Principles for Good International Engagement in Fragile States and Situations' (2007) (defining the broad range of peacebuilding and good governance work as 'state-building').

States of Disorder, Ecosystems of Governance. Adam Day, Oxford University Press.
 DOI: 10.1093/oso/9780192863898.003.0002

80 per cent is routinely misappropriated from within state institutions.[7] And the United Nations (UN) has diverted massive portions of its roughly $7 billion peacekeeping budget to statebuilding: in the Democratic Republic of the Congo (DRC), for example, the UN peace operation runs at more than $1 billion per year, accompanied by hundreds of millions of dollars in bilateral development support to governance institutions across the country. Similar amounts are spent by the UN to help the Malian government extend state authority across its territory, to supporting the Central African Republic (CAR) face down chronic rebellions, and to shoring up state capacities from Libya to Afghanistan.

However, the thirty-year project to fix failed or fragile states has remarkably little to show for it. According to Roland Paris, only two of nine UN peacebuilding interventions until 2004 were successful.[8] Doyle and Sambanis' authoritative study of the 121 civil wars between 1945 and 1999 found roughly 70 per cent of peacebuilding efforts had failed.[9] These trends have continued to this day. Despite hundreds of billions of dollars of international aid, longstanding UN peace operations, and direct assistance for decades, countries like Afghanistan, Somalia, and the DRC remain embroiled in violent conflict and have proven incapable of building the kind of effective, legitimate institutions envisaged by international interveners. In 2013, the UN was forced to abandon its ambitious statebuilding project in South Sudan following the outbreak of civil war, only two years after the country's triumphant independence. In Mali and CAR—where the UN has intervened more recently—there are few signs that state institutions will control territory effectively, protect populations, or provide services anytime soon. In fact, some evidence suggests that international interventions may work more to undermine the very state capacities they were hoping to reinforce, creating new dependencies on external support, or shoring up authoritarian regimes that tend to weaken state institutions.[10] At worst, statebuilding may emerge as a cause of state failure, rather than its cure.[11]

[7] Anthony Morland, 'The State of State-building in Somalia', *IRIN News*, 21 October 2014, http://www.irinnews.org/report/100745/analysis-state-state-building-somalia

[8] Roland Paris, *At War's End: Building Peace after Civil Conflict* (Cambridge: Cambridge University Press, 2004), 56–57.

[9] Michael Doyle and Nicholas Sambanis, *Making War, Building Peace* (Princeton, NJ: Princeton University Press, 2006), 69.

[10] Sarah von Billerbeck and Oisín Tansey, 'Enabling Autocracy? Peacebuilding and Post-conflict Authoritarianism in the Democratic Republic of Congo', *European Journal of International Relations* (2019): 1–29; Michael Barnett and Christopher Zürcher, 'The Peacebuilder's Contract: How External State-building Reinforces Weak Statehood', in Roland Paris and Timothy Sisk, eds., *The Dilemmas of Statebuilding: Confronting the Contradictions of Postwar Peace Operations* (London: Routledge Press, 2009), 23. See also Adam Day, Sarah von Billerbeck, Oisín Tansey, and Ayham al Ahsan, 'Peacebuilding and Authoritarianism: The Unintended Consequences of UN Intervention in Post-Conflict Settings', United Nations University, 2021.

[11] Susan Woodward, *The Ideology of Failed States: Why Intervention Fails* (Cambridge: Cambridge University Press, 2017), 75; Charles T. Call, 'The Fallacy of the "Failed State,"' *Third World Quarterly* 29, No. 8 (2008): 1491–1507.

Responding to these trends, this book's central question is, *Why has UN-led statebuilding so consistently failed to achieve its objectives*? Is there something inherent in the liberal orthodoxy of the state, the UN's forms of engagement, and/or the conflict settings themselves that tends to inhibit success? Or are we missing something deeper? As the following section demonstrates, experts from a range of disciplines have taken up the shortcomings of statebuilding, thus far without completely satisfactory answers. Traditional descriptions of state fragility and failure tend to be completely self-referential, almost tautological, defining stability as the capacity of state institutions to govern. These have a strong tendency to fall into neo-colonial models of statehood in which states (mainly in post-colonial settings) fall short of a fairly typical Western country's governance. But even the most robust critiques the liberal state have not been able to help us answer the question of failure; as I describe below, trends in the scholarship such as the 'local turn', hybridity, resilience, and non-state governance all provide important pieces to the puzzle, but ultimately prove unable to show us the whole picture.

This sets up my central argument: complexity theory can illuminate how change takes place in societies, offering an empirically backed explanation for why the UN has failed to transform them over the past twenty years. As I lay out in the following chapter, complexity theory allows us to map how societies change over time, giving us a sense of the underlying patterns that provide order and stability. Those forms of stability may not look familiar to Western readers: a system composed of brutal militias, criminal networks, corrupt officials, and a host of other actors may feel chaotic and unruly. But complexity thinking gives us the tools to explore how order is created in some of the wildest places on earth.

Critiques of the fragile states discourse

The concept of a 'failed state' was first popularized in 1992, when Steven Ratner referred to it as a state 'utterly incapable of sustaining itself', lacking the basic institutional capacities to govern.[12] Underpinning this is a Hobbesian social contract, where the state provides protections and services in exchange for legitimacy and acceptance by the population, generating a stable relationship.[13] Violence, corruption, predation, and various forms of political and economic exclusion are viewed

[12] Steven R. Ratner, 'Saving Failed States', *Foreign Policy* 89, No. 3 (Winter 1992–3).

[13] Thomas Hobbes, *Leviathan, or The Matter, Form and Power of a Commonwealth Ecclesiastical and Civil* (Oxford: Oxford University Press, 1996 [1651]). Some scholars attribute Hobbes' line of reasoning to Grotius. Martin Harvey, 'Grotius and Hobbes', *British Journal for the History of Philosophy* (2006): 27–50.

as symptomatic of a diminishing social contract, signalling that the governance capacities of a state are too weak.[14]

Since the early 1990s a global industry has grown around this liberal orthodoxy of state failure and fragility, where indexes now rank countries in terms of their ability to provide good governance, green indicating success and shades of orange and red moving towards failure.[15] These rankings give the veneer of mathematical accuracy—e.g. rankings from one to four on levels of transparency of a country's judiciary—and directly equate governance with stability. And they provide a sense of the threshold needed for a country to require intervention. As one Security Council member mentioned to me over a coffee in the Delegates Lounge of the UN Secretariat, 'Once we start moving from orange to red, we start getting into the realm of the UN intervening ... we need to act when we see a state falling apart'.

The liberal peace orthodoxy has come under attack on a number of fronts. Significant scholarship has pointed to the neo-colonial tendencies of importing a largely Western model of the state to post-colonial settings, underscoring that the processes of state formation in Africa in particular differed from those in Europe.[16] For example, Jean-François Bayart's well-known 'politics of the belly' suggests that post-colonial African leaders have tended to strip state resources to maintain patronage networks and legitimate their rule, necessarily weakening the institutions of the state.[17] Authors like Chabal and Daloz similarly argue that recurrent civil wars in post-colonial states have inhibited institutional capacities, rendering them more likely to fail in delivering basic governance and fall into conflict.[18] In this context, Roland Paris has cautioned against a *mission civilisatrice* by the international

[14] See, e.g., Paul Collier and Anke Hoeffler, 'On the Economic Consequences of War', *Oxford Economic Papers* 50 (1998): 563–573; James Fearon and David Laitlin, 'Ethnicity, Insurgency and Civil War', *American Political Science Review* 97, No. 1 (2003): 75–90.

[15] Finn Stepputat and Lars Engberg-Petersen, 'Fragile States: Definitions, Measurements and Processes', *Fragile Situations: Background Papers, Danish Institute for International Studies* (2008): 21–31; see, e.g., Organisation for Economic Co-operation and Development (OECD), *Conflict and Fragility: The State's Legitimacy in Fragile Situations, Unpacking Complexity* (Paris: OECD, 2010).

[16] Georg Sørensen, 'War and State Making: Why Doesn't It Work in the Third World?', *Security Dialogue* 32, No. 3 (2001): 341–354; see also Mary Kaldor, *New and Old Wars*, 2nd edition (Stanford, CA: Stanford University Press, 2007). Cf. Charles Tilly, 'War-making and State-making as Organised Crime', in Peter Evans, Dietrich Rueschemeyer, and Theda Skocpol, eds., *Bringing the State Back In* (Cambridge: Cambridge University Press, 1985).

[17] Jean-François Bayart, *The State in Africa: The Politics of the Belly* (London: Longman Press, 1993); see also William Reno, *Warlord Politics and African States* (Boulder, CO: Lynne Rienner Publishers, 1998); Mohamed Ayoub, 'State Making, State Breaking, and State Failure: Explaining the Roots of "Third World" Insecurity', in Luc van de Goor, Kumar Rupesinghe, and Paul Sciarone, eds. *Between Development and Destruction: An Enquiry into the Causes of Conflict in Post-Colonial States* (The Hague: Clingendael, 1996).

[18] Patrick Chabal and Jean-Paul Daloz, *Africa Works: Disorder as Political Instrument* (Oxford: James Currey Press, 1999); Jeffrey Herbst, *States and Power in Africa* (Princeton, NJ: Princeton University Press, 2000).

community, which has continued to push largely European models of the state into post-colonial settings around the world.[19]

The post-colonial critique of the failed states discourse has been accompanied by a vibrant and growing literature on non-state governance. This work explores how public authority is contested and fluid, constantly negotiated across different actors and institutions, rather than the sole purview of the Weberian state.[20] Raeymaekers and Menkhaus' definition captures the breadth of this conceptualization:

> Governance often discusses the active processes of administrating and managing regulation mechanisms through the allocation of certain services, goods, and rights. These include processes of describing certain rights (for example to 'public' goods such as security, but also access to resources, or citizenship) as well as the active ascription of these rights and the conflicts these generate within a particular frame or context (as exemplified in conflict resolution mechanisms, political negotiation platforms or judicial bodies).[21]

This sees governance as a verb—an 'active process'—rather than the more static formulations of 'governance institutions' or the normatively directed 'good governance'. And it avoids the tendency of many authors to conflate governance with government, instead referring to other processes, platforms, and bodies that could participate in the process. 'Doing' governance is not restricted to a specific range of actors or institutions, but is rather defined in terms of the actions of allocating rights and protections. As experts from diverse fields have convincingly demonstrated, there is no necessary limit to those who can produce governance, the list can include chiefs, patriarchs, businesspeople, militias, criminal organizations, armed groups, and ordinary citizens.[22] The lack of a single source for

[19] Roland Paris, 'International Peacebuilding and the "Mission Civilisatrice"', *Review of International Studies* 28 (2002): 637–656.

[20] Thomas Risse, *Governance without a State: Policies and Politics in Areas of Limited Statehood* (New York: Columbia University Press, 2013); Zachariah Cherian Mampilly, *Rebel Rulers: Insurgent Governance and Civilian Life during War* (Ithaca, NY: Cornell University Press, 2011); James N. Rosenau and Ernst-Otto Czempiel, *Governance without Government: Order and Change in World Politics* (Cambridge: Cambridge University Press, 2010); Paul Jackson, 'Warlords as Alternative Forms of Governance', *Small Wars and Insurgencies* 14 (2003): 131–150; Rodney B. Hall and Thomas J Biersteker, eds., *The Emergence of Private Authority in Global Governance* (Cambridge: Cambridge University Press, 2009); Christine Cheng, *Extralegal Groups in Post-Conflict Liberia: How Trade Makes the State* (Oxford: Oxford University Press, 2018).

[21] Timothy Raeymaekers and Ken Menkhaus, 'State and Non-State Regulation in African Protracted Crises: Governance Without Government?' *Afrika Focus* 21 (2008): 14.

[22] Eric Scheye and Andrew McLean, *Enhancing the Delivery of Justice and Security in Fragile States* (Paris: Organisation for Economic Cooperation and Development—Development Assistance Committee, 2006), 6; Leila Chirayath, Caroline Sage, and Michael Woolcock, 'Customary Law and Policy Reform: Engaging with the Plurality of Justice Systems', *Background Paper for the World Development Report* (2006); Peter Albrecht and Helene-Maria Kyed, 'Introduction: Non-State and Customary Actors in Development Programs', *Perspectives on Involving Non-State and Customary Actors in Justice and Security Reform* (Rome: International Development Law Organization, 2011).

governance in such settings defines its *polycentricity*, a term that captures the many competing and often unequal entities involved in the production of power.[23]

This in turn points to the fundamentally *relational* nature of governance; in conflict settings in particular, security, rights, and basic services are generated through negotiation and competition. Rather than residing in institutions, governance results from relationships; it is 'a contingent effect of power performances'.[24] Defining relationality, Morgan Brigg suggests a spectrum: 'Thin' relationality examines the relationships among entities without questioning how such entities came into being; 'thicker' relationality identifies how entities are mutually conditioned and affected through interaction; and 'thick' relationality 'gives conceptual priority to relations over entities and thus embraces a more fluid and fundamentally dynamic understanding of the social and political world of peacebuilding'.[25] In thick relationality, the relations between and among actors and entities are not merely important to a governance system, they *are* the system. Where deeply entrenched patterns of violence and civil war have prevented the growth of effective, legitimate state institutions, contestation over governance is more pronounced, and relationships are more ontologically determinative (thicker). For example, I later argue it would make sense to apply a quite thick relationality in the DRC—where endemic conflict means a range of non-state actors form a network that generates governance—while a thinner relational approach might be more appropriate in settings where the contestation over the state is less pronounced (e.g. Denmark).

Scholars have developed different terms to describe these relational, hybrid, and often contested aspects of governance. Vlassenroot and Raeymaekers write of 'complexes of power';[26] Hagman and Péclard refer to 'arenas of negotiation';[27] and Bierschenk and de Sardan suggest that governance is manufactured in a 'local political arena'.[28] Similarly, reflecting the contested realities of governance as among state and non-state actors, scholars have put forward the notions of

[23] Elinor Ostrom, 'Beyond Markets and States: Polycentric Governance of Complex Economic Systems', *American Economic Review* 100, No. 3 (2010): 641–672.

[24] Helland, Leonardo Figueroa and Stefan Borg, 'The Lure of State Failure: A Critique of State Failure Discourse in World Politics', *Interventions* 16, No. 6 (2014): 877–897.

[25] Morgan Brigg, 'Relational Peacebuilding: Promise beyond Crisis', in Tobias Debiel et al., eds., *Peacebuilding in Crisis: Rethinking Paradigms and Practices of Transnational Cooperation* (London: Routledge, 2016), 58.

[26] Koen Vlassenroot and Timothy Raeymaekers, *Conflict and Social Transformation in Eastern DR Congo* (Gent: Academia Press Scientific Publishers, 2004).

[27] Tobias Hagmann and Didier Péclard, 'Negotiating Statehood: Dynamics of Power and Domination in Africa', *Development and Change* 41, No. 4 (2010): 539–562.

[28] Thomas Bierschenk and Jean-Pierre Olivier de Sardan, 'Local Powers and a Distant State in Rural Central African Republic', *The Journal of Modern African Studies* 35, No. 3 (1997): 441–468.

'twilight institutions',[29] 'negotiated statehood',[30] 'diffuse authority',[31] 'alternative authority',[32] 'contextual authority',[33] and the 'mediated state'.[34] An entire field of scholarship is now dedicated to the notion of 'hybrid political orders', examining how state and non-state, national and local, formal and informal systems interact.[35] Common across these terms is the understanding that governance is a relational outcome of social and political exchange, where state institutions are at most only part of the story, and indeed where outside interveners too engage in an 'interactive process' with domestic actors.[36] Employing these concepts, academics have produced detailed and often ground-breaking analysis in a wide range of conflict settings, showing how rebels, criminals, clans, and businesses generate and employ governance powers.[37]

Academic inquiry into hybrid political orders has advanced several frameworks to better understand the logics and/or patterns of order that emerge in conflict settings. For example, Helmke and Levitsky developed a typology to guide inquiry into informal institutions and public order; Kraushaar and Lambach suggested a matrix to understand how effective/ineffective and formal/informal institutions converge and compete; Roger Mac Ginty has offered a four-variable framework to account for ordering in hybrid systems; and Paul Staniland has argued in favour

[29] Christian Lund, 'Twilight Institutions: An Introduction', *Development and Change* 37(4) (2006): 673–678.

[30] Hagmann and Péclard, 'Negotiating Statehood', 539–562.

[31] Bert Suykens, 'Diffuse Authority in the Beedi Commodity Chain: Naxalite and State Governance in Tribal Telangana, India', *Development and Change* 41(1) (2010): 153–178.

[32] Anne L. Clunan and Harold A. Trinkunas eds., *Ungoverned Spaces: Alternatives to State Authority in an Era of Softened Sovereignty* (Stanford, CA: Stanford University Press, 2010), 19.

[33] Jan Pospisil, *Peace in Political Unsettlement: Beyond Solving Conflict* (Cham: Springer Nature Press, 2019), 20.

[34] Ken Menkhaus, 'Governance without Government in Somalia: Spoilers, State Building, and the Politics of Coping', *International Security* 31, No. 3 (Winter 2006/7): 74–106.

[35] See, e.g., Jutta Bakonyi and Kirsi Stuvoy, 'Violence and Social Order Beyond the State: Somalia and Angola', *Review of African Political Economy* 32, No. 104 (2005): 359–382; see also Volker Boege et al., 'On Hybrid Political Orders and Emerging States: What is Failing—States in the Global South or Research and Politics in the West', *Berghof Handbook for Conflict Transformation Dialogue Series* 8 (2009): 15–35; Roger Mac Ginty, 'Hybrid Peace: The Interaction between Top-Down and Bottom-Up Peace', *Security Dialogue* 41, No. 4 (2010): 391–412; Deborah Cummins, 'A State of Hybridity: Lessons in Institutionalism from a Local Perspective', *The Fletcher Forum on World Affairs* 37, No. 1 (2013): 143–160; Richard Mallett, 'Beyond Failed States and Ungoverned Spaces: Hybrid Political Orders in the Post-Conflict Landscape', *eSharp* 15 (2010): 65–91; Roger Mac Ginty, *International Peacebuilding and Local Resistance: Hybrid Forms of Peace* (Basingstoke: Palgrave MacMillan, 2011).

[36] Christoph Zürcher, 'The Liberal Peace: A Tough Sell?' in Susanna Campbell, David Chandler, and Meera Sabaratnam, eds., *A Liberal Peace? The Problems and Practices of Peacebuilding* (London: Zed Books, 2011), 72.

[37] Zachariah Mampilly, 'Rebels with a Cause: The History of Rebel Governance, From the U.S. Civil War to Libya', *Foreign Affairs*, 13 April 2011; Ana Arjona, *Rebelocracy* (Cambridge: Cambridge University Press, 2017); Elsa González Aimé, 'Fragile States and Neoliberalism in Sub-Saharan Africa', African Studies Group University of Madrid (2008); Ken Menkhaus, 'Governance without Government in Somalia', 74–106; Christian Lund and Michael Eilenberg, *Rule and Rupture: State Formation through the Production of Property and Citizenship* (Sussex: Wiley Blackwell, 2017); Cheng, *Extralegal Groups in Post-Conflict Liberia.*

of 'wartime political orders' as an organizing concept for hybridity.[38] Of most relevance to this book, leading Africa expert Alex de Waal has developed a 'political marketplace' concept to describe and evaluate systems of power-through-bargain that arise across formal and informal networks in so-called failed or fragile states.[39] Common across these is the notion that amidst all of the diffusion, turbulence, and apparent chaos of societies in conflict, certain logics, orders, and patterns emerge that could help peacebuilders navigate effectively.

Concepts of hybridity and informal networks of power dovetail with what is called the 'local turn' in peacebuilding, where inquiry is increasingly directed at sub-national dynamics, rather than top-down national-level institutions or international actors.[40] While international peace and conflict discourse has referred to the importance of local governance for decades,[41] the 'local turn' recognizes that much of this has been more rhetorical flourish than practice, requiring that interventions more meaningfully engage with local actors as active agents in the production of public authority/governance.[42] This aligns with James C. Scott's concept of 'infra-politics of resistance' against external rule,[43] with Debiel and Lambach's argument that 'dynamics and idiosyncratic rules of local settings ... effectively determine the success or failure of state-building projects',[44] and with Ole Jacob Sending's conclusion that it is impossible to know the effects of peacebuilding without factoring in the interests, agency, and power of local actors.[45] A fairly direct rebuttal of many liberal peace models of the state, the local turn suggests indigenous sociological structures and practices should form the centre of

[38] Gretchen Helme and Steven Levitsky, 'Informal Institutions and Comparative Politics: A Research Agenda', *Perspectives on Politics* 2, No. 4 (2004): 725–740 (2004); Maren Kraushaar and Daniel Lambasch, 'Hybrid Political Orders: The Added Value of a New Concept', *Australian Center for Peace and Conflict Studies: Occasional Papers Series* 14 (2009): 1–20; Mac Ginty, *International Peacebuilding and Local Resistance*; Paul Staniland, 'States, Insurgents, and Wartime Political Orders', *Perspectives on Politics* 10, No. 2 (2012): 243–264.

[39] Alex de Waal, *The Real Politics of the Horn of Africa: Money, War and the Business of Power* (London: Polity Press, 2016).

[40] Hanna Leonardsson and Gustav Rudd, 'The "Local Turn" in Peacebuilding: A Literature Review of Effective and Emancipatory Local Peacebuilding', *Third World Quarterly* 36, No. 5 (2015): 825–839. It was first proposed in security studies by John Paul Lederach, *Preparing for Peace: Conflict Transformation Across Cultures* (Syracuse, NY: Syracuse University Press, 1995).

[41] UN Report of the Secretary-General, 'An Agenda for Peace: Preventive Diplomacy, Peacekeeping and Peace Making', A/47/277 (17 June 1992); see also John Paul Lederach, *Building Peace: Sustainable Reconciliation in Divided Societies* (Washington, DC: United States Institute of Peace, 1997), 87 ('societal spaces, practices and processes' should become the locus of inquiry).

[42] Roger Mac Ginty and Oliver Richmond, 'The Local Turn in Peacebuilding: A Critical Agenda for Peace', *Third World Quarterly* 34, No. 5 (2013): 763–783.

[43] James C. Scott, *Domination and the Arts of Resistance: Hidden Transcripts* (New Haven, CT: Yale University Press, 1998).

[44] Tobias Debiel and Daniel Lambach, 'How State-building Strategies Miss Local Realities', *Peace Review* 21 (2009): 22–28.

[45] Ole Jacob Sending, 'The Effects of Peacebuilding: Sovereignty, Patronage and Power', in Susanna Campbell, David Chandler, and Meera Sabaratnam, eds., *A Liberal Peace? The Problems and Practices of Peacebuilding* (London: Zed Books, 2011), 56.

any governance inquiry.[46] Here, local actors are the 'primary architects, owners and long-term stakeholders' of peace, and success is determined not by top-down criteria, but via 'local frameworks'.[47] The most that international/external interveners can do in such settings is facilitate and enable societies to 'self-organize', an organic process often inhibited by externally driven statebuilding interventions.[48]

Sub-national, local forms of governance have become a dominant focus for much of the peace and conflict studies and, as Mac Ginty, Leonardsson, and Rudd have demonstrated, 'the local' has become a frequently repeated keyword across development, peacebuilding, and peacekeeping interventions around the world.[49] For example, the term 'local' appears forty-six times in the landmark Brahimi Report of the UN, and 382 times in the 2011 World Development Report.[50] Local ownership has become *de rigeur* in any study of peace operations and a constant mantra of peacebuilding.[51] Oliver Richmond has argued that this recitation of the local across peacebuilding often operates as a romanticization of everyday forms of politics and society, at times imposing Orientalist visions that tend to obscure local specificity and experiences.[52] But more generally the scholarship has embraced the local turn as a solution to many of the ailments of international intervention, perhaps most notably in Séverine Autesserre's in-depth studies of local peacebuilding.[53] As I will argue in the case studies below, describing local dynamics in isolation from their broader context in national, regional, and global settings cannot fully explain the trajectories of the governance systems of South Sudan and the DRC.

Inquiry into non-state governance, hybrid political orders, and the local turn have important elements in common. First, they refuse to reduce governance to a purely state-society reciprocity.[54] Instead, they demonstrate how governance can be generated and executed among a wide range of actors, including but not limited to state institutions. Second, they share an understanding of public order

[46] Uday Singh Mehta, *Liberalism and Empire: A Study in Nineteenth Century Liberal Thought* (Chicago, IL: Chicago University Press, 1999).

[47] A. B. Fetherston and Carolyn Nordstrom, 'Overcoming Habitus in Conflict Management: UN Peacekeeping and War Zone Ethnography', *Peace & Change* 20, No. 1 (1995): 94–119; cf. Derick Brinkerhoff, 'State Fragility and Governance: Conflict Mitigation and Subnational Perspectives', *Development Policy Review* 29, No. 2 (2011): 131–153.

[48] Cedric de Coning, 'Understanding Peacebuilding as Essentially Local', *Stability* 2, No. 1 (2013): 1–6.

[49] Mac Ginty and Richmond, 'The Local Turn in PeaceBuilding', 763–783; Leonardsson and Rudd, 'The "local turn" in peacebuilding', 825–839.

[50] Mac Ginty and Richmond, 'The Local Turn in PeaceBuilding', 763–783.

[51] Sarah von Billerbeck, *Whose Peace? Local Ownership and United Nations Peacebuilding* (Oxford: Oxford Scholarship Online, 2017).

[52] Oliver Richmond, 'De-romanticising the Local, De-mystifying the International: Hybridity in Timor Leste and the Solomon Islands', *The Pacific Review* 24, No. 1 (2011): 115–136.

[53] Séverine Autesserre, *The Frontlines of Peace: An Insider's Guide to Changing the World* (Oxford: Oxford University Press, 2021).

[54] Some hybridity scholars suggest a form of legitimacy beyond the Weberian one. See, e.g., Volker Boege, Anne M. Brown, and Louise Moe, 'Addressing Legitimacy Issues in Fragile Post-conflict Situations to Advance Conflict Transformation and Peacebuilding', *Berghof Collection* (2012).

as 'emergent', constantly under negotiation, a process that 'must be consistently practiced or performed by those claiming it'.[55] Third, they resist the order/chaos binary implicit in failed states discourse, focusing instead on the ways in which contested processes create their own logic, patterns, rules, or 'variable geometry'.[56] Fourth, they insist on a localized/micro examination of how power is generated and distributed, where everyday practice is the path to well-grounded inquiry. And finally, they gravitate towards an understanding of the state as a political community that needs to be investigated empirically rather than accepted as an ideal model, thus requiring 'research capable of capturing the complexity, variety and ambiguity of the actual practices of public authorities'.[57]

While helpful in pushing back against top-down state-centric conceptualizations of governance, approaches focused on hybridity and the local have their limits and in fact tend to reintroduce many of the very binaries they hope to avoid. By definition, the term 'hybrid' refers to the mixing of two distinct entities (e.g. state/non-state), even if such entities have been previously hybridized.[58] Researchers demanding greater focus on 'everyday local' dynamics posit the local as a separate sphere or level, opposed to national, regional, and international domains existing in a separate space. There is a reason Séverine Autesserre chose the island of Idjwi in the middle of Lake Kivu for her study on highly localized peace in the DRC: it played into her argument that the local is a distinct sphere that has its own self-contained dynamics.[59] Similar dichotomies and separations of the local sphere appear in Boege and Brown's notion of 'everyday social reality',[60] Roger Mac Ginty's concept of 'indigeneity' and local practice,[61] and James C. Scott's description of 'everyday peasant resistance'.[62]

These spatial narratives of 'the everyday local'—often considered below or beyond other strata in a hierarchy as a sort of idealized village—fail to capture the dynamic ways in which public authority is distributed across social levels, through the relations among actors, entities, and institutions. Analytically, too, the 'local' is a fuzzy term that may be used in misleading ways, potentially

[55] Kasper Hoffman and Tom Kirk, 'Public Authority and the Provision of Public Goods in Conflict-Affected and Transitioning Regions', *Conflict Research Group* (2013). https://core.ac.uk/download/pdf/20050777.pdf

[56] Mac Ginty, 'Hybrid Peace, 391–412.

[57] Hoffman and Kirk, 'Public Authority and the Provision of Public Goods', 5.

[58] E.g. Menkhaus, 'Governance without Government in Somalia'; Shahar Hameiri and Lee Jones, 'Against Hybridity in the Study of Peacebuilding and Statebuilding', in Joanne Wallis et al., eds., *Hybridity on the Ground in Peacebuilding and Development* (New South Wales: Australian National University Press, 2018); see also Meera Sabaratnam, 'Avatars of Eurocentrism in the Critique of the Liberal Peace', *Security Dialogue* 44 No. 3 (2013): 259–278.

[59] Séverine Autesserre, *Peaceland: Conflict Resolution and the Everyday Politics of International Intervention*, Cambridge: Cambridge University Press, 2014.

[60] Volker M. Boege et al., 'States Emerging from Hybrid Political Orders—Pacific Experiences', *The Australian Centre for Peace and Conflict Studies, Occasional Paper Series*, 2008.

[61] Roger Mac Ginty, 'Indigenous Peace-Making versus the Liberal Peace', *Journal of Cooperation and Conflict* 43, No. 2 (2008): 139–163.

[62] James C. Scott, *Weapons of the Weak: Everyday Peasant Resistance* (New Haven, CT: Yale University Press, 1985).

ignoring broader impacts of power and dominance and/or conflating a range of sub-national phenomena.[63] Roger Mac Ginty's claim that 'everything and everyone is a hybrid',[64] or Oliver Richmond's 'local-local framework' offer little causal explanation of the phenomena they are trying to describe and beg the question of how relations, not entities or institutions themselves, produce and regulate power. Dominik Zaum, in a direct criticism of hybridity, suggests that at best it describes an obvious reality well-known to political scientists, that outcomes are the result of interactions.[65] This reality is equally obvious to those of us who have lived in these settings for extended periods: once you look under the surface, something as seemingly local as cattle rustling in rural South Sudan is quickly linked to elites in Juba who own huge cattle herds and who in turn have links to regional players in Uganda and beyond.

Similarly, the rise in popularity of the notion of resilience—which ostensibly recognizes the systemic, interrelated nature of governance—has its distinct limitations. Proponents of resilience ignore the fact that authoritarian regimes (for example) can be extraordinarily resilient in the face of external interventions, that deeply entrenched patterns of control of natural resources and violence are often deeply resistant to change, that resilience has 'both a dark and a light side'.[66] In fact, the practice of building resilience in conflict-affected settings—by the UN and others—tends to fall into the same patterns of traditional liberal peace models, focusing efforts on strong state institutions as the main intended outcome of an intervention. Jonathan Joseph captures this point adeptly, calling resilience 'embedded neoliberalism'.[67] David Chandler's hope that resilience thinking may have triggered a 'post-liberal' transformation that defies reduction to subject/object, state/society binaries is far from realized.[68] The liberal peace paradigm is alive, if not particularly well, and remains highly contagious.

In fact, maybe this is the heart of the problem: scholarship on non-state governance, resilience, and the local turn may be fascinating, but it does little for someone confronted with the question, *What should I do now*? When I wrote an internal memo to United Nations Organization Stabilization Mission in the Democratic Republic of Congo (MONUSCO) describing how an armed group

[63] See, e.g., Finn Stepputat, 'Pragmatic Peace in Emerging Governscapes', *International Affairs* 94, No. 2 (2018): 400. For an even vaguer usage, see Anne Lowenhaubt Tsing, *Friction: An Ethnography of Global Connections* (Princeton, NJ: Princeton University Press, 2005); Annika Björkdahl et al., eds., *Peacebuilding and Friction: Global and Local Encounters in Post-conflict Societies* (New York: Routledge, 2016).

[64] Mac Ginty, *International Peacebuilding and Local Resistance*, 73.

[65] Dominik Zaum, 'Beyond the Liberal Peace', *Global Governance* 18 (2012): 124; see also Kate Meagher, 'Non-state Security Forces and Hybrid Governance in Africa', *Development and Change* 43, No. 5 (2012): 1073–1101.

[66] Stepputat, 'Pragmatic Peace', 400.

[67] Jonathan Joseph, 'Resilience as Embedded Neoliberalism: A Governmentality Approach', *Resilience* 1, No. 1 (2013): 38–52.

[68] David Chandler, *Resilience: The Governance of Complexity* (New York: Routledge, 2014), 51.

called the Allied Democratic Forces (ADF) was cooperating with community leaders and Congolese army officials to traffic timber and secure resources for residents of Beni (a town in eastern Congo), my colleagues thought it was interesting, but could see no reason to change their military-driven approach to the ADF. When I wrote a paper describing how powerbrokers in Juba were linked to highly localized systems of cattle trading and resource management, it had no effect on the UN's decision to treat cattle rustling as a 'local conflict dispute'. And while many of my former colleagues in the UN today have workstreams with exciting titles like 'engagement with non-state actors' or 'non-state governance', the policies and practice of the UN have at most paid lip service to the idea that security and basic services might be produced beyond the state. Instead, across all three pillars of its work—security, development, and human rights—the UN appears to consistently equate stability with effective, legitimate state institutions.[69] And in dealing with conflicts, whether peacekeeping, peacebuilding, rule of law engagement, or mediation, the UN is similarly guided by a 'peace as governance' mindset that is overwhelmingly state-centric, echoing David Chandler's equation: peacebuilding = statebuilding = institutionbuilding.[70] As a result, despite significant efforts to make the UN's work more 'people-centric' and less monolithically focused on the state, the UN's practice over recent decades has demonstrated the enduring centrality of state institutional support to all of its work.[71]

This means that when the UN fails to achieve its goals of stabilizing fragile settings, blame usually lands on the lack of resources for institutional development. Failure to invest adequately in the UN's statebuilding project is the most frequently cited explanation for lack of progress from East Timor to Somalia.[72] The unwillingness of venal political leaders to give up their positions of power and luxury is the go-to answer for cynical UN staff members looking to explain why their programming has not delivered. And simply pointing to the need for 'national ownership' is the default way for the UN to say that the state just needs to get its act together. 'We are here for a brief while to replace the state', one senior UN leader in the DRC told me, 'and we can only leave when the state is able to again secure its people'.

[69] Zaum, 'Beyond the Liberal Peace', 121–132. See, e.g., Security Council resolution 1313 (2000) (authorizing the UN Assistance Mission in Sierra Leone to assist the government to extend state authority and restore law and order); Security Council resolution 1509 (2003) (referring to the UN Mission in Liberia's role in re-establishing national authority throughout the country); Security Council resolution 1925 (2010) (mandating the UN Stabilisation Mission in the DRC with the consolidation of state authority by the Congolese government); Security Council resolution 1542 (2004) (mandating the UN to assist the Haitian government extend state authority and support good governance).

[70] David Chandler, *Empire in Denial: The Politics of Statebuilding* (London: Pluto Press, 2006), 26–47.

[71] Michael Pugh, 'The Political Economy of Peacebuilding: A Critical Theory Perspective', *International Journal of Peace Studies* 10, No. 2 (2005).

[72] United Nations Secretary-General, 'A More Secure World: Our Shared Responsibility', United Nations High-Level Panel on Threats, Challenges and Change, 2004, para. 224; Report of the United Nations Secretary-General on Timor-Leste Pursuant to Security Council resolution 1690 (2006), S/2006/628 (2006) para. 40

But what if the state has never secured its own people? What if systems of governance have evolved for generations rendering the state but one of many players, where police stations, court houses, and commerce ministries are almost irrelevant? What if, as dozens of South Sudanese citizens told me, the army, police, and national security are the biggest threat to stability, rather than the institutions trusted to secure communities? My central argument in this book is that these complex, interrelated systems of governance hold the key to understanding how change takes place in societies, and offer the best explanation for the UN's recurrent failures at statebuilding.

Complexity and conflict—dynamical systems theory

The political economy and hybrid approaches described above begin to open the door to *complexity thinking*, a consideration of societies as part of an adaptive system that self-organizes in a non-linear fashion.[73] Thinking of the world in terms of complex systems is not new. Ancient cosmologies such as Daoism and pre-Socratic thinkers like Heraclitus saw the form of the world as composed of the relationships within it.[74] More recently, Darwin's view of evolution understood that change in life forms occurs via patterning variations in complex systems, with emergent patterns adapting to new circumstances.[75] And particularly in the fields of physics, mathematics, and economics over the past hundred years, the rise of chaos theory and other forms of systems thinking have come to dominate how the world is both described and analysed.[76] Post-modernist studies too owe an enormous debt to the concepts of complexity thinking, perhaps most clearly in the work of Jean-François Lyotard.[77]

What is complexity? A complex system is one where its constituent elements interact together to create effects different from the sum of what each element would produce on its own. Interactions in complex systems are *non-linear* and cannot be reduced to input-output models. Such systems are *open*—they interact

[73] NB: throughout this book I will use 'complexity thinking' and 'complexity theory' interchangeably as there seems little to distinguish them in the literature. I do not use 'complexity science', as authors like Walter Clemens have suggested.

[74] Jean G. Boulton et al., eds, *Embracing Complexity: Strategic Perspectives for an Age of Turbulence* (Oxford: Oxford University Press, 2015), 8–9.

[75] John Tyler Bonner, *The Evolution of Complexity by Means of Natural Selection* (Princeton, NJ: Princeton University Press, 1988), 3–25.

[76] Melanie Mitchell, *Complexity: A Guided Tour* (Oxford: Oxford University Press, 2009); Thorstein Veblen, 'Why is Economics Not an Evolutionary Science', *The Quarterly Journal of Economics*, July (1898): 373–397; Kenneth Boulding, *Evolutionary Economics* (London: Sage, 1981); Jane Boulton, 'Why Is Economics Not an Evolutionary Science?' *Emergence, Complexity and Organisation* 12, No. 2 (2010): 41–69.

[77] Jean-François Lyotard, *The Postmodern Condition: A Report on the Knowledge (Theory and History) of Literature* (Minneapolis, MN: University of Minnesota Press, 1984); Paul Cilliers, *Complexity and Postmodernism: Understanding Complex Systems* (New York: Routledge, 1998).

with their environment and are in a state of constant change. They *self-organize*, often by feeding activities back onto themselves in a way that allows for adaptation over time (called 'emergent behaviour').[78] It is helpful to think of complex systems in contradistinction to complicated ones: a car engine may have an enormous number of parts that must be fitted perfectly together, but each part performs a discrete function in a linear input-output manner. A car engine, like a traditional computer, is *complicated*, not complex. In contrast, our immune system's individual elements produce something wholly different together than they would on their own; they feed back their activities into the system in a way that allows it to adapt to new conditions and generate outcomes beyond the sum of their parts. Our immune system is complex.

Complex systems may appear chaotic, but they are not wholly without form and pattern. In the natural sciences, it has been shown that ant colonies and beehives organize into structures that appear to demonstrate a 'collective intelligence' capable of building viable structures well beyond their own individual understanding; cognitive scientists have discovered similar interrelated patterns of behaviour of neurons in the brain; and significant research has been directed at economic activity as a complex system with emergent qualities.[79] Adaptation in complex systems is non-linear, but a system's ability to self-organize—its autopoiesis—is achieved through patterns of behaviour.[80] And while systems built of human beings are not always wholly equivalent to those in the natural sciences, the modalities for self-organization operate similarly.[81]

A crucial insight for the application of complexity thinking to the social and political sciences came from Ilya Prigonine's Nobel Prize-winning research into thermodynamics: *change in complex systems is the result of the combination of the way in which existing forms and patterns interact with specific events*.[82] Systems thinking deals with patterns, while history deals with particular events; complexity brings those two together into a theory of change.[83] This has enormous implications for how we view the world, challenging longstanding Newtonian assumptions that change can be described in mechanical terms as a predictable series of interactions among discrete objects (or indeed some of the assumptions

[78] Cilliers, *Complexity and Postmodernism*, 15.

[79] Mitchell, *Complexity.*

[80] Chandler, *Resilience*, 64.

[81] For a description of agency in complex systems, see Emery Brusset, Cedric de Coning, and Bryn Hughes, eds. *Complexity Thinking for Peacebuilding Practice and Evaluation* (London: Palgrave Macmillan, 2017), 20.

[82] Ilya Prigonine et al., 'Long Term Trends and the Evolution of Complexity', in E. Lazlo and J. Bierman, eds., *Goals in a Global Community*, vol. 1: *Studies on the Conceptual Foundations* (New York: Pergamon Press, 1977); Ilya Prigonine, 'Time, Structure and Fluctuations', *Science* 201, No 4358 (1978): 777–785.

[83] Boulton et al., *Embracing Complexity*, 29; for a thorough review of the role of complexity in theories of change, see Danielle Stein and Craig Valters, 'Understanding Theory of Change in International Development', Justice and Security Research Programme, London School of Economics, 2012.

of process tracing as a research methodology, discussed below). Instead, what Jane Boulton eloquently calls complexity's 'dance between detail and structure, between science and history, between form and individualism' means that change can never be isolated as between two variables; the way complex systems self-organize is always contingent upon both the patterns in a system and the historical specificity of the moment.[84]

One of the most important ways in which systems self-organize is through 'feedback loops'. Simply put, a feedback loop is a way that information is directed back into the system to generate an effect. A positive feedback loop reinforces itself and the pattern in the system: the more people catch the flu in a community, the more will continue to catch it; the more soil erodes, the less vegetation can grow, leading to fewer root structures and greater erosion.[85] In contrast, a negative feedback loop is best thought of as a corrective, working against the process that caused it: when humans get hot, the resulting sweat cools us down; as prices in an economy increase, demand tends to decrease and stabilizes the market. In a conflict setting, interethnic animosity functions as a positive feedback loop: as tensions increase, the risk of violence between the communities grows, reinforcing enmity between the communities.[86] Corruption can also create positive feedback loops: informal networks gain traction and build relationships, undermining formal, state-owned enterprise, stripping it of resources and authority, in turn strengthening the influence of the illicit actors.

Social systems self-organize by developing patterns of thought and behaviour that tend to narrow the possible range of outcomes and stabilize the system. Over time, repeated instances of the same behaviour reinforce themselves through feedback loops, acting as 'attractors' that draw in and tend to direct behaviour. Intractable conflicts between two parties offer a good example of this dynamic: as a conflict evolves, each party's thoughts and actions tend to become attached to the idea of the other party as an enemy, thus intensifying the conflict and reinforcing the negative view of the other side.[87] Nearly anything the Palestinians do can be seen as provocative to the Israelis, and vice versa, thus reinforcing the negative perceptions of each side. Metaphorically, 'the attractor serves as a valley in the psychological landscape into which the psychological elements—thoughts, feelings and actions—begin to slide'.[88] Once trapped in such a valley, escaping over its

[84] Boulton et al., *Embracing Complexity*, 32.

[85] Examples drawn from Donella Meadows, 'Leverage Points: Places to Intervene in a System', http://donellameadows.org/archives/leverage-points-places-to-intervene-in-a-system/

[86] For an application of systemic thinking to interethnic disputes, see Dirk Splinter and Ljubjana Wustehube, 'Discovering Hidden Dynamics: Applying Systemic Constellation Work to Ethnopolitical Conflict', in Daniela Korppen et al., eds., *The Non-Linearity of Peace Processes: Theory and Practice of Systemic Conflict Transformation* (Opladen: Verlag Barbara Budrich, 2011).

[87] Peter Coleman, 'Navigating the Landscape of Conflict: Applications of Dynamical Systems Theory to Addressing Protracted Conflict', in Tobias Debiel et al., eds., *The Non-Linearity of Peace Processes: Theory and Practice of Systemic Conflict Transformation* (Opladen: Verlag Barbara Budrich, 2011).

[88] Coleman, 'Navigating the Landscape of Conflict'.

steep sides requires the kind of intention and energy that may appear impossible from within the system.

Complex social systems tend to revolve around and reinforce their strongest attractors, keeping the system stable and capable of adapting to new inputs without large-scale disruption.[89] Imagine a river that gradually carves itself into a rock, over time creating a deep canyon that captures rainfall and is unlikely to change shape without a tectonic shift. In social systems, attractors are not always the most visible feature of the terrain; latent attractors, like stereotypes and objectification of others, can exert a strong gravitational pull within a system while remaining largely below the surface. Likewise, where informal/illicit economies exist alongside formal ones, the patterns of exchange and negotiation may take place in realms typically unseen by scholars, creating what Christopher Cramer calls 'trajectories of accumulation' that invisibly drive the political economy of societies in conflict.[90] Moreover, as complex systems have high degrees of interdependence and interconnectedness, the influence of attractors is not always proximate, and effects can be felt in distant parts of the system (small correctives in economies, for example, can have significant impacts, shifting prices, demand, and the conditions of individuals in far flung areas of the system).

Taken together, the characteristics of complex systems have enormous implications for statebuilding. Unlike traditional statebuilding models, which assume that a gradual increase in institutional capacities will lead to a corresponding decrease in lawlessness and violence, a systemic approach suggests that change requires some kind of rewriting of the underlying rules. Change occurs by shifting the gravitational pull of the attractors, resulting in new ways for governance powers to be generated, negotiated, and exercised. The system must self-organize differently, finding new patterns around which to stabilize itself.[91] In protracted conflicts, this may involve the creation of new narratives that begin to undo the vicious cycles of stigmatization and hatred of the other; or it may require incentives that move actors away from illicit networks that have sustained the system for decades. In some cases, change can occur with surprising rapidity: Mohamed Bouazizi set himself on fire in Tunis in December 2010 and less than one month later protests that became the Arab Spring had snowballed (a term that refers to a rapid positive feedback loop), toppling the Tunisian head of state and spreading across the region. Similarly, severe shocks to a system can trigger an almost instantaneous leap into

[89] Luis Rios et al., 'On the Rationale for Hysteresis in Economic Decisions', *Journal of Physics, Conference Series* 811 (2015).

[90] Christopher Cramer, 'Trajectories of Accumulation through War and Peace', in Roland Paris and Timothy Sisk, eds., *The Dilemmas of Statebuilding: Confronting the Contradictions of Postwar Peace Operations* (London: Routledge, 2009), 130.

[91] For a description of self-organization in a peacebuilding context, see Cedric de Coning, 'From Peacebuilding to Sustaining Peace: Implications of Complexity for Resilience and Sustainability', *Resilience* 4, No. 3 (2016): 166–181.

a new 'phase space',[92] where patterns of behaviour are radically altered, new possibilities rapidly emerge, and the contours of the system may take time to reshape (think of the stops and starts in Egyptian rule following the Arab Spring).

In other systems, deeply entrenched patterns of behaviour can persist for generations, suffering apparent reversals and doldrums before any shift may take hold.[93] In the DRC, for example, it appears that decades of statebuilding by the UN has had little effect on the underlying patterns of patronage linking powerbrokers in Kinshasa to the peripheries of the country. Non-linearity 'requires that interveners have humility, because specific changes are often unpredictable and uncontrollable ... [it] suggests we attend to temporality and trends, not specific outcomes'.[94] Teleologically driven thinking gains little traction here because there is no end-state;[95] systems do not 'break down'—as much of the state failure literature suggests—they reorganize and reach new equilibria, sometimes at great human cost.[96]

Complexity thinking does more than merely undermine traditional notions of linearity; it offers a set of tools for researchers to map change in socio-political systems, revealing how deeply entrenched patterns in societies react to specific historical events without the kind of normative gloss that tends to appear in mainstream peacebuilding.[97] Robert Jervis' seminal work on system effects was a watershed in the application of complexity thinking to political science, including international diplomacy.[98] David Byrne drew directly from Prigonine's insights about complexity to analyse the impacts of health, education, and urban governance policies in England, while a range of other scholars have suggested complexity-driven approaches to public policy.[99] Michael Woolcock, Duncan Green, Rachel Kleinfeld, and Ben Ramalingam, among others, have drawn from complexity thinking to

[92] Kurt A. Richardson, 'Complex Systems Thinking and Its Implications for Policy Analysis', in Göktug Morçöl, ed., *Handbook on Decisionmaking* (University Park, PA: Penn State University Press, 2006): 189–221.

[93] See, e.g., Luxshi Vimalarajah, 'Thinking Peace: Revising Analysis and Intervention in Sri Lanka', in Daniela Korppen et al., eds., *The Non-Linearity of Peace Processes: Theory and Practice of Systemic Conflict Transformation* (Opladen: Verlag Barbara Budrich, 2011).

[94] Coleman, 'Navigating the Landscape of Conflict', 39.

[95] Cedric de Coning, 'Adaptive Peacebuilding', *International Affairs* 94, No. 2 (2018): 312.

[96] Mary Lee Rhodes et al., *Public Management and Complexity Theory: Richer Decision-making in Public Services* (London: Routledge, 2011), 15.

[97] Daniela Körppen, 'Space Beyond the Liberal Peacebuilding Consensus—A Systemic Perspective', in Daniela Körppen et al., eds., *The Non-Linearity of Peace Processes: Theory and Practice of Systemic Conflict Transformation* (Opladen: Verlag Barbara Budrich, 2011), 78.

[98] Robert Jervis, *System Effects: Complexity in Political and Social Life* (Princeton, NJ: Princeton University Press, 1997), 243–245.

[99] David Byrne, *Complexity Theory and the Social Sciences, An Introduction* (New York: Routledge Press, 1998); Robert Geyer and Samir Rihani, *Complexity and Public Policy: A New Approach to 21st Century Politics, Policy and Society* (New York: Routledge, 2010); Graham Room, *Complexity, Institutions and Public Policy: Agile Decision-making in a Turbulent World* (Cheltenham: Edward Elgar, 2010); Göktug Morçöl, A Complexity Theory for Public Policy (New York: Routledge, 2012); Lee Rhodes et al., *Public Management and Complexity Theory.*

suggest innovative approaches to international development and humanitarian assistance, arguing that the causal links between events must be analysed within a systemic socio-political context.[100] Bousquet and Curtis have persuasively argued for a more concerted application of complexity thinking to international relations, a call that was taken up by Emilian Kavalski in his analysis of world politics.[101] Similar applications of complexity thinking have now been suggested for international policing efforts,[102] humanitarian delivery,[103] military operations, and studies of social resilience in conflict.[104] Most relevant, de Coning, Brusset, and Hughes curated an exploratory volume on the application of complexity thinking to post-conflict peacebuilding, arguing that external attempts to 'fix' local governance systems may 'undermine and interfere with the self-organising process'.[105]

In fact, there has been a gradual shift in UN parlance towards complexity, underscored by the increasing use of the term 'resilience' in today's peacebuilding literature. In a study of dozens of policy papers on peacebuilding, Pospisil and Kühn have shown a dramatic increase in the use of the term resilience, consonant with a recognition that systemic strength is crucial to peace outcomes, that the ability of a society to withstand shocks without descending into violence is a key metric of success.[106] The UN in particular has embraced resilience as the dominant conceptual bulwark against violent conflict and instability, and the term has now permeated nearly every major international approach to conflict-affected states.[107] But though resilience is a useful concept, it is treated superficially in

[100] Michael Woolcock, 'Towards a Plurality of Methods in Project Evaluation: A Contextualised Approach to Understanding Impact Trajectories and Efficacy', *Journal of Development Effectiveness* 1, No. 1 (2009): 1–14; Duncan Green, *From Poverty to Power* (London: Oxfam e-books), https://oxfamblogs.org/fp2p/; Ben Ramalingam, *Aid on the Edge of Chaos: Rethinking International Cooperation in a Complex World* (Oxford: Oxford University Press, 2013); Rachel Kleinfeld, 'Improving Development Aid Design and Implementation: Plan for Sailboats Not Traintracks', *Carnegie Endowment for International Peace* (2015).

[101] Antoine Bousquet and Simon Curtis, 'Beyond Models and Metaphors: Complexity Theory, Systems Thinking and International Relations', *Cambridge Review of International Affairs* 24, No. 01 (2011): 43–62; Emilian Kavalski, *World Politics at the Edge of Chaos: Reflections on Complexity and Global Life* (Albany: State University of New York, 2015).

[102] Charles T. Hunt, *UN Peace Operations and International Policing: Negotiating Complexity, Assessing Impact and Learning to Learn* (London: Routledge, 2015).

[103] Ben Ramalingham and Harry Jones, 'Exploring the Science of Complexity: Ideas and Implications for Development and Humanitarian Efforts', Overseas Development Institute, Working Paper 285 (2008).

[104] Kurt Richardson, Graham Mathieso, and Paul Cilliers, 'Complexity Thinking and Military Operational Analysis', in Kurt Richardson, ed., *Knots, Lace and Tartan: Making Sense of Complex Human Systems in Military Operations Research* (Litchfield Park, AZ: ISE Publishing); Louise Wiuff Moe and Markus-Michael Müller, *Reconfiguring Intervention: Complexity, Resilience and the 'Local Turn' in Counterinsurgent Warfare* (London: Palgrave MacMillan, 2017).

[105] Brusset, de Coning, and Hughes, *Complexity Thinking*.

[106] Jan Pospisil and Florian Kühn, 'The Resilient State: New Regulatory Modes in International Approaches to State Building', *Third World Quarterly* 37, No. 1 (2016): 1–16.

[107] United Nations Development Programme, *Governance for Peace: Securing the Social Contract* (New York, 2012); Organisation for Economic Cooperation and Development, 'Supporting Statebuilding in Situations of Conflict and Fragility' (2011); World Bank, *World Development Report: Conflict, Security and Development* (2011).

peacebuilding literature and practice, considered more as a capacity of states to 'bounce back' from shocks and adjust to new risks, rather than as the deeper notion of self-organization and emergent patterns of change in complex systems.[108] It is also thought of normatively as a positive characteristic of a society, ignoring the extraordinary resilience of many predatory, venal systems that have survived for decades despite many efforts to change them. As the following section demonstrates, the language of complex systems is not a veneer, nor is it something that should be peppered into policy documents to make them appear more nuanced; complexity thinking is a lens through which to understand how change takes place in conflict settings, one more rooted in empirical reality than the more linear, teleologically driven concepts underpinning statebuilding.

[108] Chandler, *Resilience*.

2
Into the black hole—applying complexity

What does it meant to apply complexity to settings like eastern Congo or South Sudan? What specifically does complexity thinking offer that other scholarship does not? Here I take the common shortcomings of hybridity and the local turn as a starting point, arguing that distinctions like local/international are less important than the types of relationships that organize a given system.[1] When examining the role of a traditional authority figure in a conflict setting, for example, I focus less on the hybrid status of the individual and more on how governance authority is distributed across others around them through symbiotic relationships, including within local/rural communities, state officials, military actors, and non-governmental organizations (NGOs). The relations are what define the systems of governance examined in this project, they exhibit Morgan Brigg's 'thick relationality' discussed above.[2] How relations shift over time allows for an understanding of the patterns that shape governance, including the UN's attempts to build capacities in areas with weak state institutions.

Moreover—and central to this book—scholarship to date tends to ignore how the UN becomes part of a governance system itself. Experts like Susan Woodward compellingly argue that international statebuilding fails *because* it never truly engages with local or national authorities, developing the statebuilder's capacities rather than entering a country's bloodstream or leaving anything useful behind.[3] Séverine Autesserre's excellent critiques of the UN's engagement in places like the Democratic Republic of Congo (DRC) are brutal indictments of the UN's failure to make meaningful contact with the people and institutions of the country; driving around in heavily reinforced ivory Landrovers, UN peacekeepers are described as

[1] I have previously taken a similar line when analysing the stabilization work of the United Nations (UN): Adam C. Day and Charles T. Hunt, 'UN Stabilisation Operations and the Problem of Non-Linear Change: A Relational Approach to Intervening in Governance Ecosystems', *Stability International Journal of Security and Development* 9(1) (2020): 1–23.

[2] Morgan Brigg, 'Relational Peacebuilding: Promise beyond Crisis', in Tobias Debiel et al., eds., *Peacebuilding in Crisis: Rethinking Paradigms and Practices of Transnational Cooperation* (London: Routledge, 2016), 58.

[3] Susan Woodward, *The Ideology of Failed States: Why Intervention Fails* (Cambridge: Cambridge University Press, 2017).

States of Disorder, Ecosystems of Governance. Adam Day, Oxford University Press.
 DOI: 10.1093/oso/9780192863898.003.0003

the epitome of a disconnected external actor, living in a superficial 'peaceland' that never comes into contact with local realities.[4] Even where the impact of the UN is considered, it is typically through the lens of the UN as an exogenous factor, an intervention that generates consequences, intended or otherwise.[5] Ole Jacob Sending has referred to this as an 'Archimedean' view of Western intervention, where interveners see themselves as above and disinterested in the settings in which they act.[6]

Indeed, UN interventions create consequences, but these are better understood from the point of view of the UN as *part of the system*, as one of the endogenous nodes of power that relates to others in a given setting. UN statebuilding is not separate from the systems that produce governance; in fact, as Berdal and Zaum have demonstrated, the UN is often intimately involved within the political economy of statebuilding, better understood as part of the local system than apart from it.[7] Building on this political economy foundation, I propose to consider the UN within a system characterized by emergent properties, asking how systems adapt to the UN's activities and how the underlying rules, patterns, and characteristics may impact the goals of statebuilding. This approach also allows for an examination of how a UN mission itself may adapt (or indeed be shaped) within a system, though the starting point is Susanna Campbell's insight that UN interventions typically fall short of the kinds of adaptation needed to achieve their objectives.[8]

But what, specifically, does complexity thinking offer to an investigation into statebuilding? Unless this project is exact in its use of complexity thinking, there is a risk that it will merely rebrand other concepts with new vocabulary, potentially obscuring more than it explains. Here, the key value added of complexity thinking is that it offers a way to understand how change occurs over time without reliance on linear notions of progress; rather, it explains how change is the emergent outcome of systemic patterns interacting with specific events.

[4] Séverine Autesserre, *Peaceland: Conflict Resolution and the Everyday Politics of International Intervention* (Cambridge: Cambridge University Press, 2014).

[5] Chiyuki Aoi et al., eds., *The Unintended Consequences of Peacekeeping* (Tokyo: United Nations University Press, 2007); Page Fortna, *Does Peacekeeping Work? Shaping Belligerents' Choices after Civil War* (Princeton, NJ: Princeton University Press, 2004); Håvard Hegre, Lisa Hultman, and Håvard Mokleiv Nygård, 'Evaluating the Conflict-reducing Effect of UN Peacekeeping Operations', *The Journal of Politics* 81, No. 1 (2019): 215–232.

[6] Ole Jacob Sending, 'The Effects of Peacebuilding: Sovereignty, Patronage and Power', in Susanna Campbell, David Chandler and Meera Sabaratnam, eds., *A Liberal Peace? The Problems and Practices of Peacebuilding* (London: Zed Books, 2011), 63.

[7] Mats Berdal and Dominik Zaum, eds., *Political Economy of Statebuilding: Power after Peace* (London: Routledge Press, 2013).

[8] Susanna Campbell, 'Routine Learning? How Peacebuilding Organisations Prevent Liberal Peace', in Susanna Campbell, David Chandler, and Meera Sabaratnam, eds., *A Liberal Peace? The Problems and Practices of Peacebuilding* (London: Zed Books, 2011), 89–105.

Self-organization, feedback loops, strong attractors

The following case studies are analysed using three core concepts of complexity thinking, all aimed at the question of how a given system self-organizes: symbiotic relationships, feedback loops, and strong attractors. First, complex systems are by nature relational; they are composed of symbiotic exchanges that create patterns and tendencies within a given system.[9] Each case study will explore how the underlying relationships that formed the governance systems changed over time, often creating new tendencies and patterns within the system. These changes are described in terms of feedback loops, where the system either is able to regain equilibrium through negative feedback or change rapidly via positive feedback. Over time, patterns emerge and create what are called strong attractors, which can be thought of as the gravitational pulls within a system, the recurrent forms of feedback that tend to direct a system back to the same state.[10] In many instances, ethnicity appears to act as a strong attractor, a kind of organizing force to which societies return; in other cases, a system may have a strong pull towards the geographic centre of the capital city, as resources, power, and people appear drawn inwards ineluctably. Violence, paradoxically, acts as a stabilizing element of many governance systems, creating predictable, if highly dangerous, patterns. Attractors can be overcome, but it tends to require some rewriting of the underlying rules and patterns for lasting change to take place, something that appears well beyond the capabilities of the UN in these settings.

In order to enable comparison, each case study will follow the same overall approach (1) describe the system of governance in a given setting, using a historical inquiry that highlights how certain patterns have arisen and evolved over time; (2) map the patterns within the system at the moment of the UN intervention, using the concepts of complexity thinking; (3) identify the goals and approaches taken by UN statebuilding; (4) describe how the system of governance reacted to the intervention, identifying the ways in which existing patterns contributed to the outcomes over time; (5) review and reject alternative explanations for the outcome; and (6) present the strongest explanation why a particular course of events unfolded, identifying the ways in which the UN intervention may have contributed to it. This approach roughly aligns with process tracing, in terms of building a historically rooted argument and focusing on causality at key moments, but it begins with a broader description of the system as a crucial context for analysis that informs the examination of the particular.[11] Rather than assume a linear path can be charted by

[9] For a more in-depth background on symbiosis, see Day and Hunt, 'UN Stabilisation Operations', 1–23.

[10] Peter T. Coleman et al., 'Attracted to Peace: Modeling the Core Dynamics of Sustainably Peaceful Societies' (unpublished, on file with author).

[11] Andrew Bennett and Jeffrey T. Checkel, *Process Tracing: From Metaphor to Analytic Tool* (Cambridge: Cambridge University Press, 2015).

linking events seamlessly together, it suggests that the causal mechanism is better thought of in broad systemic terms as a set of patterns that carry across individual events, influencing them in similar ways over time. This does not ignore the need to explain particular events, but offers a broader context for them.

It is worth flagging three additional points here. The first is the importance of mapping relationships in this project. Complexity thinking places interrelatedness at the heart of systemic inquiry; it suggests that the connections across actors matters more than their formal status.[12] Bruno Latour's Actor-Network Theory offers an early example of relational scholarship, helpfully describing the types of mapping required to apply systems thinking to social inquiry.[13] Norbert Elias' figurational sociology does as well, considering 'patterns which interdependent human beings, as groups or as individuals, form with each other.'[14] For the purposes of statebuilding, Finn Stepputat's notion of 'governscapes' offers a somewhat helpful description of 'landscapes with different constellations of authority and governance that form and spread unevenly within and beyond national boundaries.'[15] Catherine Boone's well-known political topographies of power in Africa offer a similar concept.[16]

Complexity suggests these landscapes are dynamic and change over time, meaning that notions of sovereign governance are 'deeply relational' rather than static.[17] In the case studies that follow, I map how different relationships constitute the governance systems in conflict settings, whether it is among key actors (e.g. traditional authorities, soldiers, and community leaders) or across institutions (e.g. the presidency and NGOs), or a combination of both. My core argument here is that the UN has not taken into account the fundamental relationality of governance systems in these settings, instead presuming that state institutional structures are per se the appropriate vehicles of authority. This blindspot has meant UN interventions proceed unaware of the fact that they too become part of the complex interrelated systems of governance, and are thus easily absorbed into pre-existing patterns.

Relationality also offers a way out of shortcomings of the 'local turn', which tends to glorify local-level experience and treat it in isolation from national, regional, or international actors. As one of my South Sudanese interviewees told me, 'nothing here is just local, everything is connected, the cows by the river mean something

[12] Brigg, 'Relational Peacebuilding', 23.

[13] Bruno Latour, *Reassembling the Social: An Introduction to Actor-Network Theory* (Oxford: Oxford University Press, 2005).

[14] Norbert Elias, 'The Retreat of Sociologists into the Present', *Theory Culture Society* 4, No. 2 (1987): 85. Note that Alex Veit's approach to DRC (covered in Chapter 6 of this book) adopts Elias' figurational approach.

[15] Finn Stepputat, 'Pragmatic Peace in Emerging Governscapes', *International Affairs* 94, No. 2 (2018): 400.

[16] Catherine Boone, *Political Topographies of the African State: Territorial Authority and Institutional Choice* (Cambridge: Cambridge University Press, 2003).

[17] Boone, *Political Topographies of the African State*, 402.

to the politicians in Juba.'[18] He understands that South Sudan is a complex system, where interconnections matter more than the formal status of entities or the level at which they exist; the United Nations Mission in the Republic of South Sudan (UNMISS), with its bifurcated political and civil affairs divisions operating in separate silos, did not.

In fact, complexity redefines 'local' in a way that avoids the more romantic undertones of the local turn and allows for more empirically rigorous analysis. Scholars like Mac Ginty, Boege, and Autesserre see 'the local' in territorial and hierarchical terms: it is the village level, the 'everyday practice' of average citizens going about their work.[19] In Gearoid Millar's description, local actors are those whose influence is bounded by their own geography, whereas national and global actors have greater influence.[20] These notions of locality implicitly presume that local actors individually have shorter reach, less impact on the trajectory of events within a country, even while arguing that local dynamics are in many ways constitutive of the country. This is on the one hand patronizing of a particular class of people, and also lacking in empirical backing. Instead, complexity thinking offers a reconceptualization where 'local' is the most immediate set of impacts and connections between one node and the others within a system. The actions of the president of a country may have a localized impact, while a village chief may trigger a chain of events that can start a civil war on a national scale. The more important question is not about level (local/national) but about how, within a complex system, localized relationships interact and aggregate into patterns, allowing the system to adapt to new stimuli.

It may be worth offering a brief example from my research: In Beni, eastern DRC, an armed group called the Allied Democratic Forces (ADF) entered into relationship with some community leaders to help them fight for scarce land and resources. The ADF also had relationships with elements of the Congolese army and municipal politicians, collaborating to illegally export timber across the DRC/Uganda border. Those municipal powerbrokers in turn had 'patrons' in Kinshasa who protected their positions in exchange for rents on the natural resources. The ADF thus became a 'local node' bringing together widely disparate actors into a symbiotic relationship that generated revenues, protection for some communities, violence against others, and a very fluid arrangement vis-à-vis the state. When the UN decided to conduct joint military operations with the Congolese army against the ADF, it was on the assumption that the group was a violent,

[18] Interview with UNMISS national staff, Juba, 13 December 2018.

[19] Roger Mac Ginty, 'Hybrid Peace: The interaction between top-down and bottom up peace', *Security Dialogue*, 41(4) (2010): 391–412; Volker M. Boege, et al, 'States Emerging from Hybrid Political Orders – Pacific Experiences', *The Australian Centre for Peace and Conflict Studies, Occasional Paper Series*, 2008.

[20] Gearoid Millar, 'Respecting Complexity: Compound friction and unpredictability in peacebuilding', in *Peacebuilding and Friction: Global and local encounters in post-conflict societies*, eds. Annika Bjökdahl et al (New York: Routledge, 2017), 32.

disruptive force in the area (it was indeed very violent) that needed to be neutralized. To date, these military operations have failed to end the ADF's presence in North Kivu. Seen through the lens of purely local dynamics, or seen as merely an armed group, the ADF's persistence is difficult to explain. Why haven't the dozens of military campaigns by the Congolese army and the UN together been able to drive out this armed group? By examining the role of the ADF as a node, as a point at which many actors were brought together in a complex, interrelated system, we can begin to understand why the military campaign against the ADF did not work. In addition to its roles as a brutal armed group capable of mass atrocities (indeed in part because of it), the ADF was crucial to resource generation, intercommunal conflicts, and political dynamics stretching from Beni to Kinshasa and Kampala. Military campaigns against the group disrupted that underlying system and triggered its 'strong attractors', the patterns that helped it to stabilize over time. The result was a ripple effect: when the ADF was attacked, surrounding communities repositioned themselves around new opportunities and risks, members of the Congolese army stepped in to help the ADF secure their access to the illicit timber trade, politicians jostled for influence with Kinshasa, the system adapted.

This example brings up the second point, the treatment of the UN as part of the system of governance in conflict settings. Critiques of liberal peacekeeping almost inevitably describe the international community as divorced, sequestered, out of touch with the realities of the conflicts they are trying to solve. Susan Woodward lambasts statebuilding as an externally driven activity that serves mainly to shore itself up; Berdal and Zaum rightly point to the ways in which local elites resist and the 'external intrusion' of UN statebuilders; and Autesserre, Hagman, and Thelen all suggest that international intervention fails to make meaningful contact with local realities.[21] These lines of inquiry are useful in exposing Western actors as misaligned and often destructive towards those they are purporting to assist. A systemic approach, however, refuses the notion of exogeneity. So-called outside actors 'are in fact very much part of the conflict system', playing a role in the contestation over power and rights, even if uncomprehending of it.[22] UN statebuilding participates in the political economy which it is trying to affect, it is 'privy to the logics of the political marketplace.'[23] Western approaches may be at odds with local dynamics, but they operate within the same system, mapped onto the same

[21] Woodward, *The Ideology of Failed States*; Autesserre, *Peaceland*; Tobias Hagmann and Markus Hoehne, 'Failures of the state failure debate: Evidence from the Somali territories', *Journal of International Development* 21 (2012); Tatjana Thelen et al., *Stategraphy: Toward a relational anthropology of the state* (New York: Berghahn Press, 2018).

[22] Luxshi Vimalarajah, 'Thinking Peace: Revising Analysis and Intervention in Sri Lanka', in *The Non-Linearity of Peace Processes: Theory and Practice of Systemic Conflict Transformation*, eds. Daniela Körppen et al (Opladen: Verlag Barbara Budrich, 2011).

[23] Tatiana Carayannis, Koen Vlassenroot, Kasper Hoffmann and Aaron Pangburn, 'Competing networks and political order in the Democratic Republic of Congo: a literature review on the logics of public authority and international intervention', *Conflict Research Programme, London School of Economics* (2018); see also, Berdal and Zaum, *Political Economy of Statebuilding*, 117.

terrain. The UN's military campaign against the ADF was not separate from the underlying system of governance in North Kivu, it became an element of it.

My approach incorporates the perspectives of Mac Ginty and Boege, who treat concepts like local, indigenous, liberal, exogenous and international as 'composites, or amalgamations resulting from long-term processes of social negotiation and adaptation',[24] but also offers the tools to map and describe how these negotiations absorb the UN. At times UN statebuilding may seem to 'go with the grain' of the system, amplifying and potentially gaining momentum from the patterns in play; in others, the patterns will work as a sort of undercurrent against UN programming; there are even instances where the UN is able to adapt itself to achieve more within a system.[25] Simply put, this project approaches UN statebuilding as part of the system of contested governance, not apart from it.

Finally, complex systems are extremely difficult to reduce to legible narratives, often requiring a bit of literary flare to give readers a sense of the environment. In his introduction to complexity thinking, David Byrne suggests that the entire application of chaos theory to political and social science is a form of metaphor, and he encourages researchers to employ literary tropes if they deepen analysis.[26] Charles T. Hunt has drawn from nature to illustrate how complex socio-political systems can rest on symbiotic relations across different actors, using fungi and sharks as analogues for social relations,[27] an approach I also took with him when analysing UN stabilization operations.[28] Claude Combes likewise comments upon the global arms race in terms of parasitic relationships found in nature.[29] I use these tropes with caution, as they may be misleading or distracting; but with metaphors there is also the possibility of illuminating elusive ideas succinctly.[30] In the case studies of this book, it is often helpful to employ metaphor, to imagine governance systems as schools of fish, scattering and reshaping themselves around the bulk of a potentially dangerous statebuilding shark, at times finding shelter in the shadow of the same large fish.[31] Indeed, in many instances, the UN's statebuilding intervention is more like a sunken boat, around which the shoal swims with hardly a glance.

[24] Mac Ginty, 'Hybrid Peace', 391–412.

[25] For a good description of the notion of 'going with the grain' in a political marketplace, see Alex de Waal, 'Inclusion in Peacemaking: From Moral Claim to Political Fact', in Pamela Aall and Chester A. Crocker, eds., *The Fabric of Peace in Africa: Looking Beyond the State* (Ontario: Center for International Governance Innovation, 2017), 176–177.

[26] David Byrne, *Complexity Theory and the Social Sciences, An Introduction* (New York: Routledge Press, 1998), 55.

[27] Charles T. Hunt, 'Beyond the Binaries: Towards a Relational Approach to Peacebuilding', *Global Change, Peace & Security* 29, No. 3 (2017): 209–227.

[28] Day and Hunt, 'UN Stabilisation Operations', 1–23.

[29] Claude Combes, *The Art of Being a Parasite* (Chicago: University of Chicago Press, 2005).

[30] Donald Davidson, 'What Metaphors Mean', in Sheldon Sacks, ed., *On Metaphor* (Chicago: Chicago University Press, 1978), 32–33.

[31] For a discussion of various symbiotic relations in complex systems, see Day and Hunt, 'UN Stabilisation Operations', 1–23.

PART II
EXPERIENCES IN STATEBUILDING

The overarching question of this book is, *Why has UN statebuilding failed to meet its objectives*? Part One, by exploring the fragile states literature and dominant approaches to statebuilding, suggests that scholarship to date has provided unsatisfactory explanations in part because much of it tends to follow the same linear logic of statebuilding itself. Instead, I propose an approach drawn from complexity thinking to guide the case-specific analysis, one focused on understanding how systems of governance evolve in conflict settings, and how the United Nations (UN)'s activities can be seen as part of the system itself.

Part Two now puts the analytic framework into action, comparing two prominent UN statebuilding missions to understand how and why they have not achieved their goals. Chapter 3 explores the governance system that evolved in South Sudan over a twenty-year war and subsequent five-year peace process, demonstrating that an ethno-military network had come to dominate the social, political, and economic landscape of South Sudan by its independence in 2011. Chapter 4 builds on that analysis and traces the statebuilding efforts of the UN Mission in South Sudan (UNMISS) from 2011 until the outbreak of civil war in 2013, arguing that the UN's overriding focus on building up state institutions actually contributed to the start of the civil war, rather than helping to stabilize the country. Chapters 5 and 6 follow the same approach with the Democratic Republic of the Congo (DRC), first identifying the key characteristics of the governance system and then exploring how the UN's engagement produced unintended consequences. Across both case studies, I employ the core concepts and tools of complexity thinking, including the ways in which symbiotic relations, feedback loops, self-organization, strong attractors, and phase space influence the trajectories of statebuilding. Ultimately, these cases demonstrate that the very different systems of governance that evolved in the DRC and South Sudan over decades (indeed over hundreds of years) proved highly resilient against the kinds of linear change anticipated by the UN statebuilding missions on the ground.

3

'A new dawn'

South Sudan's brief experiment with statebuilding

Upon South Sudan's independence in 2011, President Salva Kiir proclaimed, 'The Republic of South Sudan is like a white paper—*tabula rasa*!'[1] Across the international community too, there was a sense that the world's newest country was embarking on a fresh start. President Obama spoke of a 'new dawn'[2] after a period of darkness, while the World Bank summarized the challenge: 'As a new nation without a history of formal institutions, rules or administration accepted as legitimate by society, South Sudan must build its institutions *from scratch*. Core administrative structures and mechanisms of political representation are only beginning to emerge.'[3] Building the state of South Sudan was comparable to filling a void, writing into a blank space where the state's capacities to provide order were utterly absent. The newly established UNMISS was given a billion-dollar mandate to fill this institutional vacuum, to constitute and strengthen state governance capacities.[4] Taking the helm of UNMISS in 2011, Hilde Frafjord Johnson wrote that the UN's task was 'literally building a country'.[5]

Only two years later, any optimism about South Sudan evaporated as the country descended into a brutal civil war, resulting in the death of nearly 400,000 people and the displacement of more than four million.[6] It quickly became clear that state security services were prime actors in this conflict, driving large populations from their homes, killing, looting, and raping civilians, and obstructing humanitarian

[1] President Salva Kiir's Martyr's Day Speech, 30 July 2011, available at https://paanluelwel.com/2011/07/31/president-kiirs-speech-in-the-6th-martyrs-day-30-7-2011/

[2] Statement of President Barack Obama Recognition of the Republic of South Sudan, 9 July 2011, available at: https://obamawhitehouse.archives.gov/the-press-office/2011/07/09/statement-president-barack-obama-recognition-republic-south-sudan; Statement of UN Secretary-General Ban Ki-Moon on the Independence of the Republic of South Sudan, 9 July 2011, available at: https://news.un.org/en/story/2011/07/381102

[3] World Bank, 'South Sudan Overview', 2013, available at www.worldbank.org/en/country/southsudan/overview (emphasis added).

[4] United Nations Security Council Resolution on South Sudan, S/RES/1996 (8 July 2011), para. 3.

[5] Hilde F. Johnson, *South Sudan: The Untold Story from Independence to Civil War* (London: I.B. Tauris, 2016), 98.

[6] Franceso Checchi et al., 'South Sudan: Estimates of Crisis-Attributable Mortality', London School of Hygiene and Tropical Medicine, September 2018, available at https://crises.lshtm.ac.uk/wpcontent/uploads/sites/10/2018/09/LSHTM_mortality_South_Sudan_report.pdf

States of Disorder, Ecosystems of Governance. Adam Day, Oxford University Press.
 DOI: 10.1093/oso/9780192863898.003.0004

aid to vulnerable populations.[7] In response, the UN Security Council immediately halted the statebuilding mandate of UNMISS, cutting off enormous resources that had been dedicated to supporting state institutions across the country, instead demanding that UNMISS focus on protecting civilians caught up in the conflict.[8] In mere months, the UN had pivoted from the role of building the state to one of protecting the people from it. Statebuilding had failed.

Reflecting on the international community's inability to prevent the 2013 civil war, the UN and its partners agreed: the problem was not enough statebuilding. Specialrepresentative of the secretary-general (SRSG) Johnson argued that capacity development of the South Sudanese state had been conducted in a 'patchy and uncoordinated' manner, 'not done in the comprehensive and systematic way needed to build a functioning state'.[9] The World Bank found that massive dysfunction in the institutions of the state—including clear evidence of corruption—meant that public expenditures had not delivered the kind of institutions needed to prevent the war.[10] Capturing a sentiment held across many in the donor community, Richard Dowden suggested that South Sudan had become independent *too early*, before the international community had been able to help it build effective state institutions that would be resilient in the face of ethnic divisions.[11]

The following two chapters offer an alternative—and in many ways directly opposing—explanation for the UN's failure to prevent South Sudan's descent into civil war. The central argument advanced is that governance in South Sudan is best understood in systemic terms as the outcome of negotiated, contested processes among a range of state and non-state actors. By mapping relations within the system, it is possible to observe the emergence of dominant patterns over time, an 'attractor landscape' that strongly tends to direct behaviour.[12] In the case of South Sudan, this landscape was characterized by a centre/periphery relationship mediated through traditional authorities, over time becoming subordinated to the military needs of the Southern People's Liberation Movement / Southern People's Liberation Army (SPLM/SPLA). This system had become highly adaptive over decades of war, capable of self-organizing around new interventions, including UNMISS' statebuilding efforts. By examining how the system absorbed and in

[7] Letter dated 20 November 2017 from the Panel of Experts on South Sudan addressed to the president of the Security Council, S/2017/979 (2017).

[8] United Nations Security Council resolution, S/RES/2155 (2014).

[9] Hilde F. Johnson, *South Sudan: The Untold Story from Independence to Civil War* (London: L.B. Tauris, 2016), 17.

[10] Kimo Adiebo et al., 'Public Expenditures in South Sudan: Are They Delivering?' *World Bank Economic Brief*, Issue 2, February 2013.

[11] Richard Dowden, 'South Sudan's Leaders Have Learnt Nothing from 50 Years of Independence in Africa', *African Arguments*, 22 January 2014.

[12] Peter Coleman et al., 'Intractable Conflict as an Attractor: A Dynamical Systems Approach to Conflict Escalation and Intractability', *American Behavioral Scientist* 50, No. 11 (2007): 1454–1475.

many ways thrived on the work of UNMISS, I offer an explanation for the UN's failed statebuilding.

As a starting point, this chapter maps governance in South Sudan as a set of relationships, illustrating how power has been distributed across key actors, institutions, and entities from the pre-colonial period to today. I argue that the legal, political, and cultural ways in which power has been negotiated as between the central authorities and the peripheries of the South have been strongly influenced by governance as a tool of extraction and war, rather than as a modality for civil administration. Within this, the role of traditional leaders was often defined by their ability to translate and reciprocate needs between the state and communities, a role that became increasingly subordinated to the military over the two civil wars preceding independence. The result was a governance system built upon ethno-military patronage, where resources and loyalty were exchanged across formal/informal, state/non-state, local/national divides, and where resort to violence was a form of communication within the system. This systemic understanding of South Sudan forms the analytic basis for Chapter 4, which describes how UNMISS became part of the governance landscape from 2011 until the 2013 civil war.

A mapping of de- and recentralization of governance in southern Sudan

South Sudan did not recover from its nineteenth century experience.

(Edward Thomas)

Governance in South Sudan at the moment of independence in 2011 was a palimpsest, written over earlier systems of authority. In each major epoch of the region's history, from pre-colonial times to present, authorities and their communities have grappled with fundamental questions concerning how the centre would relate to (and often exploit) the periphery, modifying older structures of authority to suit their purposes. Drawing on Catherine Boone's well-known concept of 'political topography'—which offers a range of ways in which centre/periphery relations have been ordered in Africa—this section explores the major systems of governance that have evolved through the pre-colonial, colonial, post-colonial, and post-independence South Sudan.[13] It interrogates how the relationships among central authorities and largely rural communities have changed over time, typically as a result of differing approaches to decentralization.[14] By mapping the ebbs and flows of public authority from pre-colonial times

[13] Catherine Boone, *Political Topographies of the African State: Territorial Authority and Institutional Choice* (Cambridge: Cambridge University Press, 2003).

[14] For a more in-depth analysis of the philosophical underpinnings of this issue in South Sudan, see Douglas H. Johnson, 'Federalism in the History of South Sudanese Political Thought', in *Struggle for*

to South Sudan's independence, three key patterns emerge: (1) the gravitational pull of ethnicity as an ordering force in southern Sudan, a conduit for channelling resources and power; (2) economic dependency of the periphery on the centre, even as nominal decentralization was implemented; and (3) the militarization of governance through two civil wars, resulting in what Clémence Pinaud has called a 'military aristocracy' in South Sudan.[15] Within all three patterns, chiefs and so-called 'traditional leaders' have operated as intermediaries, liminal figures drawing authority and identity from their ability to move across state/non-state, centre/periphery, and legal/customary divides. Taken together, these dynamics will offer topographical texture to the system of governance in post-independence South Sudan explored in Chapter 4.

Pre-colonial 'ordered anarchy' and 'divine kings'

During the pre-colonial period (prior to the Turco-Egyptian regime that took power in 1821), there was a variety of governance systems across southern Sudan. Within the Nuer and Dinka communities, socio-political ordering was achieved absent a highly centralized authority; instead, elders managed relations within and across communities without recourse to formal legislative or executive institutions.[16] Edward Evans-Pritchard famously referred to this system as 'ordered anarchy', but it is perhaps more helpfully understood as an acephalous—headless—governance structure with heavy reliance on kinship and lineage as its principal ordering mechanisms.[17] In contrast, the Shilluk kingdom was governed by a 'divine king' possessed of near absolute executive and judicial powers,[18] while the Azande people established several centrally administered, lineage-based kingdoms on the back of military expansion and assimilation of other ethnic groups.[19]

While these systems differed significantly in the degree to which they centralized authority, they shared a reliance on kinship, lineage, and intra-ethnic custom as the foundation for governance. As the following periods will demonstrate, these ethnically based systems never fully disappeared, showing resilience against colonial and post-colonial attempts to emplace other systems of authority in their

South Sudan: Challenges of Security and State Formation, eds. Luka Biong Deng Kuol and Sarah Logan (London: I.B. Tauris, 2019), 103–123.

[15] Clémence Pinaud, 'South Sudan: Civil War, Predation and the Making of a Military Aristocracy', *African Affairs* 113, No. 451 (2014): 192–211.

[16] Luka Biong Deng Kuol and Sarah Logan, eds., *The Struggle for South Sudan: Challenges of Security and State Formation* (London: I.B. Tauris, 2019), 82–103.

[17] Edward Evans-Pritchard, *The Nuer: A Description of the Modes of Livelihood and Political Institutions of a Nilotic People* (Oxford: Oxford University Press 1940), 12.

[18] David Graeber, 'The Divine Kingship of the Shilluk: On Violence, Utopia, and the Human Condition', in David Graeber and Marshal Sahlins, eds., *On Kings* (Chicago: Hau Books, 2017), 65–139.

[19] Kuol and Logan, *Struggle for South Sudan*, 82–103; Edward Evans-Pritchard, 'The Ethnic Composition of the Azande of Central Africa', *Anthropological Quarterly* 31, No. 4 (1958): 95–119.

stead. Even as other structures were developed to regulate security, justice, and basic services, ethnicity continued to function both as a kind of foundational reference point and also a currency in the system, allowing power-brokers to channel authority and maintain loyalty.

Colonial assimilation vs. decentralization

The colonial period saw the pendulum swing twice, first towards a centralized governance system under the Turco-Egyptian and Mahdiyya regimes (1821–98), and then in the direction of decentralization under the Anglo-Egyptian regime that ruled until 1956. Southern Sudan emerged from this period with a strong economic dependency on the North, deepened reliance on ethnicity as a modality for channelling authority, and a growing constellation of urban 'nodes' of governance across the region.[20]

Both the Turco-Egyptian and Mahdiyya control over Sudan were motivated by the slave and ivory trades: the militarized, centralized system of governance developed during this period was designed more for the efficient plunder of the region than any kind of meaningful administration or development of a civil service.[21] Arab groups in the North were vested with greater authority than the communities in the South, consolidating power in a centralized Islamic state predicated on religious allegiance and a stigmatization of the southern hinterlands.[22] This period saw the emergence of the North—Omdurman and Khartoum—as the administrative and political centre of Sudan, while southern Sudan as a whole became an economic and political periphery. Slave raids into southern territories by Arab nomads and Turco-Egyptian forces were the most obvious way in which the northern capital extracted from the peripheries, with brutal consequences: according to David Graeber, attacks by Mahdiyya forces halved the Shilluk population in just a few decades, while other communities were equally ravaged.[23] Rather than fundamentally transforming the kinship-based governance structures within southern Sudan, however, this period tended to consolidate the traditions of the pre-colonial period. As Luka Biong Deng notes, many groups tended to turn to their traditional, ethnically based governance structures as a form of resistance and self-protection against the slave raids.[24] Resort to ethnic affiliation reappears

[20] A note on terminology is needed here. In the period up to the 2005 Comprehensive Peace Agreement (CPA), the southern region of Sudan was referred to as 'southern Sudan', reflecting its status as a mere territory within Sudan. The CPA offered the region greater autonomy and I will follow academic custom here by referring to it as 'southern Sudan' in this period. From 2011 onwards, I refer to the Republic of South Sudan as 'South Sudan'.

[21] Kuol and Logan, *Struggle for South Sudan*, 82–103.

[22] Douglas H. Johnson, *The Root Causes of Sudan's Civil Wars* (Oxford: James Currey Press, 2003), 7.

[23] Graeber, 'The Divine Kingship of the Shilluk', 89.

[24] Kuol and Logan, *Struggle for South Sudan*, 82–103.

in later eras in the South as an underlying pattern for the system to reorganize when under pressure.

The slave and ivory trade also forged new networks of power across the territory of southern Sudan, creating loci of authority at the intersections of the trading routes. As Edward Thomas describes, 'The slavers' forts were slowly constituted as nodes of state power that gradually extended authority into ungoverned hinterlands ... [they] established a state system that emphasized the spatial unevenness of development—more development at the nodes and less in the hinterland.'[25] In these growing villages, chiefs became intermediaries between the foreign regime and the local communities, participating in trade where possible while also working to protect their own communities from the violence of colonial powers. This role of intermediary positioned the chiefs in relational terms between state and non-state realms, with their identity and authority largely drawn from their movement between the two. The relational characteristic of South Sudan's chiefs persists to the present and will be a conspicuous feature of the mapping of governance later in this section.

The subsequent Anglo-Egyptian rule of Sudan (1898–1956) was driven by the notion of 'native administration', or 'indirect rule', where local customary governance systems were left in place but subordinated to the demands of the colonial power.[26] Here, the local customary practices of each community were reinforced via a policy to build up 'self-contained racial or tribal units' as the most effective means to legitimize the colonial regime's authority and organize tax collection.[27] Intercommunal communication or sharing of traditions was strictly punished during this period in an attempt to ensure that no coherent political grouping could form in the South, while the northern influence of Islam was mainly confined to the towns.[28] This precipitated a shift in the role of community chiefs into what Edward Thomas calls 'neo-traditional' leadership, where local leaders were given police powers and weapons to implement a coercive economic policy of the colonizer, including forced labour, compulsory payment of crops, and forced movement into villages.[29] The extractive economic policy of the Anglo-Egyptian regime thus deployed tribalism as the means to regulate access to land, resources, and justice, while also deepening the developmental and cultural divides between North and South. It also emplaced a set of highly unequal symbiotic relationships between urban and rural areas that carried through as a pattern to the modern day.

[25] Edward Thomas, *South Sudan: A Slow Liberation* (London: Zed Books, 2015), 58.

[26] Johnson, *The Root Causes of Sudan's Civil Wars*, 9–21.

[27] Kenneth D. Henderson, *Sudan Republic* (London: Benn Press, 1965); see also Johnson, *The Root Causes of Sudan's Civil Wars*, 9–21.

[28] Johnson, *The Root Causes of Sudan's Civil Wars*, 13.

[29] Thomas, *A Slow Liberation*, 96.

Anglo-Egyptian rule created fundamentally relational systems of governance within southern Sudan, where actors were defined in relation to each other rather than based solely on their formal identity or position. On one hand, decentralization produced a bolstering of the traditional governance systems that had preceded colonial times but had been driven underground during the Turco-Egyptian and Mahdiyya periods, giving them newfound coercive powers. But the policy of native administration placed these traditions into a relationship between the local and the colonizer. So-called 'traditional chiefs' were no longer merely the product of the lineage of their own communities, they were also state-recognized mediation points between the communities of southern Sudan and others, including colonial powers, traders, and the Arab peoples of northern Sudan. They possessed 'the capacity to render the government more predictable, [based on] the claim that a chief knows how to turn the arbitrary forces of state power into a source of protection for persons and property.'[30] Traditional authorities emerged as instruments of the colonial state, vested with responsibilities of taxation and rule of law on the ruler's behalf, while also expected to legitimize colonial rule by their continuity as kinship-driven leaders. The traditional authority's identity this became partially constituted within the colonial encounter itself.

The Anglo-Egyptian policy towards southern Sudan also meant that inequality was experienced in both ethnic and geographical terms. Broadly, investment in development was focused in the North, while the South was considered a source of extraction and taxation, feeding the colonial centre in Khartoum/Omdurman. Across the territory of southern Sudan, nodes of the slave trade were expanded into larger towns, places where chiefs were expected to raise revenues for the colonial powers and transmit them up the main artery to the North. As Cherry Leonardi describes, towns became the place where the mediation role of the chief played out:

> [A] whole range of people in and around the towns have made claims upon the state and/or their chief, often employing notions of a contract, transaction or reciprocal deal to demand guarantees of their rights in property or persons. In its most basic expression ... this was a bargain of protection from the threat of the same state from which the guarantee was obtained.[31]

In this dynamic, the distinction between *governance* and *government* is important. In southern Sudanese terms, government is often referred to as *aciek* ('manufactured' or 'artificial'), in the sense that it takes on the outer appearance of traditional leadership without being an inherited, communally based form of

[30] Cherry Leonardi, *Dealing with Government in South Sudan: Histories of Chiefship, Community and State* (Oxford: James Currey Press, 2015), 2.

[31] Leonardi, *Dealing with Government in South Sudan*, 3.

governance.[32] Traditional leaders were able to simultaneously embody this manufactured state role while retaining recognition as legitimate inheritors of authority according to their indigenous customs. A 'traditional leader' thus should be distinguished from a mere 'chief'—the former is empowered by the state to act with administrative authority. The governance system of Anglo-Egyptian period can be considered as an attempt by the colonial authorities to inject their own rule through the personhood of the chief, instrumentalizing the role of traditional leader as the vehicle for imposition of colonial power. From the perspective of the colonized communities, their rights and resources had to be negotiated via the traditional authority, who embodied both the legitimate kinship-based role of community leader and the power of the state.

As a result of the colonial instrumentalization of local customary roles, wealth and administrative authority were inextricably linked to the ethnic affiliation of the traditional leader. Access to resources was negotiated as between a community and the colonial power through the intermediary of the traditional authority, who maintained local legitimacy through kinship. This dynamic aligns with Volker Boege et al.'s research on other settings where traditional authorities 'adopt an ambiguous position with regard to the state, appropriate state functions and "state talk," but at the same time pursu[e] their own agenda under the guise of state authority and power.'[33]

Moreover, the presence of traditional authorities primarily in the urban areas across southern Sudan meant that the topography of power became concentrated in the same nodes that had formed during the slave and ivory trade, with the deeper hinterlands largely isolated from the political economy of southern Sudan. As Edward Thomas' research has shown, '[t]he spatial differences between moneyed towns and cashless hinterlands have played out in social differences', where ethnic groups affiliated with the urban centre benefitted from the largesse of the state.[34] Lacking a landed aristocracy in the rural areas, no European style feudalism developed, instead leaving ethnicity and community relations as a crucial ordering mechanism between centre and periphery, a dynamic that carried over into subsequent periods as well.

[32] Simon Harragin, 'Waiting for Pay-day: Anthropological Research on Local-level Governance Structures in South Sudan', *Save the Children Report*, 2007, available at http://southsudanhumanitarianproject.com/wp-content/uploads/sites/21/formidable/Harragin-2007-Waiting-for-pay-day-Anthropological-Research-on-Local-level-Governance-Structures-in-South-Sudan2-annotated.pdf

[33] Volker Boege et al., 'On Hybrid Political Orders and Fragile States: State formation in the context of fragility', *Berghof Research Center*, October 2008.

[34] Thomas, *A Slow Liberation*, 22.

Post-colonial Sudan: The gravitational pull of the centre

Governance in Sudan's post-independence period (1956–2011) was largely shaped by the two civil wars and the agreements that ended them. In simplified terms, it tracked the efforts of Khartoum to exercise some form of assimilationist rule over the peoples of southern Sudan, and the southerners' attempts to resist assimilation and establish greater autonomy. While the many experiments in different forms of rule during this period are the subject of significant academic inquiry,[35] I here focus on three key characteristics of the systems of governance that emerged over this period: (1) deepened reliance on ethnicity within southern Sudan as a result of Khartoum's divide-and-rule policy; (2) patterns of economic dependency on the centre by the peripheries in the South; and (3) the militarization of governance functions by the SPLA. Taken together, these characteristics form the basis for the ethno-military patronage network that became the dominant governance system at the time of South Sudan's independence.

At the close of Sudan's first civil war, the 1972 Addis Ababa Agreement granted southern Sudan regional autonomy, partially decentralizing executive and legislative powers to Juba, and for the first time giving southern Sudan formal political representation in Khartoum. This political influence of the southern bloc in Khartoum was a significant factor in the decision by Sudanese President Nimeiri to divide the South into three regions via a process widely known by its Bari translation, *kokora*.[36] The administrative division was welcomed by some of the southern leaders, who had been concerned that a Dinka-dominated southern government might exclude their interests from the political processes in Khartoum. And by offering three of the major ethnic groups administrative units in which they were a majority, *kokora* did assuage some of those concerns. But beneath the veneer of decentralization, it appeared Nimeiri had intentionally sown the seeds for deeper interethnic tensions in the South; groups finding themselves minorities in the new *kokora* districts began pressing the southern leadership for further subdivision around their own ethnic interests. *Kokora*, rather than bolstering southern influence in Khartoum, 'prevented the creation of a unified southern regional government that would have been more able to challenge Khartoum's agenda.'[37]

Kokora not only offers an example of how Khartoum worked to divide southerners along ethnic lines, but also an illustration of how patterns perpetuate themselves across epochs of South Sudan. More than thirty years later in 2013, some leaders from the Equatorian states in the South revived anti-Dinka sentiment

[35] E.g. Johnson, 'Federalism in the History of South Sudanese Political Thought', 103–123.

[36] Alex de Waal and Naomi Pendle, 'Decentralisation and the Logic of the Political Marketplace in South Sudan', in Luka Biong Deng Kuol and Sarah Logan, eds., *Struggle for South Sudan: Challenges of Security and State Formation* (London: I.B. Tauris, 2019), 172–194.

[37] de Waal and Pendle, 'Decentralisation and the Logic of the Political Marketplace in South Sudan', 176.

by referring to federalism in terms of *kokora*, a terminological slippage that appears to equate administrative authority with ethnicity.[38] Douglas Johnson has pointed to this as an example of 'ethnic federalism', which historically has been used to bolster central authority by aligning ethnic groups against each other in a struggle for the limited resources of the periphery.[39] Indeed in my 2018 interviews with South Sudanese Azande leaders in Yambio, the failure of the government to provide adequate development for their communities was listed as a principal cause of their taking up arms in the 2013 civil war. One of the most enduring patterns in South Sudan—and one that will reappear in the post-independence period at the core of this case study—is the blurring of the ethnic and the administrative, where relations of power between the centre and periphery are deployed in ethnic terms.

Khartoum's manipulation of southern Sudan via administrative boundaries in the three decades before the Comprehensive Peace Agreement (CPA) of 2005 was accompanied by a policy of keeping the South economically dependent upon the North, an example of Catherine Boone's concept of 'institutionalised power-sharing'.[40] Here, local elites were permitted significant governance roles across southern Sudan, but were held in perpetual economic dependence upon the North. In fact, from the 1880s until 2005, no southern administration was permitted to maintain any budgetary surplus at all, instead relying entirely on the North for fiscal (often erratic and incomplete) transfers.[41] This left the southern leadership with few incentives to generate revenue from taxation or expansion of the agricultural sector. For example, a 1981 study found that tax revenue only accounted for 15 per cent of total government revenue, compared with 82 per cent in neighbouring Kenya.[42] Edward Thomas refers to this relationship euphemistically as the 'government's autonomy from the productive efforts of its people', but it can also be thought of in relational terms as an exchange of nominal self-rule for economic dependency: Khartoum provided the façade of decentralization in the form of administrative boundaries, but in return withheld the economic capacity of the South to govern itself. A second decentralization initiative in 1994—expanding the number of states in the South—aptly demonstrated this dynamic, as a financial crisis at the time meant many of the newly created states received no resources whatsoever.[43]

Throughout most of the twentieth century, the most reliable way for southern Sudanese to attract resources from the centre was not through the budgetary

[38] Peter Kopling, 'Peaceful Coexistence: How the Equatorians Got It Right!', *South Sudan Nation*, available at: www.southsudannation.com/peaceful-coexistence-how-the-equatorians-got-it-right/.

[39] Johnson, 'Federalism in the History of South Sudanese Political Thought', 103–123.

[40] Boone, *Political Topographies*.

[41] Thomas, *A Slow Liberation*, 67.

[42] Terje Tvedt, 'The Collapse of the State in Southern Sudan after the Addis Ababa Agreement: A Study of Internal Causes and the Role of the NGOs', in Sharif Harir and Terje Tvedt, eds., *Short Cut to Decay: The Case of Sudan* (Uppsala: Nordiska Africkainstitut, 1994).

[43] De Waal and Pendle, *Struggle for South Sudan*, 177.

structures of decentralization, but rather by obtaining a governmental post, often on the basis of ethnicity. Analysis of nearly a century of budgets has indicated that up to 96 per cent of expenditures in southern Sudan went on government salaries and wages.[44] This created a highly dependent and ethnically stratified set of relationships shaping the administration of southern Sudan. Local government positions—distributed along traditional kinship lines—were the exclusive recipients of resources from the centre, creating what Edward Thomas has called the 'ethnic homogeneity of administrative units' given their strong tendencies to distribute resources within their own communities.[45] And when Khartoum experienced economic downturns, the government transmitted the costs first and foremost to the southern peripheries, increasing southern dependency on the North over time. For example, as late as 2003, the International Monetary Fund found that peripheral dependency on the centre was still increasing, even as the southern government had created ostensible governance capacities across the southern territory.[46] This heightened the tendency for southern communities to protect themselves with whatever resources they could garner.

The centre-periphery dynamic between Khartoum and southern Sudan was replicated within the South itself, as cities and towns grew into the loci of economic activity. Here, it is important to understand that many of the rural communities of southern Sudan have traditionally lived as cashless societies, utilizing a complex system of bridewealth, cattle, and barter as the major forms of economic exchange.[47] As towns grew into centres of power through the colonial and postcolonial periods, cashless rural societies were drawn towards urban areas where traditional authorities were able to resolve disputes, secure rights to resources, and participate in economic development. But rural communities also saw urban economies as a foreign imposition, a violent penetration of their moral and physical space. Cherry Leonardi's in-depth research into this dynamic demonstrates that rural societies understood a 'binary distinction between the values of an idealised moral economy of kinship and reciprocity, and the immoral, individualistic cultures of money and town.'[48] Particularly around land rights, but also across a wide range of governance powers that had been customarily addressed within the kinship networks of communities, rural populations found themselves in the uncomfortable position of needing traditional authorities as mediator between their own everyday reality and the realm of the state.[49] Communities were drawn to

[44] Thomas, *A Slow Liberation*, 93.

[45] Thomas, *A Slow Liberation*, 131.

[46] International Monetary Fund, 'Sudan: Selected Issues Paper', no 12/299, November 2012, available at https://www.imf.org/external/pubs/ft/scr/2012/cr12299.pdf

[47] Cherry Leonardi, 'Paying "Buckets of Blood" for the Land: Moral Debates over the Economy, War and State in Southern Sudan', *Journal of Modern African Studies* 49, No. 2 (2011).

[48] Leonardi, 'Paying "Buckets of Blood"', 216.

[49] For a comprehensive analysis of how centre-periphery dynamics played out in land disputes, see Nasseem Badiey, *The State of Post-conflict Reconstruction: Land, Urban Development and State-building*

urban centres for resources, but also saw themselves as morally and politically distinct from the towns. For example, when examining how rural communities related to urban centres and traditional authorities concerning land issues in southern Sudan, Naseem Badiey points to communities' 'continuing desire to preserve a *distance* from the state' and protect their moral identity as the corrupting influences of the centre.[50] This vacillation of rural communities between proximity to and distance from the state, centred around the fluid role of the traditional authority, is a pattern that will repeat over the next era of the South its civil war with the North.

Sudan at War: The militarization of governance through the second civil war

Sudan was in a state of civil war for the majority of the period between its independence in 1956 and the signing of the CPA in 2005, meaning that the centre-periphery dynamics within the country were contested on the battlefield and via the military chains of command. The role of the SPLM/SPLA[51] through the second civil war (1983–2005) played a determinative role in reshaping governance systems in the South in two important and related ways: (1) through the subordination of traditional authorities into the service of the SPLA itself; and (2) via the rise of ethnic factionalism, in which fomenting rebellions became the primary way in which southern communities could voice dissatisfaction with the southern leadership and negotiate greater resources and power.

Observers of modern day South Sudan often highlight the unity across the region in the lead-up to the 2011 referendum, pointing to the overwhelming vote in favour of secession as evidence that the SPLM had succeeded in bringing key southern constituencies within its 'big tent'.[52] Indeed, even in 1983 the SPLM was founded upon a common southern platform of frustration at underdevelopment and marginalization in the South and a progressive vision of economic and political autonomy from Khartoum (though certainly the movement had no goal of independent statehood at the time).[53] The SPLA achieved far more cohesive territorial control than its predecessor—the Ananyana rebellion—building greater unity across different constituencies through the war. However, this narrative of the SPLA's hegemony elides the long history of divisions within the SPLM/SPLA

in Juba Southern Sudan (Oxford: James Currey, 2014) ('land debates may mask concerns over the destabilizing processes unleashed by the expanding presence of the state').

[50] Badiey, *The State of Post-conflict Reconstruction*, 218 (emphasis added).

[51] Throughout, I make little distinction between SPLM and SPLA, reflecting the lack of distinction within the group between its political and military leadership. In fact, this blurring is crucial to the later analysis of how the SPLA became a central node in the governance system of southern Sudan.

[52] James Alic Garang, 'The Question of Big Government and Financial Viability: The Case of South Sudan', *Sudd Institute*, 1 February 2013.

[53] Johnson, *The Root Causes of Sudan's Civil Wars*, 64.

and southern communities; in fact, most of the civil war was fought on southern territory, among southern groups and proxies of the North.[54] Examining how the SPLM/SPLA worked to prevent its own disintegration through the governance system of southern Sudan, this section describes the construction of an ethno-military patronage network, where pre-existing centre-periphery relations were subordinated to the overriding cause of the rebellion.

From birth, the SPLA considered itself a movement aspiring to alter how Sudan was governed as a whole, not as a future government of a southern Sudanese state. In fact, prior to the CPA period in 2005, it had never set up the kind of shadow ministries or provisional government structures typical to an autonomous region, but instead had largely assumed the structures of the Anglo-Egyptian native administration.[55] Even the 1998 decision to set up the Civil Authority in New Sudan represented a largely pro forma administrative structure in the region, subordinated to SPLA commanders at the *payam* and *boma* ('sub-county' and 'village') levels.[56] Traditional chieftaincies continued to be recognized as the custodians of customary law within communities, and they were expected to perform state-like activities such as tax collection and infrastructural projects on behalf of the SPLA. However, customary authorities were subjected to the military exigencies of the movement in a variety of ways: SPLA officers often played a supervisory role over the chiefs, including the selection of chieftaincies; in rural areas SPLA commanders carved out fiefdoms where they overruled community leadership and extracted resources; and rural communities were forced to contribute to SPLA upkeep via taxes in kind, such as grains, livestock, and cattle.[57] A South Sudanese expert described this pseudo-governmental role of the SPLA as 'plunder, pillage, and destructive conquest' of its own people, but in less dramatic terms it meant traditional governance roles were embedded within and reliant upon the military structures of the SPLA.[58] John Garang's famous promise to 'take the towns to the people' was expressed as a form of mediation: towns were the sites where the rights and resources of the rural communities interfaced with the SPLA.[59]

The SPLA's governance role created a symbiotic relationship between the rebel group and the communities, mediated by traditional authorities.[60] On the one hand, the SPLA gained material resources—food, shelter, recruits, and different

[54] Johnson, *The Root Causes of Sudan's Civil Wars*, 91.

[55] Johnson, *The Root Causes of Sudan's Civil Wars*, 105.

[56] Zacharia Mampilly, *Rebel Rulers: Insurgent Governance and Civilian Life during Civil War* (Ithaca, NY: Cornell University Press, 2011), 130; Sukanya Podder, 'Mainstreaming the Non-state in Bottom-Up State-building: Linkages between Rebel Governance and Post-conflict Legitimacy', *Conflict, Security and Development* 14, No. 2 (2014): 277.

[57] Pinaud, 'South Sudan: Civil War', 192–211.

[58] Peter Adwok Nyaba, *Politics of Liberation in South Sudan: An Insider's View* (Kampala: Fountain Publishers, 1997), 51.

[59] Leonardi, 'Paying "Buckets of Blood"', 49.

[60] For an in-depth use of symbiotic relations in peacebuilding, see Charles T. Hunt, 'Beyond the Binaries: Towards a Relational Approach to Peacebuilding', *Global Change, Peace & Security* 29, No. 3 (2017): 209–227.

forms of rent—via their territorial control of many parts of southern Sudan. Operating through traditional authorities allowed the SPLA to maintain some degrees of legitimacy within communities; there were even instances where traditional authorities were given SPLA military ranks to ensure compliance and guarantee that SPLA presence was seen as part of the community governance structure.[61] The ethno-military aspect of the SPLA allowed it to provide to its communities as well: because the network was maintained along ethnic lines, the SPLA was seen as a protector of community interests, directing land, natural resources, and representation at the centre in favour of the community in which they were deployed. Again, traditional chiefs were a mediation point, articulating community needs and demands upwards while expressing the SPLA's power downwards. This symbiotic relationship operates as a strong pattern that became even more entrenched during and after the CPA period.

One outcome of the militarization of the governance system in southern Sudan was the lack of attention to economic development in the region (showing the opposite of Tilly's 'war makes states' argument in the South Sudan context). Roads, government offices, communications, and basic services, none of which was particularly well-delivered at any point in the South's history, fell into further disrepair. While some experts have blamed the SPLA for the erosion of basic infrastructure and ineffective governance during this period,[62] it is more accurate to think of the decline as the outcome of the war itself, the isolating tactics of Khartoum, and the repurposing of southern Sudan's resources for military objectives. 'The nucleus of the political system', Sukanya Podder writes, 'was confined to garrison towns ... while the rural areas served as the base for planning and launching war operations.'[63] As chieftaincy structures were incorporated into the SPLA's military chain of command in these garrison towns—and indeed as the SPLA took on a more direct role in appointing chieftaincy positions—local governance was redirected in support of the rebellion rather than providing for the communities of the region. Resource flows reflected this dynamic as communities received very little in exchange for the food, taxes, and resources provided to the SPLA.[64]

The SPLA's failure to deliver basic services to the territories under its control created the conditions for one of the largest international relief efforts in history, mostly directed at rebel-held areas in southern Sudan. From 1989 to 1999, nearly $2 billion of relief aid under Operation Lifeline Sudan was directed into non-governmental organizations (NGOs) and their networks across the South, burgeoning into some of the largest agricultural, educational, and employment

[61] Podder, 'Mainstreaming the Non-state', 213–243.
[62] Tvedt, 'The Collapse of the State in Southern Sudan'.
[63] Podder, 'Mainstreaming the Non-state', 213–243.
[64] Matthew Le Riche, 'Conflict Governance: The SPLA, Factionalism, and Peacemaking', in Steven E. Roach, eds., *The Challenges of Governance in South Sudan* (London: Routledge 2018), 30.

programmes in the world.[65] There is strong evidence that many of the local NGOs' aid delivery was repurposed to support the SPLA's war effort in the early years, and the fact that the SPLA was not expected or required to provide basic services certainly meant that it could focus on the rebellion over its responsibilities to communities.[66] The establishment of the South Sudan Relief Agency—and later the Relief Association of Southern Sudan—was widely seen by donors as an SPLA-driven instrumentalization of the aid effort, given that both organizations had their activities and access controlled by the SPLA. Similarly, an SPLA decision in 2000 to require that NGOs seek SPLA permission before interacting with local communities—paying administrative fees to the SPLA at the same time—meant that the massive aid effort was largely channelled through the SPLA's lines of authority.[67] At the same time, large-scale 'gap-filling' by NGOs in crucial governance areas meant that the weak technical and administrative capacities of the southern Sudanese institutions never improved, creating a deep culture of dependency on external aid that continues to this day.

In the context of massive international aid, the dual role of the chiefs—as both vehicles for SPLA authority and representatives of their respective communities—was more visible than ever. Naomi Pendle and Chirrilo Madut Anei's in-depth case studies of the interpositional character of chiefs are particularly illuminating here: one chief managed relations between local traders and the SPLA, while also raising taxes for the SPLA and securing humanitarian relief for his community directly from international agencies.[68] Chiefs were, in Simon Harragin's anthropological study of southern Sudan, 'the means by which the most remote rural locations were taxed and governed' by the SPLA; their identity was constituted within the relationship between the SPLA and the communities, and increasingly also as a guarantor for humanitarian aid from NGOs.[69] By pouring massive humanitarian resources into the southern Sudanese system, international donors contributed to a centre-periphery relationship where resource flows and community protections were mediated through traditional leaders, often to the benefit of the SPLA's war effort. Moreover, the SPLA's well-guarded ability to 'bring the UN in' and save lives in rural communities created a state-like role for the SPLA, though largely absent formal institutional capacities and resources.

[65] Øystein Rolandsen, 'Guerrilla Government: Political Changes in Southern Sudan during the 1990s', Nordic Africa Institute, Uppsala (2005), 128.

[66] Mark Duffield, 'Post-modern Conflict: Warlords, Post-Adjustment States and Private Protection' *Civil Wars* 1 (1998): 5–102.

[67] Volker Riehl, *Who is Ruling in South Sudan?: The Role of NGOs in Rebuilding the Socio-Political Order* (Uppsala: Nordic Africa Institute, 2001).

[68] Naomi Pendle and Chirrilo Madut Anei, 'Wartime Trade and the Reshaping of Power in South Sudan', South Sudan Customary Authorities Project, Rift Valley Institute, 2018, available at https://riftvalley.net/download/file/fid/4966

[69] Harragin, 'Waiting for Pay-day'.

The SPLA's failure to govern effectively or fairly is one of the most cited reasons for the series of splits and infighting that characterized southern dynamics in the civil war from the mid-1980s through the 1990s. Anne Walraet's research has shown that a combination of predatory practices of the SPLA—including its forcible takeover of lucrative agricultural resources, forced taxation, and looting—deepened distrust and fomented rebellions within the South.[70] Stripped of the means to govern effectively other than by the authority vested in them by the SPLA, local governors and chiefs were thus caught between their roles as representatives of the communities and as recipients of patronage from above. Cherry Leonardi describes this role in bargaining terms, where people in and around towns in southern Sudan entered into deals with chiefs to secure guarantees around land rights and also protection from predation by the state itself.[71]

Here, it is important to highlight the nexus between the economic and the security aspects of governance in southern Sudan, as it demonstrates early patterns that later became the country's deeply entrenched patronage network. As noted above, the SPLA largely assumed the Anglo-Egyptian structures of customary authorities, but placed chieftaincies within the SPLA's military chain of command. This meant that traditional mechanisms of governance were repurposed for war aims, allowing for high degrees of predation and abuse by the SPLA, especially in rural areas. But it also led the SPLM/SPLA leadership to use the military network across southern Sudan to maintain coherence in the face of splits, rebellions, and mutinies by communities during the war with Khartoum. This coherence was achieved, in blunt terms, by purchasing loyalty. Faced with divisions and rebellions by southern communities, SPLM leader John Garang tended to offer integration into the SPLA and/or leadership positions within the movement, where a secure pay cheque hedged against future disloyalty. Given that Khartoum's principal method for weakening the rebellion was to foment discord within the SPLA, preventing the collapse of the group was often Garang's overriding strategic objective. As Matthew le Riche notes, 'managing the political economy of factional dynamics in the region became the main vehicle through which Garang and many of his commanders conducted the war.'[72] The military chain of command, laid over the traditional authority structures from the colonial era, thus became the conduit to maintain the communities of southern Sudan in a unified fight against the North.

This meant that communities wishing to express dissatisfaction with the SPLM/SPLA found that the most expedient act was armed rebellion. Groups capable of threatening the SPLM/SPLA leadership with violence could establish a bargaining position, extract concessions for ending their uprising, and create new economic opportunities for their communities. Those without the ability to

[70] Anne Walraet, 'Governance, Violence and the Struggle for Economic Regulation in South Sudan: The Case of Budi County (Eastern Equatoria)', *Afrika Focus*, 2008.

[71] Leonardi, *Dealing with Government in South Sudan*, 8.

[72] Le Riche, 'Conflict Governance', 22–26.

confront the military strength of the SPLA were either quashed or ignored. Major insurrections—such as the uprising of the Nasir faction in 1991—not only exhibited the willingness of Khartoum to instrumentalize ethnic divisions within the South, but also presaged a sort of continual disintegration and reintegration of the SPLM/SPLA over decades, including through the CPA period. Dozens of insurrections appeared across southern Sudan, with some commanders defecting so frequently it became a joke in Juba trying to count the number of rebellions by a single leader.[73] As John Garang himself wrote, 'the marginal cost of rebellion in the South became very small, zero to negative; that is, in the South it pays to rebel.'[74]

However, as Matthew le Riche's authoritative study on factionalism in southern Sudan has uncovered, the continual process of fracturing and reconstituting the SPLA was not a purely military venture. Le Riche found that the levels of violence did not determine whether a rebellion would be rewarded with an integration deal; instead, it was the combination of some military threat along with a high degree of political authority that created bargaining position.[75] This points to one of the dominant patterns that emerged through the SPLA's role in governance: southern communities expressed their political needs militarily. Describing a dynamic that spans the periods before and after the CPA, le Riche writes: 'Governance in South Sudan is a continual process of negotiating, brokering and mediating between a wide range of leaders and between communities, many of whom have well-armed followers that either are, or could be, a threat to the state, at least in a localized area.'[76] Here, governance is expressed, not merely as a relationship in which legitimacy is exchanged for protections and services, but as a mode of survival. In order to resist the attempts of Khartoum to fracture the SPLM/SPLA along ethnic lines, its leadership continually brokered deals with communities via military integration. With its leaders integrated into the SPLA, a community could be assured of basic protections (though also subjected to the predations of the troops) while disenfranchised communities would rebel in the hopes of gaining more resources via the next integration deal.

The outcome of the continual disintegration and reintegration of the SPLA was the growth of a patronage network expressed through the military chain of command, layered over existing traditional governance structures. Here, the mode of negotiation between communities and the SPLA was insurrection, where bargains were struck in accordance with the political and military threat posed by a local leader. Largesse was dispensed militarily, in the form of integration deals

[73] In 2010, for instance, the commander Peter Gatdet had defected more than a dozen times, each time receiving a reintegration deal back into the SPLA.

[74] Atta El-Batahani, Ibrahim A. Elbadawi, and Ali Abdel Gadir Ali, 'Sudan's Civil War. Why Has It Prevailed for so Long?', in Nicholas Sambanis and Paul Collier, eds., *Understanding Civil War: Evidence and Analysis*, vol. 1: *Africa* (Washington, DC: World Bank 2005), 193.

[75] Le Riche, 'Conflict Governance', 22–26.

[76] Le Riche, 'Conflict Governance', 38.

that included the right to SPLA command positions over specific territories. As Sukanya Podder notes, a form of 'wartime governance' arose during this period, privileging and legitimizing the rebel SPLA in ways that allowed it to permeate the social and economic spheres of southern Sudan, becoming what Clémence Pinaud has called a 'military aristocracy' in the South.[77] This blurring of the military and economic generated a consolidation of elite power within the SPLA that, as I will explore in the next section, strengthened the centre-periphery symbiotic relationships that had begun in the colonial and post-colonial periods.

Peace floods the system

The 2005 CPA ended the twenty-year civil war in Sudan and brought to a close a fifty-year period where war had dominated the governance system of southern Sudan. In a single day, the SPLM transformed from a rebel group into an internationally recognized regional government. The CPA offered south Suda[78] a high degree of legislative and judicial autonomy from Khartoum, representation at the vice-presidential level in the Sudanese national Government, and most importantly, the rights to 50 per cent of the oil revenues generated from the southern territories.[79] The peace agreement initiated a five-year period in which Khartoum and Juba could build on this new relationship, the SPLM could bolster its capacities for self-governance, and the underlying dissatisfaction at the economic and political marginalization of the South could begin to be addressed. At the end of this period, the CPA required a referendum, where the southern population could decide whether sufficient steps had been taken to 'make unity attractive', voting to remain part of a united Sudan or become an independent state. Despite the transformational aspiration of the CPA, I here argue that the centre-periphery patterns of governance from the post-colonial period if anything grew stronger during the CPA period, marking the political topography of south Sudan even more noticeably with the features of ethno-military patronage. These patterns acted as strong attractors in the southern Sudanese system, directing energy and resources towards networks of authority that ran largely along ethnic lines and via the SPLA.

This section explores how the huge outpourings of cash introduced into south Sudan during the CPA period flowed like water through the existing governance landscape, deepening the channels of power along ethno-military lines. The result was a southern government synonymous (literally) with the rebel group that preceded it, an SPLM/SPLA that deployed its new administrative authority in service of a sprawling patronage system; here, territorial boundaries

[77] Podder, 'Mainstreaming the Non-state', 213–243; Pinaud, 'South Sudan: Civil War'.
[78] See note 20 on usage of 'southern Sudan' and 'South Sudan'.
[79] Comprehensive Peace Agreement, Wealth Sharing Agreement, articles 4.5 and 4.3, available at http://www.usip.org/ publications/peace-agreements-sudan

and government posts were distributed to further consolidate power rather than offering meaningful development to the people of the South.

In the year following the 2005 CPA, Juba's annual budget jumped a hundredfold, from $14.5 million to $1.3 billion, based on the more than $100 million per month in oil revenues that were shared between North and South.[80] For the first time, the governing SPLM controlled this budget, and duly spent it overwhelmingly on maintaining its army.[81] Post-war spending on security-sector wages outstripped even Afghanistan's, with a near total dependency on oil revenues to maintain salary rates.[82] Of this, military wages constituted nearly 70 per cent of government salaries, with soldiers receiving roughly $150 per month (far more than neighbouring countries).[83] These almost euphoric outlays were in part driven by dramatic increases in oil production from the 1990s through the early 2000s, and a (misplaced) sense among the southern leadership that revenues would continue to grow.[84] In 2006, SPLM eagerness to pour resources into wages meant that it overspent its annual revenues by more than $200 million.[85] This fiscal policy, which appeared to violate nearly every accepted norm for dealing with resource windfalls,[86] demonstrated the SPLM's overriding prioritization of its own military strength, and its use of military structures to maintain loyalty across south Sudan. In simplified terms, the SPLM as a movement was not distinguished from the SPLA as its army when it came to administering south Sudan.

As the SPLM garnered greater authority over its own resources, decentralization within the South became a crucial question. Both the 2005 interim constitution and the 2009 Local Act established formal relationships between central, state, and local government within the South, carving out local judicial and administrative authorities for chiefs as empowered state actors.[87] But the SPLM/SPLA tended to override these spheres of authority, instead maintaining a highly centralized system of government, controlling the peripheries via the army rather

[80] Jill Shankleman, 'Oil and State-building in South Sudan', United States Institute of Peace, July 2011.

[81] This chapter intentionally makes little distinction between the SPLM and its army (SPLA), reflecting the blurred lines between the two in South Sudan. But for the purposes of this section, it is worth noting the administrative distinction, to illustrate that the SPLM chose to channel its resources to its army rather than to administrative structures on the civilian side.

[82] Luka Biong Deng Kuol, 'The Federalism-Decentralisation-Peace Nexus in South Sudan', in Luka Biong Deng Kuol and Sarah Logan, eds., *The Struggle for South Sudan: Challenges of Security and State Formation* (London: I.B. Tauris, 2019), 228.

[83] Kuol, 'The Federalism-Decentralisation-Peace Nexus in South Sudan', 231.

[84] Shankleman, 'Oil and State-building in South Sudan'; Luke Patey, 'Crude Days Ahead? Oil and the Resource Curse in Sudan', *African Affairs* 109, No. 437 (2010): 617–636.

[85] Overseas Development Institute Briefing Paper, 'Planning and Budgeting in South Sudan: Starting from Scratch', October 2010, available at https://www.odi.org/sites/odi.org.uk/files/odi-assets/publications-opinion-files/6093.pdf

[86] Frederick van der Ploeg and Anthony J. Venables, 'Harnessing Windfall Revenues: Optimal Policies for Resource Rich Developing Economies', Oxcarre Research Paper No. 9, Oxford University, 2008, revised July 2010, available at http://www.oxcarre.ox.ac.uk/images/stories/papers/ResearchPapers/oxcarrerp2008.09.pdf

[87] Leonardi, *Dealing with Government in South Sudan.*

than meaningful economic empowerment of local authorities.[88] Marieke Schomerus' study of federalism in southSudan highlights that centralized governance, combined with a focus on the security services, 'resulted in situations in which decentralized authorities, even though officially in charge of security within their territory, [were] overruled by agencies that [were] under a different chain of command.'[89] Clémence Pinaud argues that 'a form of "solidaristic graft" emerged following the signing of the CPA, in which the new military elite extended post-war benefits to its kin.'[90] Decentralization was not a bureaucratic process achieved through institutions, but rather a political relationship between Juba and the peripheries, mediated through the SPLA's ethnically based control of much of south Sudan.

The distribution of largesse via ethno-military networks rather than institutionalized administrative authorities created a heavily dependent periphery within the governance system of south Sudan. Stripped of any capacity to meaningfully collect taxes, and without funding from the centre, local institutions beyond the major towns relied almost entirely on Juba for their existence and communicated those needs through the SPLA. According to the World Bank, most southern counties could cover less than 20 per cent of their budgets from their own tax revenues, while the SPLA rapidly encroached upon local roles of administrating land and cattle markets.[91] The result was a reinforcing (positive) feedback loop within the governance system of south Sudan: over time the states' ability to generate revenue declined, making them less able to develop institutional infrastructure or maintain staff, leading to a further decline in their revenue generation.[92] Consequently, the formal state structures were only somewhat involved in the distribution of power and resources across south Sudan, more like rocks in a stream dampened by the flows around them but unable to influence the current.

Governance via ethno-military networks was the basis for what Alex de Waal has called 'the hegemonic power of the SPLM-SPLA patronage-coercion nexus'.[93] At its heart, this network relied on a pattern of exchange built over decades: loyalty to the SPLM in return for the right to draw benefits from a position within the SPLA. When the oil boom began in the early 2000s, these benefits were easily

[88] Adam Branch and Zachariah Cherian Mampilly, 'Winning the War, but Losing the Peace? The Dilemma of SPLM/A Civil Administration and the Tasks Ahead', *Journal of Modern African Studies* 43, No. 1 (2005): 1–20.

[89] Marieke Schomerus and Lovise Aalen, 'Considering the State: Perspectives on South Sudan's Subdivision and Federalism Debate', Overseas Development Institute, August 2016.

[90] Pinaud, 'South Sudan: Civil War', 192–211. The term 'solidaristic graft' was taken from Ernest Harsch, 'Accumulators and Democrats: Challenging State Corruption in Africa', *The Journal of Modern African Studies* 31 (1993): 31–48.

[91] World Bank, 'Southern Sudan: Enabling the State: Estimating the Non-Oil Revenue Potential of State and Local Governments', Washington, DC, 2010; Thomas, *A Slow Liberation*, 228.

[92] International Monetary Fund, 'Sudan: Selected Issues Paper'.

[93] Alex de Waal, 'When Kleptocracy becomes Insolvent: Brute Causes of the Civil War in South Sudan', *African Affairs* 113, No. 452 (2014): 349.

expressed in cash terms; political accommodation within the 'big tent' of the SPLM was a rambunctious but relatively predictable affair where the many rebellions, defections, and disagreements were quieted by pay-outs. However, the system did not merely run on cash: ethnicity was a crucial currency that also flowed through it, lubricating relations when money was short. Ethnicity was how the patronage network extended from the urban centres to the largely cashless hinterlands, ensuring that those beyond the reach of pay-outs were nonetheless incorporated into the system.[94] 'Tribalizing' issues was a cheap modality to ensure loyalty, as evidenced by the widespread practice of SPLA soldiers marrying within the families of their chain of command.[95] When SPLA General Paulino Matiep died, for example, his forty-seven wives and 102 children were not just a sign of his status and wealth within south Sudan, but also a network of soldiers and loyalists with a clear function in the southern governance system.[96]

In the background, the governing SPLM faced a dilemma: In concentrating on political accommodation and maintenance of the ethno-military network as the key mechanism for stability across the South, southern resources were never channelled into functioning administrative institutions.[97] Instead, the SPLM focused on cash disbursements within their personal and communal networks: Salaries for the state security services constituted more than 40 per cent of Juba's budget and in places like Upper Nile State often approached 80 per cent, while funding for formal administrative structures in those locations hovered close to zero.[98] In order to get to the 2011 referendum with the SPLM in one piece and prove that the South could achieve statehood, Garang's successor, Salva Kiir, paradoxically was compelled to deprive state institutions of any chance of success. Indeed, part of the SPLM's strategy from 2005 onwards appeared to be to ensure that unity with the North was *not* made attractive, which meant limiting development in the short-term in the hopes that a deeply disaffected southern population would continue to blame the North and vote for independence.[99]

The result was the accelerated decline during the CPA period of much of south Sudan's already anaemic formal administration, even as international partners' rhetoric grew louder in favour of building the SPLM's governance capacity. In 2007, two years after the CPA period began, no resources had been set aside by the SPLM to pay salaries for key posts at the county level, while appointed state

[94] Pendle and Anei, 'Wartime Trade and the Reshaping of Power in South Sudan' (noting that the patronage network grew weaker as it extended beyond urban centres).

[95] Pinaud, 'South Sudan: Civil War', 192–211.

[96] *Sudan Tribune*, 'Paulino Matip Nhial Nyaak, General', August 2012, available at http://www.sudantribune.com/spip.php?mot1948

[97] Wolfram Lacher, 'South Sudan: International State-Building and Its Limits', *German Institute for International and Security Affairs*, available at, https://www.swp-berlin.org/fileadmin/contents/products/research_papers/2012_RP04_lac.pdf

[98] Lacher, 'South Sudan'.

[99] Le Riche, 'Conflict Governance', 42.

and county officials spent the bulk of their time chasing their own salaries.[100] Fifteen government institutions representing 80 per cent of the government's payroll at the time could present no records of their staff.[101] By the end of the interim period in 2011, half of the statutory positions within ministries of south Sudan still had not been filled, while the region ranked near or at the bottom of every governance indicator worldwide.[102] Oil revenues instead serviced what Morris Szeftal has termed the 'prebendal state', where state officials used their position enrich themselves and their communities.[103] In this sense, the SPLA's ethno-military dominance of the governance system created positive feedback loops around elite control of resources as they were diverted into elite coffers, strengthening the patterns of peripheral dependency on the centre. More resources perversely meant even less potential to build stable institutions.

This dynamic has been described—with reason—as the kind of corruption typical of resource-rich post-colonial states in Africa.[104] Transparency International's description of south Sudan captures this view: 'Corruption permeates all sectors of the economy and all levels of the state apparatus and manifests itself through various forms, including grand corruption and clientelistic networks along tribal lines.'[105] This characterization of the systemic nature of corruption is borne out statistically: 67 per cent of south Sudanese surveyed believed that corruption had increased during the 2005–11 period; roughly the same percentage reported having paid bribes during that period; and at the end of the interim period, President Kiir accused seventy-five of his own ministers of embezzling more than $4 billion out of the country.[106] Corruption also exposed the extent to which formal administrative structures were subordinated to the SPLM/SPLA chain of command; in the April 2010 elections, for example, the SPLM imposed its chosen candidate, despite a clear win by an independent politician.[107] 'Corruption is how the government works, it is why the government needs to control all the key positions, without corruption the system breaks down', one South Sudanese expert explained to me in Juba.[108]

[100] Harragin, 'Waiting for Pay-day'.
[101] Johnson, *South Sudan: The Untold Story*, 30.
[102] Johnson, *South Sudan: The Untold Story*, 30; Magali Mores, 'Overview of Corruption and Anti-corruption in South Sudan', Transparency International, 4 March 2013.
[103] Morris Szeftel, 'Between Governance and Underdevelopment: Accumulation and Africa's "Catastrophic Corruption"', *Review of African Political Economy* 27, No. 84 (2000): 302. See also Morris Szeftel, 'Political Graft and the Spoils System in Zambia—the State as a Resource in Itself', *Review of African Political Economy* 9, No. 24 (1982): 4–21.
[104] Jean-Francois Bayart, Stephen Ellis, and Beatrice Hibou, *Criminalization of the State in Africa*, 2nd edition (Bloomington, IN: Indiana University Press, 2009), 39.
[105] Mores, 'Overview of Corruption and Anti-corruption in South Sudan'.
[106] Transparency International, Global Corruption Barometer, 2011, available at, https://www.transparency.org/gcb201011; David Smith, 'South Sudan President Accuses Officials of Stealing $4 bn of Public Money', *The Guardian*, 5 June 2012.
[107] Human Rights Watch, 'Democracy on Hold: Human Rights Violations in the April 2010 Sudan Elections', 30 June 2010.
[108] Interview with head of South Sudanese NGO, Juba, 13 December 2018.

In the face of this clear evidence of widespread corruption and misuse of funds, south Sudan's major donors nonetheless dramatically increased their own funding of the SPLM during the CPA period. Immediately after the signing of the CPA in 2005, donors pledged $4.5 billion for a two-year period, followed by a second pledge of the same amount in 2008.[109] From 2005 to 2007, $4.1 billion in overseas development assistance was reported, with countries like the US providing hundreds of millions for capacitybuilding of the SPLA.[110] The number of international NGOs increased by 300 per cent, from forty-seven in 2005 to 155 in 2010.[111] According to some estimates, the UN and NGOs provided 80 per cent of South Sudan's basic services during this period, including water, healthcare, sanitation, and education.[112] Major disarmament, demobilization, and reintegration (DDR) programming by the UN Mission in Sudan (UNMIS) funnelled significant resources into the SPLA in the hopes of transitioning away from the inflated troop numbers built over the twenty-year civil war; much of this was redirected by the SPLA into its patronage network.[113] UNMIS' other support to the regional government in the South—in particular its support to justice institutions—failed to curb these excesses, as Baker and Sheye point out in their criticism of the UN's approach to rule of law in the CPA period.[114]

Massive financial outlays to southSudan in this period were designed to bolster nascent institutions, a precursor to the statebuilding that followed independence. Capacitybuilding support relied upon the assumption that, as formal administrative capacities increased, they would act as a curb on the kind of pervasive corruption that characterized the interim period, empowering licit structures of power that would eventually compete with illicit ones for a monopoly of governance in southSudan. As this section has demonstrated, however, the rapid growth of resources participated in a feedback loop, reifying and strengthening the centre-periphery patterns that had grown out of the civil war, and bolstering an ethno-military elite that related to rural communities via a combination of financial dependency and ethnic affiliations. These dynamics set the stage for the further increase of resources into the newly independent country, and the UN's attempts to channel support into viable state institutions. Failing to take into

[109] World Bank, 'Report to the Southern Sudan Multi-Donor Trust Fund', Second Quarter Report, 1 April–30 June 2010; Jort Hammer and Nick Grinstead, 'When Peace Is the Exception: Shifting the Donor Narrative in South Sudan', Clingendael Policy Brief, June 2015.

[110] 'Resource Flows to Sudan: Aid to South Sudan', Global Humanitarian Assistance Report, July 2011, available at http://devinit.org/wp-content/uploads/2011/07/gha-Sudan-aid-factsheet-2011-South-Sudan-focus.pdf

[111] South Sudan NGO Forum, available at http://southsudanngoforum.org/ngos-in-southern-sudan

[112] Podder, 'Mainstreaming the Non-state', 232.

[113] Small Arms Survey, 'Failures and Opportunities, Rethinking DDR in South Sudan', Issue Brief, Geneva, 2011; Jairo Munive, 'Invisible Labour: The Political Economy of Reintegration in South Sudan', *Journal of Intervention and Statebuilding* 8, No. 4 (2014): 224–356.

[114] Bruce Baker and Eric Scheye, 'Access to Justice in a Post-Conflict State: Donor-Supported Multidimensional Peacekeeping in Southern Sudan', *International Peacekeeping* 16, No. 2 (2009): 171–185.

account the existing governance system, UN programming assumed the need to build governance 'from scratch', considering existing channels of power as distractions and deviations, rather than the system into which their programming would soon become absorbed.[115]

I probably should have seen this coming more clearly. In 2010, on an overcast day in Malakal, I sat with a national staff member of UNMISS, a tall, lanky man with a narrow head and long elegant hands that wrapped around his third Coke bottle of the afternoon. We had been sitting in the market area of town, talking about the politics of Upper Nile State while waiting for a delayed meeting. I kept coming back to what Malakal might be like after independence: what would be different, how would the town change once South Sudan became a country?

'You see all these people in the market', Charles said, accepting another Coke from the ice bucket.

> They are Nuer, Dinka, Shilluk, all together here in the market. Some of us have spent hundreds of years competing with each other over land, cattle, the river. That all seemed to change when the [civil] war broke out and the SPLM was born. Then we all became SPLA, fighting the north, feeding our rebels. Sometimes I think this market could only be like this because of the SPLA. We can only all come together because we had a common enemy. But we are still Shilluk, Nuer and Dinka, we still have our allegiances. So now, when you ask me what will happen after independence, when the SPLA is supposed to be dissolved, when we are supposed to create something called a 'nation' with things like an army and police for everyone. Well, I think it will be very difficult to change what we have all grown used to. What we have now is the way we feed ourselves. Who will volunteer to stop being fed?

The answer, we found out only a few years later, was no one. The system that had evolved around the creation and sustainment of the rebel SPLA movement had become too deeply entrenched to be transformed by a UN statebuilding mission. The ways the South Sudanese people had developed to feed and protect themselves were strongly resistant to the kind of institutional changes the international community had in mind.

[115] Johnson, *South Sudan: The Untold Story*, 98; Overseas Development Institute Briefing Paper, 'Planning and Budgeting in South Sudan'.

4
Myopia and mirages: The unmaking of UNMISS

In January 2010, I was based in Juba, co-authoring the United Nations (UN)'s 'Conflict Assessment of South Sudan', an in-country evaluation of the political and security trajectory of the country entering the final year of the Comprehensive Peace Agreement (CPA) that would later be used as a planning basis for UN Mission in South Sudan (UNMISS).[1] Our conclusions about the challenges facing the country as it prepared for independence were telling:

> Decades of neglect and a 20-year civil war mean that little if any state infrastructure exists, and as of 2009 the GoSS [government of South Sudan] administrative and rule of law structures barely permeate beyond Juba and the State capitals. The failure of the central state to extend into the periphery in Southern Sudan has been a direct cause of violence, especially in remote areas in Jonglei State that have received little or no protection or services from the state or central government.[2]

The UN's (and my) focus on the absence of viable state institutions in the peripheries of south Sudan was typical of assessments of the region around the time of independence, as was the link between weak state capacity and endemic violence. The World Bank, alongside the so-called 'Troika' of the United States (US), the United Kingdom (UK), and Norway, all agreed that critical shortfalls in state institutional capacity were the foremost challenge to the new country.[3]

In the eyes of Western donors and the Security Council, South Sudan was 'in start-up phase',[4] not equipped with the basic capacities to effectively govern itself and thus in need of a transformational level of statebuilding support.[5] This

[1] During the 2009–11 period, I served as a Political Affairs Officer on the Sudan Integrated Operational Team in the UN Department of Peacekeeping Operations. I was the co-author of the Conflict Assessment used as the basis for planning UNMISS.

[2] Fabrizio Hochschild and Adam Day, 'Southern Sudan Assessment', UN Department of Peacekeeping Operations, January 2010 (on file with author).

[3] Greg Larson, Peter Biar Ajak, and Lant Pritchett, 'South Sudan's Capability Trap: Building a State with Disruptive Innovation', Harvard Kennedy School, 2013.

[4] United Nations, 'Report of the United Nations Secretary-General on South Sudan', S/2011/678 (2011).

[5] Diana Felix da Costa and Cedric de Coning, 'United Nations Mission in the Republic of South Sudan (UNMISS)', in Joachin Koops et al., eds., *The Oxford Handbook of United Nations Peacekeeping Operations* (Oxford: Oxford University Press, 2015), 831–840.

States of Disorder, Ecosystems of Governance. Adam Day, Oxford University Press.
© Adam Day (2022). DOI: 10.1093/oso/9780192863898.003.0005

view aligns with Marieke Schomerus' observation, '[w]hen South Sudan became independent in 2011, there had been no conclusive preparation for the system of governance the country might adopt.'[6] Paradoxically, the perceived absence of governance required *rebuilding* a state that never was, employing the Western orthodoxy of post-conflict *re*construction in a setting experiencing statehood for the first time.[7]

However, by focusing on what South Sudan lacked at the moment of independence, those who designed the UN's statebuilding interventions (myself included) neglected the presence of a firmly entrenched ethno-military system of governance with roots stretching back to the pre-colonial period. This very real system of governance in South Sudan had already shown itself extraordinarily adept at co-opting large resource flows into its own networks; resources fed strong feedback loops that tended to strengthen centre-periphery patterns of dependence over the CPA period. At the same time, key members of the South Sudanese elite had benefited from decades of speaking the language of responsible institutional governance to international donors, contributing to the perception of a common and achievable trajectory towards traditional statebuilding.

Examining the core assumptions of the UN and its partners around the founding of UNMISS, this chapter argues that the enormous gaps between rhetoric and reality in South Sudan set the stage for UNMISS' failure. Across Security Council mandates, UN strategic planning, and views of the UN leadership at the time, South Sudan was viewed via a generic template of statebuilding common to the orthodox failed states discourse. Here, the UN's approach was based upon a normatively driven assumption that a gradual improvement in the governance capacities of the state institutions would lead to a corresponding reduction in the forms of corruption, patronage, and militarized factionalism that were seen as deviations from the kind of state South Sudan should become. Seen against the mapping of governance from the previous chapter, however, this vision of the state was a mirage, obscuring the actual governance landscape beneath.

Rather than think of UNMISS as an intervention from outside, I argue that UNMISS' statebuilding work from its inception was part of the South Sudanese system, subject to the patterns within it. By examining the related projects of institutional capacity building and security sector reform (SSR), I offer evidence that UNMISS' statebuilding efforts were co-opted into the ethno-military network of relations that resulted from decades of war, predation, and foreign control. The result was a clear failure by UNMISS to help build viable state institutions as intended; if anything the intervention deepened pre-existing patterns of governance

[6] Marieke Schomerus and Lovise Aalen, 'Considering the State: Perspectives on South Sudan's Subdivision and Federalism Debate', Overseas Development Institute, August 2016.

[7] Larson, Ajak, and Pritchett, 'South Sudan's Capability Trap'.

that kept state institutions from taking hold. In contrast to the prevailing Western view of statebuilding in South Sudan, a different vision emerges from this chapter, one where the UN's efforts to reinforce the state were not only extremely unlikely to achieve their objectives regardless of the amount of resources, but where UNMISS' role in South Sudan's governance system appears to have contributed to the 2013 civil war itself.

UNMISS' statebuilding logic

At the highest level, UNMISS was designed to support a transformation of South Sudan into a viable state, 'strengthening the capacity of the Government of the Republic of South Sudan to govern effectively and democratically.'[8] This would be achieved by large-scale reform—especially within the security sector—and massive capacity building.[9] A key objective of major donors to South Sudan therefore was to fill the government's 'capacity gap' via one of the most ambitious projects in history.[10] Here, capacity building was roughly synonymous with statebuilding, defined by the World Bank as 'a range of objectives from the broadest one of state-building to the specific training of civil servants.'[11] And the capacitybuilding needs were enormous: US Agency for International Development (USAID) recommended that the number of so-called 'capacity builders'—experts who would directly advise the government and replace lack of experience in the short-term—be 'significantly bolstered' around independence, subsequently spending more than $23 million on 'good governance' in 2011 alone.[12] By independence, South Sudan was receiving development assistance from thirteen bilateral and eight multilateral sources, totalling more than $1.4 billion per year.[13] Hundreds of South Sudanse government officials received training in anti-corruption; thousands of civil servants received fiscal and management skills training; dozens of institutions were refurbished in the hopes that South Sudan would begin to function more like a state.[14]

[8] United Nations Security Council resolution on the situation in South Sudan, S/RES/1996 (2011), para. 3.

[9] Office of the Secretary-General, 'Special Report of the Secretary-General on the Sudan', S/2011/314, United Nations Security Council, UNMIS (17 May 2011), para. 41(e).

[10] Larson, Ajak, and Pritchett, 'South Sudan's Capability Trap'.

[11] World Bank Report, 'South Sudan Governance Analysis (P156685): Building Sustainable Public Sector Capacity in a Challenging Context', January 2017 available at http://documents.worldbank.org/curated/en/439881495817910529/pdf/South-Sudan-Capacity-Building-ASA-P156685.pdf

[12] Management Systems International (MSI). 'Government of Southern Sudan: Functional Capacity Prioritization Study'. USAID, 3 December 2009.

[13] Larson, Ajak, and Pritchett, 'South Sudan's Capability Trap'; Fiona Davies, Gregory Smith, and Tim Williamson, 'Coordinating Post-conflict Aid in Southern Sudan', Overseas Development Institute, September 2011.

[14] Larson, Ajak, and Pritchett, 'South Sudan's Capability Trap'; Davies, Smith, and Williamson, 'Coordinating Post-conflict Aid in Southern Sudan'.

UNMISS' initial mandate in 2011 aligned with this overriding focus on building up the state, setting the core priority as statebuilding through institutional capacity development.[15] Across political, security, and rule of law arenas, UNMISS was tasked to provide support to the institutions of state, with clear benchmarks for measuring its success, including the state's demonstrated capacity to reintegrate 150,000 former rebel soldiers, develop of a functioning police service, and regulatory frameworks for rule of law institutions, and to implement a national strategy for SSR.[16] Within the civilian section of the mission, a staggering 1,100 staff were identified within the mission's budget as supporting state capacitybuilding programming.[17] UN agencies followed suit with the UN Development Programme referring to the overarching need to 'put state-building first', and spending millions on a programme of support to the government of South Sudan.[18]

Crucially, UNMISS was designed to support the extension of state authority from urban areas into the rural peripheries, in recognition of the longstanding absence of formal institutional capacities beyond the larger towns. In this sense, the mission design paralleled the state/county model of the government, setting up offices in state capitals and 'county support bases' to build state governance capacities in isolated parts of the country.[19] The theory behind these bases was for UNMISS' statebuilding work to have a 'portal' to local communities, gradually identifying key governance needs and extending state capacity into rural areas. As articulated by the secretary-general, UNMISS was to support the presence of state capacities across the country, until national authorities were able to build effective institutions.[20]

UNMISS staff were of course aware of local governance capacities beyond state actors, and the mission possessed some of the most knowledgeable analysts in South Sudan, many of whom had spent decades engaging with community actors.[21] But the mission tended to treat local issues within a different sphere.

[15] United Nations Security Council resolution on the situation in South Sudan, S/RES/1996 (2011), para. 3.

[16] United Nations, 'Budget for the United Nations Mission in South Sudan for the Period from 1 July 2011 to 30 June 2012: Report of the Secretary-General', A/66/532 (2011).

[17] United Nations, 'Budget for the United Nations Mission in South Sudan for the Period from 1 July 2011 to 30 June 2012', 41.

[18] United Nations, 'Country Programme Action Plan Between the Government of the Republic of South Sudan and the UN Development Programme (2012–2013)', available at http://www.ss.undp.org/content/dam/southsudan/library/Reports/southsudanotherdocuments/UNDP%20South%20Sudan_CPAP%202012-2013%20Fin%20%20Signed.pdf

[19] Da Costa and de Coning, 'United Nations Mission in the Republic of South Sudan', 831–840; United Nations, 'Report of the United Nations Secretary-General on the Situation in South Sudan', S/2012/746 (8 October 2012), para. 5.

[20] United Nations, 'Secretary-General's Remarks at Security Council Open Debate on Trends in United Nations Peacekeeping', 11 June 2014.

[21] During the conflict assessment I co-authored in 2010–11, I worked directly with the head of civil affairs, who had spent twenty years working in southern Sudan and who had an extraordinarily rich understanding of local dynamics. Unfortunately few, if any, of her insights were reflected in any of the finished planning documents put forward by the UN.

Structurally, the mission was divided into civil affairs (focused mainly on local conflict resolution) and political affairs (focused on national political issues). This contributed to a bifurcation within the mission: at a local level, civil affairs analysis focused on intercommunal issues, such as cattle rustling, land disputes, and longstanding cycles of violence; at the national level, political affairs dealt with issues like the constitutional provisions around decentralization and consolidation of the peace. On a research trip to Malakal with the acting head of civil affairs 2010, I asked her about this distinction. 'One of the problems', she said, 'is that we in civil affairs understand far better what the South Sudanese people expect in terms of governance, but political affairs is what feeds the UN. What this means is everything is couched in terms of institutions of the state, even if they don't really exist.'[22]

Indeed, when the UN and its partners referred to governance issues at the local level, it was almost uniformly in terms of bolstering state capacities. For instance, the UN Development Programme (UNDP) wrote of needing to understand 'the links between county, state and central levels of government in order to be able to operate optimally within these new *state structures*.'[23] Similarly, the EU priority at the sub-national level was to 'increase the capacity of local governments'.[24] Aligned with this view of the state as the solution to insecurity in the peripheries, the UN secretary-general repeatedly suggested that intercommunal violence, cattle raiding, land disputes, and other tensions should be addressed via 'effective rule of law and state authority'.[25] The panacea to the many ills of South Sudan was statebuilding.

Overall, UNMISS was an extraordinarily ambitious mission possessed of a uniquely strong mandate in support of state institutions. But in many respects, it was also similar to UN missions elsewhere; peace operations in Afghanistan, Mali, Democratic Republic of Congo (DRC), and Somalia all possess nearly identical mandates regarding the need to shore up and extend state authority from the centre to the periphery. Like UNMISS, all were founded upon the assumption that strengthened state institutions would provide the kind of governance and stability necessary to transition from failed to successful states. UNMISS' trajectory may follow the most precipitous decline from optimism to war, but it is by no means a unique set of failings. As the next section will explore, UNMISS' myopia when it came to governance meant that its lofty aims of increasing state capacity were quickly absorbed into the patterns of authority across the country.

[22] Notes from the South Sudan Conflict Assessment (on file with author).
[23] United Nations, 'Country Programme Action Plan'.
[24] 'EU Single Country Strategy (Response Strategy) for South Sudan 2011–2013 Aligned with and in Support of South Sudan's 2011–2013 Development Plan', available at https://ec.europa.eu/europeaid/sites/devco/files/single-country-strategy-south-sudan-2011-2013_en.pdf
[25] E.g. United Nations, 'Report of the United Nations Secretary-General on the Situation in South Sudan', S/2012/486 (2012), para. 98.

UN statebuilding within South Sudanese governance system

This chapter's central argument is that UNMISS was tasked to support the South Sudanese state to build and extend effective governance institutions, but instead it became part of the existing system, subject to the strong gravitational pulls of a deeply entrenched ethno-military network and thus unable to execute its mandate as expected. Thus far, I have laid out the key characteristics of South Sudan's governance system, followed by a description of the starkly different assumptions upon which UNMISS was designed. Here I bring the two together, arguing that the rules of the South Sudan governance game dictated the impact of UNMISS' work, distorting the trajectory of the UN away from its intended goals of strong, effective, widely dispersed state institutions. I examine this phenomenon in two related areas: (1) the UN's financial and human resources employed for capacitybuilding within the South Sudanese state; and (2) attempts to reform the Southern People's Liberation Army (SPLA) into a traditional (and right-sized) army. In both areas a similar pattern emerged: while the rhetoric of statebuilding continued to follow an orthodox narrative of international support to state institutions, authority and resources in fact fed into the ethno-military network instead. In the language of complexity thinking, UNMISS' work participated in a positive feedback loop, strengthening the tendency of the system to pursue its existing patterns rather than changing them.

A finger on the scales: Capacitybuilding and 'corruption'

As described above, UNMISS, along with major donors, relied upon a linear logic of change in South Sudan, where gradual increases in capacities by the state institutions would result in improved and territorially expanded governance across the country. Following independence, the government of South Sudan appeared to follow suit, establishing the South Sudan development plan for 2011–13, which articulated statebuilding goals in an uncannily similar way to the UN and major donors. Referring to itself a 'the nation's response to core development and state-building challenges', the plan highlighted governance as a key priority and allocated 25 per cent of the annual budget to building state capacity for good governance.[26] South Sudan's development planning, however, was described by a Harvard study as a form of 'isomorphic mimicry' in which state actors adopted the forms of traditional state structures while actually pursuing different objectives.[27] By speaking in the same terms as international partners, the government was able

[26] Government of the Republic of South Sudan, 'South Sudan Development Plan (2011–2013): Realising Freedom, Justice, Equality, Prosperity and Peace for All', August 2011.
[27] Larson, Ajak, and Pritchett, 'South Sudan's Capability Trap'.

to 'tick the boxes'[28] for international donors and secure continued support, despite its direction of the resources elsewhere. One donor described this mimicry in vivid terms, noting that the government maintained a 'fake ministry' that dealt with international actors and reported on progress according to the development plan, while the 'real ministry' funnelled resources elsewhere.[29] Evidence of misappropriation, when it came to light, was often spectacular. In 2012, for example, President Kiir sent an open letter to seventy-five of his current and former ministers demanding that they return roughly $4 billion that was 'unaccounted for or, simply put, stolen'.[30] However, the massive scale of graft tends to obscure the fact that the 'real ministries' were part of the ethno-military network in South Sudan; so-called 'corruption' was the system of governance persisting and evolving to new inputs.

Evidence that South Sudan's system of governance differed from UNMISS' assumptions was perhaps most visible in attempts to decentralize authority to the state and county level. UNMISS was mandated to help to build institutional capacities beyond the major urban areas, including by improving the state's rule of law capacities across the country. Deploying 900 police to the ten states of South Sudan with a mandate to train the state's security services, the mission dedicated a majority of its civilian resources to capacity building. While the government's development plan—on paper—aligned almost flawlessly with UNMISS', in practice state resources were instead directed away from institutions and towards salaries, especially for individual units of the SPLA.[31] Government austerity measures in 2011, for example, made cuts of roughly 30 per cent to consumption, development, and transfers to the states, but maintained the wage levels of all public officials.[32] In fact, Alex de Waal tracked a *rise* in salaries to the SPLA in the immediate post-independence period, a continuation of the patterns of patronage created during the CPA period and before.[33] Cuts to fiscal transfers to formal institutions at the state level, combined with increases in the salaries of the SPLA in the same areas, clearly point to the use of the military rather than to rule of law institutions (police, judicial) as the primary vehicle for governance even in the post-independence period. To the extent they received resources, decentralized administrative structures 'function[ed] above all as patronage instruments', rather than meaningful efforts

[28] John A. Snowden, 'Work in Progress: Security Force Development in South Sudan through February 2012', *Small Arm Survey* (2012): 16.

[29] Larson, Ajak, and Pritchett, 'South Sudan's Capability Trap'.

[30] Philip Aleu, 'South Sudan Ministers Invited to Answer Questions on $2 Billion Missing Grain Scandal'. *Sudan Tribune*, 16 June 2011.

[31] See, e.g., South Sudan Ministry of Foreign Affairs, 'Multi Annual Strategic Plan South Sudan 2012–2015', 2011, available at http://extwprlegs1.fao.org/docs/pdf/ssd148386.pdf (emphasizing capacitybuilding as a core task).

[32] Magali Mores, 'Overview of Corruption and Anti-corruption in South Sudan', *Transparency International*, 4 March 2013.

[33] Alex de Waal, 'When Kleptocracy becomes Insolvent: Brute Causes of the Civil War in South Sudan', *African Affairs* 113, No. 452 (2014): 349.

to establish institutions in the peripheries.[34] Failure to fund such institutions was not a new dynamic but rather a continuation of deep patterns; for decades the state had been defined by the relationship between the SPLA and its communities, most often functioning as a channel to reinforce elite power along ethnic lines.

A resident of Malakal (a town in Upper Nile States) described this dynamic to me in 2011:

> [President] Kiir has been holding together his big tent by paying out through the SPLA. That stops rebellions and lets the SPLA commanders feed their people. If humanitarian aid comes from the UN, that is fine, because the SPLA decides how that gets spent. But then the UN comes along and starts talking about new institutions, new buildings, new people who will be involved in deciding how money is spent. This is a threat to how the SPLA has been working for the last 20 years, and you will see that those new initiatives will quickly become part of the SPLA, in one way or another.[35]

By pouring resources and political legitimacy into state institutions, UNMISS thus participated in and influenced the relationships between the Southern People's Liberation Movement (SPLM) / SPLA and the local communities, tending to reinforce the top-down, centre-periphery dynamic. 'UNMISS put its finger on the scales, it only helped the Dinka. That's what capacity development means to us', one South Sudanese expert stated.[36] In speaking to dozens of South Sudanese, I heard a frequently reiterated view that UNMISS' capacitybuilding work from 2011 to 2013 was directed at a government controlled by President Kiir (a Dinka) and employed in the service of shoring up Dinka interests across South Sudan.[37] Sukanya Podder similarly argues that external efforts to reform the political structures of South Sudan appeared to result in the 'progressive consolidation of an elite-centred and Dinka-dominated decision-making structure that remains top-down and personality driven.'[38] Interestingly, Øystein Rolandsen's study of UNMISS's negligible financial impact within South Sudan's communities offers another part of this picture: rather than offset the ingrained patterns of largesse by distributing resources directly into communities, UNMISS' resources remained at the elite level, crystallizing elite control over state institutions.[39] It is worth noting that this

[34] Wolfram Lacher, 'South Sudan: International State-Building and Its Limits', German Institute for International and Security Affairs, 2012, available at https://www.swp-berlin.org/fileadmin/contents/products/research_papers/2012_RP04_lac.pdf

[35] Interview, Malakal, January 2011.

[36] Interview with head of South Sudanese non-governmental organization (NGO), Juba, 13 December 2018.

[37] Interviews, Juba, 1–15 December 2018.

[38] Sukanya Podder, 'Mainstreaming the Non-state in Bottom-Up State-building: Linkages between Rebel Governance and Post-conflict Legitimacy', *Conflict, Security and Development* 14, No. 2 (2014): 213–243.

[39] Øystein H. Rolandsen, 'Small and Far Between: Peacekeeping Economies in South Sudan', *Journal of Intervention and Statebuilding* 9, No. 3 (2015): 353–371.

consolidation was not necessarily the direct intention of President Kiir—who had put in place a remarkably ethnically balanced cabinet in 2011—but can be considered the result of entrenched power systems that tended to channel authority into a small circle of elite.[40] This centralization of power in the hands of a small circle of Dinka elite can be defined as a form of corruption, but it is more usefully understood as the way in which the governance system of South Sudan had been functioning for decades, an example of a well-evolved attractor rather than a deviation from the norm.

One of the most important ways in which UNMISS' capacitybuilding work participated in South Sudan's governance system was the issue of land. In the immediate post-independence period, the combined effect of increased urbanization and returns of large numbers of people previously displaced by the war laid enormous pressures on land ownership as communities scrambled to lock in their claims with the state. State recognition of land ownership was (and remains) one of the most common areas of dispute across the communities of South Sudan, especially as the SPLA often treated land rights as a natural spoil of the war won on behalf of the South.[41] In fact, according to Nasseem Badiey, 'authority over land had become the primary vehicle of political action in Southern Sudan, and "ethnic" identity the main avenue through which to assert and /or exercise land rights.'[42] Here, the patterns of South Sudan's governance system were on full display: traditional chiefs' roles in land disputes were defined in relationship between formal state institutions and the communities contesting ownership; chiefs were able to exercise control over land disputes via their ability to channel state authority and simultaneously speak on behalf of community interests when it came to land allocation from the state.[43] But while the roles of traditional authorities within land regulation were formalized in the Land Act of 2009 and the transitional constitution, state-level planning on land tended to ignore the delicate contestation processes over land, especially in the suburban areas near major towns. As Badiey concisely notes, state planning 'completely disregarded local land politics'.[44]

UNMISS' capacitybuilding work bolstered the role of state institutions in the realm of land disputes, but instead of resulting in better governance capacity, it often fed tensions between the state and communities, and appeared to contribute to abuse by SPLA commanders. One South Sudanese land advocate interviewed noted, 'UNMISS trained all the state bureaucrats in how to apply the laws, but that just told us that the SPLA take our land for their people. We already knew

[40] 'Kiir Forms First Cabinet of the Independent South Sudan', *Sudan Tribune*, 27 August 2011.

[41] Cherry Leonardi, 'Paying "Buckets of Blood" for the Land: Moral Debates over the Economy, War and State in Southern Sudan', *Journal of Modern African Studies* 49, No. 2 (2011).

[42] Nasseem Badiey, *The State of Post-conflict Reconstruction: Land, Urban Development and State-building in Juba Southern Sudan* (Oxford: James Currey, 2014).

[43] E.g. Cherry Leonardi, *Dealing with Government in South Sudan: Histories of Chiefship, Community and State* (Oxford: James Currey Press, 2015), 195.

[44] Badiey, *The State of Post-conflict Reconstruction*, 142.

that.'[45] While the UN advocated for and supported a stronger state—and indeed a state capable of imposing rule of law on the communities around it—the mission ignored a crucial reality: in many respects the state was the SPLM/SPLA, and as such it was an active participant in intercommunal contestation over land in South Sudan. Extending state authority and capacity beyond the urban areas may have sounded appealing during the planning phases of UNMISS, but it masked 'destabilizing processes unleashed by the expanding presence of the state' in the area of land ownership.[46] In fact, 'alienation of land by government, was the greatest common grievance among the marginalized people of Sudan', where 'members of the land-owning clans complain that they are increasingly disregarded in land transactions' as they became dictated solely by the government.[47] Badiey's key finding when examining land issues in post-independence South Sudan—that local land dynamics are symptomatic of resistance against the imposition of state authority—point to a possible conclusion that UNMISS' support to the state may have created greater local resistance.[48]

On the face of it, bolstering the state's role in land regulation may appear to be a statebuilding success, given UNMISS' objective of extending state authority over the territory of the country. However, land regulation too appears to fall into a form of mimicry: state institutions were granted the *de jure* authority to regulate land across South Sudan, but the *de facto* patterns of power persisted, adapting themselves to new inputs. When the World Bank conducted a country-wide study of land regulation in South Sudan in 2014 it found a remarkably comprehensive failure of formal institutions: less than 10 per cent of rural land had actually been registered with the state and was instead regulated by traditional mechanisms, while more than 50 per cent of the urban population also resided on unregistered land.[49] Other in-depth studies of land regulation made similar findings, with one noting that the rush to titling land by the state had 'interrupted traditional patterns of land use and created opportunities for both rent-seeking and inequitable distribution of land.'[50] By supporting the state, UNMISS did not achieve its objective of effective state control of territory, but instead played into the dynamic negotiation between urban and rural actors, where longstanding resistance to state imposition over traditional structures increased as the state attempted to exert itself. Again, UNMISS acted more to strengthen existing patterns than to shift the rules of the game.

[45] Interview, Juba, 12 December 2018.
[46] Badiey, *The State of Post-conflict Reconstruction*, 110.
[47] Leonardi, 'Paying "Buckets of Blood"', 224.
[48] Badiey, *The State of Post-conflict Reconstruction*, 110.
[49] World Bank, 'Land Governance in South Sudan: Policies for Peace and Development', Report 86958, 14 May 2014.
[50] Tiernan Mennan, 'Customary Law and Land Rights in South Sudan', Norwegian Refugee Council, March 2012.

Reforming the security services—a Sisyphean task

Prior to independence, there had been no formal transformation of the SPLA into a traditional army, though as described earlier in this chapter the army played an outsize role in all areas of governance.[51] Reform of South Sudan's security sector was therefore a central objective of the UN's statebuilding project, mentioned three times in the initial mandate for UNMISS and overtly at the heart of much of the rule of law and capacitybuilding work of the mission.[52] In line with the overall argument of this book, I here examine how UNMISS' approach to SSR failed to deliver on its stated objectives due to the patterns within the South Sudanese governance system.

The SPLA was not merely a former rebel movement turned national army, it was an ethnically charged vehicle for securing and maintaining loyalty among the peripheries and a vicious tool for the elite to keep its hold on power. During the 2011–13 period, risks of large-scale insecurity and fractures along ethno-political lines meant that SSR programming coexisted and competed with these three operational prerogatives of the SPLA, with a strong tendency for the UN to be pulled into centre-periphery dynamics. Presuming that change could be achieved by top-down, legislatively driven processes, UNMISS and its partners found themselves caught up in patterns where the push for a right-sized, professional, traditional army appeared to encounter strong resistance.

UNMISS' approach to SSR was driven by advocacy for legislative reforms, downsizing through disarmament, demobilization, and reintegration (DDR), and professionalization through training.[53] The mission planned to help reduce the size of the army by 80,000 troops during the post-independence period,[54] with training on offer for up to 150,000 demobilized soldiers wishing to return to civilian life.[55] A freshly established rule of law unit within UNMISS oversaw much of the reform on the legislative and capacitybuilding side, staffed with dozens of trained civilians.[56] This work aligned with the government's own SSR plan,[57] which was

[51] Richard Rands, 'In Need of Review: SPLA Transformation in 2006–10 and Beyond', Small Arms Survey Working Paper No. 23, November 2012.

[52] United Nations Security Council Resolution on South Sudan, S/RES/1996 (8 July 2011).

[53] Jonathan Blackham, 'Situation Report: SSR and DDR in the Sudans', Security Sector Reform Resource Centre, Centre for Security Governance, 11 December 2013.

[54] United Nations Mission in South Sudan (UNMISS), 'Disarmament Demobilization and Reintegration', 17 July 2014, available at http://unmiss.unmissions.org/Default.aspx?tabid =4055&language=en-US

[55] UNMISS, 'Disarmament Demobilization and Reintegration', 17 July 2014.

[56] United Nations Mission in South Sudan (UNMISS), 'Rule of Law and Security Institutions Support', 1 July 2014, available at http://unmiss.unmissions.org/Default.aspx?tabid=4056

[57] Department for International Development (DFID), 'Annual Review Security Sector Development & Defence Transformation', Report No. 200329 Development Tracker, 16–27 July 2012, available at http://iati.dfid.gov.uk/iati_documents/3644468.odt

budgeted at $1.3 billion overall, with more than $250 million to be spent during the first two years after independence.[58] Donors anticipated large-scale investment in SSR, with the UK prioritizing development spending on security sector development and defence transformation.[59] Remarkably, UNMISS' planning predicted that the security sector could be reformed extremely quickly; in its 2011–12 budget, the Mission suggested that within three years resources for SSR were likely to be essentially redundant![60]

On paper, the government appeared to achieve significant progress towards the central goals of SSR during its first two years. A DFID study, for example, found that between 2011 and 2013, indicators of progress included: the government's passage of a draft National Security Plan; a Training Strategy under which the SPLA conducted its own basic military training; a logistics capacity for the army; and an information technology (IT) training facility.[61] On the police side, hundreds of trainings for newly recruited police offered hope that internal security might indeed gradually shift away from the army to the police, while newly passed legislation on the security sector (including important reforms to prisons and rule of law institutions[62]) suggested that South Sudan might be moving in a positive direction.[63] UNMISS regularly reported on its support for these reforms, highlighting the advice it gave to the legislative processes and the capacitybuilding it was conducting with the security services.[64]

However, this apparent progress towards the stated goals of both UNMISS and the government belied the actual trajectory of the security services in South Sudan, in particular their continued role in an ethnically driven patronage system. Crucially, instead of shrinking the army in line with established plans, SPLA ranks swelled before and immediately following independence.[65] In Unity State alone, the SPLA conscripted roughly 7,000 new recruits following independence, ostensibly to ward off their incorporation into local militias.[66] Promotion of

[58] Snowden, 'Work in Progress'.

[59] Department for International Development (DFID), 'Project Completion Review (PCR)', Development Tracker, 2012, available at http://iati.dfid.gov.uk/iati_documents/4511971.odt

[60] United Nations, 'Budget for the United Nations Mission in South Sudan for the period from 1 July 2011 to 30 June 2012', para. 14.

[61] DFID, 'Annual Review', 16–27 July 2012.

[62] United Nations Mission in South Sudan (UNMISS), 'ROLSISO—What We Do', 17 July 2014.

[63] UNMISS, 'Rule of Law and Security Institutions Support', 1 July 2014.

[64] United Nations, 'Report of the United Nations Secretary-General on the Situation in South Sudan', S/2012/486 (2012), paras 71–73; United Nations, 'Report of the United Nations Secretary-General on the Situation in South Sudan', S/2013/140 (2013), para. 58. Not all were so positive, see, e.g. Mark Malan and Charles T. Hunt. 'Between a Rock and a Hard Place: The UN and the Protection of Civilians in South Sudan'. *International Strategic Studies Paper* 275 (2014).

[65] Annette Weber, 'Transformation Backlog in South Sudan: Security Sector Reforms Stall in the Face of Growing Autocracy', German Institute for International and Security Affairs, SWP Comments 20 (July: 2013); Alex de Waal, 'Peace and the security sector in Sudan, 2002–11', *African Security Review* 26:2 (2017): 180–198.

[66] Snowden, 'Work in Progress'.

dozens of new major and brigadier generals added to the already top-heavy structure of the army, at a time when the government was publicly calling for massive reductions.[67] Moreover, in 2011, all SPLA personnel received a near doubling of their salaries, meaning that soldier salaries accounted for over 80 per cent of the government's defence budget after independence.[68]

The dissonance between planning and reality was more than just numbers: within months of South Sudan's independence, it became clear that the government intended to use the internationally funded DDR programme to offload its elderly, sick, or disabled soldiers, ensuring that those unfit for duty would nonetheless receive funds. As John Snowden points out, DDR programming by the UN and its partners acted more as a means to allow the SPLA to replenish its healthy troops than a meaningful downsizing of the army.[69] By 2013, the World Bank estimated that the SPLA and southern militias accounted for more than 300,000 troops, a near doubling of the figure during the CPA period and a clear sign that downsizing was a mirage.[70] The creation of the South Sudan National Police Service (SSNPS) offered further evidence that SSR was not resulting in a shift in the rules of the game: dramatically underfunded and clearly unable to replace the army as the providers of internal security, the newly formed police was most notable for its overwhelmingly Dinka leadership.[71] Other evidence, such as the deployment of the SPLA across the entire territory of South Sudan rather than areas of most acute violence, pointed to the inescapable conclusion that the security services remained what it had been for decades: a means to ensure that the centre could generate the loyalty of the periphery.

Why did SSR fail to take hold in the first two years of South Sudan's independence? Many experts have pointed to growing insecurity as a key cause: in 2011 alone, 3,000 people were killed and 300,000 displaced, requiring emergency deployment of large portions of the SPLA.[72] With special representative of the secretary-general (SRSG) Johnson calling for increased UN troops to support the state's protection responsibilities, downsizing the army may not have been a viable reform between 2011 and 2013.[73] Other experts have pointed the finger at corrupt government officials whose interests conflicted with those of SSR; Wolfram Lacher's suggestion that the objectives of the SPLA 'diverge[d] considerably' from

[67] Rands, 'In Need of Review: SPLA Transformation'.

[68] Snowden, 'Work in Progress'.

[69] Snowden, 'Work in Progress'.

[70] International Development Association and International Finance Corporation, 'South Sudan—Interim Strategy Note for FY2013–2014', Report No: 74767-SS, World Bank, 30 January 2013, 5

[71] Snowden, 'Work in Progress'.

[72] United Nations, 'Report of the United Nations Secretary-General on the Situation in South Sudan', S/2012/140 (March 2012); Written Evidence of UK International Development Committee, 11 April 2012, available at https://www.publications.parliament.uk/pa/cm201012/cmselect/cmintdev/1570/1570we08.htm

[73] Hilde Johnson, 'In South Sudan, Old Feuds Test a New State', *Sudan Tribune*, 1 February 2012.

those of international partners euphemistically captures this viewpoint.[74] These explanations would maintain statebuilding as a worthwhile task that was merely derailed by insecurity, underfunding, or individual greed.

In contrast, a systemic understanding of governance offers greater explanatory power, and even a suggestion that these other narratives have missed the mark. The SPLA was not a monolithic entity that could be reformed via legislation and training, because it was largely defined within the centre-periphery relationship, acting more to consolidate the SPLM's power across communities than to secure and provide for the population. Edward Lino's claim that 'there was nothing called "SPLA", it was divided and shredded into tribal formations adhering to individual commanders'[75] captures part of this notion of the SPLA as caught between its ethnic/communal identities, its role in consolidating elite control of the peripheries, and its longstanding identity as a rebellion against an oppressive regime to the North. When I asked a former South Sudanese minister about the reform of the SPLA, he laughed and told me, 'you can't reform our way of communicating ... the SPLA is the way Juba negotiates with the many tribes in this country.'[76]

In systemic terms, governance in South Sudan had come to depend on the SPLA as the conduit for influence from the centre to the periphery. Integration into the SPLA was the way in which Juba addressed potential rifts in its network, meaning that efforts to downsize the army ran against well-established patterns that acted to stabilize the system. As Matthew le Riche notes, armed group integration was a 'cyclical political process' rather than a linear statebuilding one, extremely unlikely to result in the development of functioning institutions.[77] As South Sudan underwent successive shocks to its system—in particular the 2012 oil shut-off—reliance on the SPLA to hold the network together became even more urgent. Austerity was passed on to the formal institutions, not the SPLA network; generals were promoted rather than retired; patterns of purchasing loyalty proved too deep to be overcome by superficial legislation and occasional training regimes.[78] Insecurity and corruption offer only small glimpses into why SSR failed: reform never took hold because it never fundamentally altered the rules of the game.

If anything, these dynamics demonstrate that UNMISS' support to SSR may have invigorated existing governance patterns across the country. The combination of a Juba-focused, legislatively driven attempt to build formal institutions

[74] Lacher, 'South Sudan: International State-Building and Its Limits'.

[75] Edward Lino, 'There Was No Coup in Juba', 9 February 2014, available at https://paanluelwel.com/2014/02/09/edward-lino-there-was-no-coup-in-juba/

[76] Interview with former South Sudanese minister, December 2018.

[77] Matthew Le Riche, 'Conflict Governance: The SPLA, Factionalism, and Peacemaking', in Steven E. Roach, eds., *The Challenges of Governance in South Sudan* (London: Routledge, 2018), 19.

[78] Le Riche, 'Conflict Governance', 45.

appeared to contribute to what Sukanya Podder has called 'the progressive consolidation of an elite-centred and Dinka-dominated decision-making', and an embedding of the elite's dependence upon the SPLA to maintain its web of control.[79] In dozens of interviews conducted with South Sudanese—including former government officials and members of civil society—there was a consistent theme around the topic of SSR: UN support to the government ran with the grain of patronage, not against it, offering resources and political support that were channelled into the existing network rather than changing how it functioned.[80] 'There was no "reform" in SSR', one expert told me, 'only more money for Kiir to pay his commanders'.[81]

Conclusion

This chapter has explained the failure of the UN's statebuilding engagement in South Sudan for the first two years of the country's independence. It has shown how the system of governance evolved over time, and how its particular centre-periphery patterns made South Sudan resistant to the kinds of change envisioned within UNMISS' mandate. In the interrelated areas of institutional capacity-building and SSR, I have argued that the UN's undeniable failure to achieve the anticipated outcomes was the result of the dominant patterns within this system: pouring resources and political energy into a top-down, institutionally focused set of statebuilding activities was extremely unlikely to generate the kind of national-level change anticipated in UNMISS' mandate. This is in part due to a conceptual failing of the UN and its partners: South Sudan did not need to be 'built from scratch', nor should the mission's task have been 'literally building a country'.[82] The lack of formal administrative institutions across the country was misleading, contributing to a model of statebuilding that assumed the need to extend state capacity into a disordered periphery. But instead of encountering a *tabula rasa*, UN statebuilding found itself caught up in a web of relations involving communities, traditional chiefs, military commanders, and politicians, a set of patterns that proved extraordinarily resistant to systemic change. In this, UNMISS' statebuilding did not fail, per se, but rather became part of the system, subject to the systemic rules that had evolved over decades, and at times reinforcing them. The UN's failure in this case was one of vision, of imagining South Sudan as a surface upon which the state could be written.

[79] Podder, 'Mainstreaming the Non-state', 213–243.

[80] Adam Day, 'Assessing the Effectiveness of the UN Mission in South Sudan', Norwegian Institute of International Affairs, March 2019, available at https://effectivepeaceops.net/unmiss/

[81] Interview with senior member of South Sudanese think tank, Juba, 13 December 2018.

[82] Hilde F. Johnson, *South Sudan: The Untold Story from Independence to Civil War* (London: I.B. Tauris, 2016), 98.

As the following chapters will explore, this dynamic is not exclusive to South Sudan. Across UN statebuilding, governance systems that pre-dated the UN's arrival tend to be ignored in favour of a generic approach that looks to expand state authority into a chaotic periphery. And though these systems differ significantly from that of the ethno-military patronage in South Sudan, they share a common capacity to adapt to and distort UN statebuilding from its intended results. It is largely the inability of the UN to adapt in turn that contributes to its perennial failures.

5
The Congolese 'black hole'

The Democratic Republic of the Congo (DRC) has been called many names: a lame Leviathan; a dinosaur on the brink of extinction; collapsed, disintegrated, corrupt; a façade obscuring the private accumulation of wealth; and a forsaken black hole filled with calamity, chaos, and confusion.[1] These descriptions underscore general agreement across scholarship that Congo is the paradigmatic example of a failed state, devoid of the widely recognized attributes of statehood and overwhelmingly prone to high levels of structural violence.[2] Yet despite its near total lack of Weberian features, and indeed through long periods of apparent institutional failure, Congo's political system has survived and adapted. The country's resilience—the way in which statehood paradoxically appears to thrive on its own institutional weakness—has given rise to the Congolese saying, *l'état est moribond, mais pas mort*, constantly on the brink of death but still alive.[3]

This chapter argues that Congo's recurrent institutional shortcomings are not symptomatic of fragility or instability per se, but are better understood as outcomes of a complex system of governance in which a wide range of actors negotiate and contest governance powers.[4] This contestation among interdependent nodes means that governance is emergent, the product of self-organization rather than a static power residing within institutions. As described in the opening chapters of this book, complex systems follow patterns of adaptation, feeding back in ways that create path dependencies and exhibit what Peter Coleman has called 'strong

[1] Theodore Trefon, *Reinventing Order in the Congo: How People Respond to State Failure in Kinshasa* (London: Zed Books, 2005); Timothy Raeymaekers, *Violent Capitalism and Hybrid Identity in the Eastern Congo: Power to the Margins* (Cambridge: Cambridge University Press, 2014); Jason Stearns, *Dancing in the Glory of Monsters: The Collapse of the Congo and the Great War of Africa* (New York: Perseus Books, 2011); Thomas Turner, *The Congo Wars: Conflict, Myth and Reality* (London: Zed Books, 2006).

[2] See, e.g., Lionel Cliffe and Robin Luckham, 'Complex Political Emergencies and the State: Failure and the Fate of the State', *Third World Quarterly* 20, No. 1 (1999): 27–50; William Reno, 'Congo: From State Collapse to "Absolutism", to State Failure', *Third World Quarterly* 27, No. 1 (2006): 43–56; René Lemarchand, *The Dynamics of Violence in Central Africa* (Philadelphia, PA: University of Pennsylvania Press, 2009), 191–260.

[3] Trefon, *Reinventing Order in the Congo*.

[4] Christian Lund, 'Twilight Institutions: An Introduction', *Development and Change* 37, No. 4 (2006): 673–684 (describing 'active sites of political negotiation and mediation' over the distribution of power and public authority).

States of Disorder, Ecosystems of Governance. Adam Day, Oxford University Press.
 DOI: 10.1093/oso/9780192863898.003.0006

attractors' towards certain kinds of behaviour.[5] In the DRC, these patterns of adaptation have meant that, over time, governance has evolved into a system that tends to strip state institutions of capacity, build centres of authority in the periphery, and rely heavily on violence as a (paradoxically) stabilizing element of the system.

The application of complexity theory to the governance systems of the DRC draws on political economy and historical analysis of the country, and in many ways aligns with the findings that the DRC's trajectory has been driven by a combination of exploitative, violent, and neglectful political leadership over the past seventy years. By providing a systemic lens, and via the tools of complex systems analysis, complexity theory augments these findings, identifying underlying patterns that stretch across long periods of time and organize the system even through periods of intense change. Drawing on my extensive time living, working, and researching in the DRC, I also demonstrate how complex systems are more than an abstract set of concepts; they are, as Jane Boulton has written, 'a description of the way things are'.[6] The day-to-day reality for the Congolese people reflects the complex system visibly at work: they understand interdependence and emergence, even if the United Nations (UN) does not.

The chapter is organized around three eras in the DRC's post-colonial history: Mobutu Sese Seko's thirty-year rule following independence (1965–97); the First and Second Congolese Wars (1996–2003); and the post-war period in which Joseph Kabila's presidency dominated the political arena. Each era began with a shock to the system, a moment where the underlying rules appeared momentarily thrown into uncertainty and where new modes of governance seemed possible. Examining how the system returned to a form of equilibrium following these shocks—and focusing on how the relationships among the various governance actors shifted over time—I make three broad claims regarding the emergence of Congo's governance system.

First, I argue that the Mobutu era was characterized by two impulses: an attempt to vest complete authority over the country in the individual of the president and a near total relinquishment of governance functions on behalf of the state. Over time, this allowed for the emergence of 'strongmen' empowered by their connections to Mobutu and able to funnel resources outside of formal state institutions. Rather than a liberal governance structure where a national budget is disbursed to fund state institutions in the periphery, the Mobutu era thus witnessed a hollowing out of institutional capacity. Here, the system evolved via a set of positive feedback loops: encouraged to ignore formal state institutions, strongmen and private citizens diverted resources through informal networks, further stripping the state of capacity and thus requiring still greater reliance on non-state forms of governance.

[5] Peter Coleman et al., *Attracted to Conflict: Dynamic Foundations of Destructive Social Relations* (New York: Springer, 2013).

[6] Jean G. Boulton et al., eds, *Embracing Complexity: Strategic Perspectives for an Age of Turbulence* (Oxford: Oxford University Press, 2015), 8–9.

Second, the onset of Congo's two civil wars shocked the system, eliminating Mobutu from the centre and temporarily disrupting the patronage network that drew resources in from the population. Rather than fundamentally transform how governance was produced, however, the wars can be thought of as introducing violence to it: strongmen in the peripheries came to rely upon a range of militias and regional armies to guarantee their role as governance actors. Here, a form of symbiosis can be observed among communities, armed groups, and businesses, all of which were necessary to protect their common interests.[7]

Finally, I describe how the centre returned to the DRC in the post-war era as Joseph Kabila re-established a patronage network *à la* Mobutu, demanding loyalty in exchange for protection. However, through the wars, the system had become deeply reliant on violence as an organizing force; governance was inextricably linked to the various roles played by armed groups across eastern Congo. Repeating a pattern from the Mobutu era, these violent forms of governance tended to strip the state of capacity, creating instead a militarized protection racket where both the centre and the periphery relied upon armed groups to secure the relationship.

Across these three eras, Congo has displayed a set of strong attractors towards protectionist relationships between centre and periphery. Through several shocks, the system demonstrated a powerful tendency to return to these relationships, albeit in different forms. Importantly, it has shown a capacity to stabilize itself by maintaining hollow, disempowered, instrumentalized state structures, ones which display a strong resilience against the kind of top-down, institutionally driven changes the UN attempted for decades.[8]

Système D—the Mobutu era and contested political orders

Mobutu Sese Seko's 'mafia-like enterprise' that soon followed Zaire's independence has been held up as the epitome of repression, exploitation, and kleptocratic rule.[9] Over a thirty-year period, he erected an absolutist model of political control atop

[7] Koen Vlassenroot and Timothy Raeymaekers, 'New Political Order in the DR Congo? The Transformation of Regulation', *Africa Focus* 21, No. 2 (2008): 39–52.

[8] See, e.g., Tom De Herdt and Claudine Tshimanga, 'War and the Political Economy of Kinshasa', in Stefaan Marysse and Filip Reyntjens, eds., *The Political Economy of the Great Lakes Region in Africa* (New York: Springer Press, 2005); Theodore Trefon, 'Public Service Provision in a Failed State: Looking Beyond Predation in the Democratic Republic of Congo', *Review of African Political Economy* 36, No. 119 (2009): 9–21; Michael Nest, François Grignon, and Emizet F. Kisangani, *The Democratic Republic of Congo: Economic Dimensions of War and Peace* (Boulder, CO: Lynne Rienner Press, 2006); Tatiana Carayannis, Koen Vlassenroot, Kasper Hoffmann and Aaron Pangburn, *Competing Networks and Political Order in the Democratic Republic of Congo: A Literature Review on the Logics of Public Authority and International Intervention* (London: London School of Economics, 2018).

[9] René Lemarchand, 'The Democratic Republic of Congo: From Collapse to Potential Reconstruction', in Robert Rotberg, ed., *State Failure and State Weakness in a Time of Terror* (Washington, DC: Brookings Institution Press, 2003), 29–70.

a sprawling military and administrative bureaucracy, the sole purpose of which was to arrogate power to the centre.[10] In many respects, Mobutu built on existing colonial patterns and structures designed for the pillage of the country, maintaining the central role of customary chiefs in administering localities and continuing the practice of mercantilist economic production for his own personal benefit.[11] From 1965 onwards, he concentrated the state's authority in an army and administrative bureaucracy that responded solely to his own commands.[12]

However, while he glorified the state in his speeches, Mobutu's rule was based upon a *de facto* withdrawal of state institutions from the day-to-day administration of Zaire, relying on citizens to fend for themselves for their own protection and well-being. Instead of using state resources to build schools, police stations, judiciaries, or public utilities beyond the capital, he relied on former colonial notions of indirect rule where local leaders governed their respective communities.[13] Here, Mobutu demanded that traditional authorities generate revenues for the state, but otherwise left them largely to their own devices.[14] Importantly, this approach kept potential challengers at bay, never allowing a sufficiently weighty node of authority to form within government.[15]

Mobutu's rule was thus based on a network of redistribution, where the elite were linked vertically with local power-brokers such as traditional authorities and provincial politicians, most of whom were officially renamed members of Mobutu's own political party.[16] These networks were underfed, offering local opportunities for predation rather than salaries as an incentive to remain loyal, alongside regular purges and threats of violence against those who stepped out of line.[17] On a daily basis, thousands of 'gatekeepers' exchanged access to state authority for money extracted from Congolese citizens. Soldiers took bribes at checkpoints; customs officials skimmed tolls to offset their paltry, erratic salaries; a vast range of public officials saw their roles as a costly bargain with the state that could only offer survival if local citizens were made to pay illicit rents.[18]

[10] Timothy Raeymaekers and Koen Vlassenroot, 'Reshaping Congolese Statehood in the Midst of Crisis and Transition', in Ulf Engel and Paul Nugent, eds., *Respacing Africa* (New York: Brill, 2010), 140.

[11] Raeymaekers, *Violent Capitalism*, 70.

[12] Raeymaekers, *Violent Capitalism*, 72.

[13] Alex Veit, Intervention as Indirect Rule: Civil War and Statebuilding in the Democratic Republic of Congo (New York: Campus Verlag, 2011), 90.

[14] For a description of Mobutu's attempts to reform the chieftaincy system, see Crawford Young and Thomas Turner, *The Rise and Decline of the Zairian State* (Madison, WI: University of Wisconsin Press, 1985), 236.

[15] See Joel Migdal, *Strong Societies, Weak States: State-Society Relations and State Capabilities in the Third World* (Princeton, NJ: Princeton University Press, 1988) (describing policies to weaken state institutions as a way to keep challengers from gaining an upper hand).

[16] Vlassenroot and Raeymaekers, 'New Political Order in the DR Congo?', 39–52.

[17] Denis M. Tull, *The Reconfiguration of Political Order in Africa: A Case Study of North Kivu (DR Congo)* (Hamburg: Institut für Afrika-Kunde, 2005), 277.

[18] Raeymaekers, *Violent Capitalism*.

The symbol of Mobutu's kleptocratic rule became his mantra, *débrouillez-vous*, a call to fend for yourself in the absence of any meaningful state role in governance or economic development outside the capital. Here, unfettered extraction of rents from the local population was not only tolerated, it became the principal modality for sustaining the patronage network.[19] Civil servants and other state agents were provided with unpaid positions and expected to feed profits upward in order to maintain their protected roles. Luca Jourdan describes this as a 'social pact' between state and society, allowing the state to retire from its governance functions while leaving the population to act unlawfully.[20] In addition to personal gain, communities were told to protect their own ethnic base via Mobutu's notion of *géopolitique* by which national institutions and public positions were based on ethnic quotas and local positions were occupied by so-called native officials.[21]

Système D, as Mobutu's fend-for-yourself ideology was called, evolved via a series of positive feedback loops that acted to decentralize governance and further strip the state of capacities, eventually rendering Zaire a 'decentralized centralized state'.[22] Public authority became a contested resource—something competed over by both state and non-state actors—but which did not in itself generate any revenues for state institutions. Instead, those asked to govern were expected to extract from the population and feed resources upwards, enriching Mobutu and his coterie but never establishing a national budget that could be used to build schools, police stations, or courthouses.[23] Poorly performing formal state institutions in the country's peripheries—especially the resource-rich Kivus in the East—left room for other actors to step in, particularly those with strong links to the patronage network. The more Mobutu encouraged private actors to fend for themselves, the weaker the state became, opening even greater space for private enterprise: a positive feedback loop that meant governance was increasingly decided by private accumulation drawn from the resource-rich periphery.

This feedback loop gradually transformed Zaire into a highly decentralized network of informal governance mechanisms that largely escaped formal administrative control.[24] Through the 1970s and 1980s, the meagre infrastructure and administration that had existed at independence dissolved as state coffers were used for personal enrichment rather than public services. Likewise, the army became decrepit, 'a mirage', incapable of fighting an armed enemy, a vehicle for

[19] Vlassenroot and Raeymaekers, 'New Political Order in the DR Congo?', 39–52.

[20] Cited in Koen Vlassenroot and Timothy Raeymaekers, eds., *Conflict and Social Transformation in Eastern DR Congo* (Ghent: Conflict Research Group and Academia Press, 2004), 226.

[21] Carayannis, Vlassenroot, Hoffmann, and Pangburn, *Competing Networks and Political Order*.

[22] Carayannis, Vlassenroot, Hoffmann, and Pangburn, *Competing Networks and Political Order*.

[23] Michael Schatzberg, *The Dialectics of Oppression in Zaire* (Bloomington, IN: Indiana University Press, 1988).

[24] Vlassenroot and Raeymaekers, 'New Political Order in the DR Congo?', 39–52.

patronage with a reputation for theft, extortion, and violence against the population.[25] As a result, public authority was not exercised by the state but became the outcome of transaction and competition among a range of power-brokers attempting to protect themselves from predatory agents of the central government while also seeking to benefit from its largesse. Stephen Jackson has referred to this in Foucauldian terms, analysing the 'non-governmentality' of eastern Congo, where non-state actors competed to be responsible for the bulk of governance roles and where the local citizenry exhibited little respect for state-run rule of law.[26]

The transactional nature of governance meant that the state was only necessary insofar as it could reciprocally offer protection in exchange for resources. As opportunities for private accumulation allowed local strongmen and non-governmental organizations to develop autonomous arrangements in the peripheries, the role of state institutions shrunk still further.[27] By the 1980s, essentially all of Zaire's healthcare and education were delivered by civil society groups and religious organizations who often competed with each other for the right to provide services.[28] Lacking consistent national investment in the mining industry, central control of mines declined and artisanal mining became the accepted norm, leaving natural resources under greater local non-state control.[29] In many communities in eastern Zaire, local defence militias emerged to protect their communities and secure mining revenues, collecting taxes in the name of the state without paying into it.[30] By the end of Mobutu's rule, nearly 75 per cent of the land that had been declared state property following decolonization had been subsequently possessed by local entrepreneurs, stripping the state of vital economic resources.[31] These syncretic forms of governance—created by a mixture of private, state, and communal actors—were the outcome of a proliferation of gatekeepers under Mobutu.[32] They operated in positive feedback loops, establishing and reinforcing a pattern where power gradually transferred to the periphery, further stripping the state of direct authority and capacity, and opening more space for non-state governance.

[25] Stein Sundstol Eriksen, 'The Liberal Peace Is Neither: Peacebuilding, Statebuilding and the Reproduction of Conflict in the Democratic Republic of Congo', *International Peacekeeping* 16, No. 5 (2009): 652–666; see also Thomas Callaghy, *The State-Society Struggle* (New York: Columbia University Press, 1984), 294.

[26] Stephen Jackson, 'The State Didn't Even Exist: Non-Governmentality in Kivu, Eastern DR Congo', in Tim Kelsall and Jim Igoe, eds., *Between a Rock and a Hard Place: African NGOs, Donors and the State* (Durham, NC: Carolina Academic Press, 2004).

[27] Vlassenroot and Raeymaekers, 'New Political Order in the DR Congo?', 39–52.

[28] Vlassenroot and Raeymaekers, 'New Political Order in the DR Congo?'.

[29] Veit, *Intervention as Indirect Rule*, 93.

[30] Kasper Hoffmann, Koen Vlassenroot, and Gauthier Marchais, 'Taxation, Stateness and Armed Groups: Public Authority and Resource Extraction in Eastern Congo', *Development and Change* 47, No. 6 (2006): 1434–1456.

[31] Raeymaekers, *Violent Capitalism*, 94.

[32] For the notion of syncretic governance, see Tatiana Carayannis, José Bazonzi, and Aaron Pangburn, 'Configurations of Authority in Kongo Central Province: Governance, Access to Justice and Security in the Territory of Muanda', Social Science Research Council, JSRP Working Paper No. 31 (2017).

Ironically, Mobutu's authoritarian tendencies to centralize all authority in himself thus had the eventual result of rendering the peripheries the most important aspect of Zaire's governance system. With many natural resources concentrated in the eastern reaches of the country, local actors had little incentive to channel their resources to Kinshasa, preferring instead the proximate and more lucrative markets in Rwanda and Uganda. As Zaire's domestic production stalled in the 1980s, the importance of accessing the international market for locally mined goods like gold, diamonds, and other minerals grew, empowering cross-border gatekeepers to play increasingly state-like roles such as customs, border control, taxation, and even basic infrastructure. Stephen Jackson insightfully describes this in electronic circuitry terms, suggesting that only a limited number of actors were able to 'complete the circuit' of trade, placing them in the role of needing to govern the borderlands to protect their business interests.[33] An example of this was the Nande community in the Kivus, which evolved a highly sophisticated transborder trade of natural resources that allowed them *de facto* governance over a significant territory, one that lasts to this day.[34]

Broadly, *Système D* transformed Zaire's vast territory into a something of a doughnut, with populations and resources clustered around its outer borders and a largely empty interior.[35] This reflects the way in which the governance system self-organized, over time leaving the political centre in Kinshasa bereft of power while local brokers in the periphery took control. Mobutu was able to maintain power only insofar as he could offer meaningful protection via the vertical network he had established between the centre and the peripheries, or by threat of indiscriminate violence against his opponents. Amidst a financial crisis in the late 1980s, however, his patronage dried up, allowing for the emergence of even more autonomous nodes of power that did not depend as much on the largesse of the president.[36] When, in 1990, Mobutu announced that all natural resources would be nationalized, it set a ripple through a system that had adapted to highly decentralized rule and transborder flows of resources.[37] Mobutu's failure do more than occasionally suppress rebellions had allowed armed groups to flourish in the East, creating ripe conditions for much larger scale armed confrontation.[38] As national support for Mobutu dwindled, the power-brokers in the East and Zaire's neighbours realized that the centre could not hold—they moved to take control.

[33] Stephen Jackson, 'Borderlands and the Transformation of War Economies: Lessons from the DR Congo', *Conflict, Security & Development* 6, No. 3 (2006): 425–447.

[34] Raeymaekers, *Violent Capitalism*.

[35] Jackson, 'Borderlands and the Transformation of War Economies', 425–447.

[36] Judith Verweijen, 'Stable Instability: Political Settlements and Armed Groups in the Congo', Rift Valley Institute, 2016.

[37] Raeymaekers, *Violent Capitalism*, 74.

[38] Veit, *Intervention as Indirect Rule*, 101

War recalibrates the system

From 1996 to 2002, Congo was wracked by two wars triggered by foreign efforts to expel Mobutu and secure control over Congo's vast resources. The wars were a chaotic and staggeringly violent competition for power among the armies of the region and their respective proxies within Congo, resulting in millions dead, large-scale displacement, and what has been described as a fundamental transformation of the political constellation of Congo.[39] In complex systems terms, however, the wars can be understood as the Congolese system adapting to the growth of violence as a principal means to contest power, resulting in the gradual militarization of existing governance networks rather than a wholesale transformation. As national armies and other armed groups competed over Congo's natural resources, violent groups increasingly took on state-like roles; rather than fundamentally altering the system, violence became incorporated into it.

Following Rwanda's 1996 invasion of what was then called Zaire, the country quickly became overrun with foreign troops as Uganda, Burundi, Angola, and Eritrea joined the fight against Mobutu. Persistent foreign military presence effectively created three political-military networks of power with links to Rwanda, Uganda, and Kinshasa, with local militias in their pay.[40] These networks fed off control of key sites of revenue generation, including artisanal mines, marketplaces, border posts, and outright plunder. The power networks thus played two related roles: parties in an international war driven by national capitals, and nodes in highly localized competition over land, ethnic rights, and resources.[41]

The presence of large armed groups on Congolese territory further shifted the locus of governance powers away from Kinshasa and linked it more closely with ethnic communities. From the outset of the war, the national armies of Rwanda and Uganda had occupied lucrative territories in eastern Congo, pillaging natural resources and further entrenching the illicit transborder trade routes out of the country. Rather than needing to channel the authority of Mobutu's state, these forces obtained their power more locally, relying on local ethnic groups to shore up control of territory.[42] Timothy Raeymaekers describes the process as armed groups 'institutionaliz[ing] their role as brokers of local development by weaving their claims to political authority into existing complexes of power.'[43] Mobutu's concept of *géopolitique*, which had placed ethnicity in a pre-eminent role

[39] Stearns, *Dancing in the Glory of Monsters*.

[40] Philippe le Billon, 'Diamond Wars? Conflict Diamonds and Geographies of Resource WarCs', *Annals of the Association of American Geographers* 98 (2008): 345–372.

[41] Koen Vlassenroot, 'Reading the Congolese Crisis', in Koen Vlassenroot and Timothy Raeymaekers, eds., *Conflict and Social Transformation in Eastern DR Congo* (Ghent: Conflict Research Group and Academia Press, 2004).

[42] Raeymaekers, *Violent Capitalism*, 94.

[43] Raeymaekers, *Violent Capitalism*, 92.

in shaping governance structures, became the vehicle for armed factions to assert their own authority locally.

If Mobutu's *Système D* was organized around protection by the patriarch, the emergence of militarized governance during the Congolese Wars demonstrates that system's evolution rather than its end. War perpetuated the reliance on ethnicity as a means to channel power, instrumentalizing traditional authorities to secure legitimacy in the periphery, but rendering their authority dependent upon violent groups. Here, the various armed groups that appeared on the Congolese landscape mobilized locally, feeding off the same traditional structures that had sustained Mobutu's long rule. Regional strongmen and their militias were able to perform state-like functions without any relationship to formal state institutions based in Kinshasa, relying instead on the traditional leaders and/or local defence militias to exert their power.

A prime example of this was taxation. Community-based armed groups with links to the regional armies rapidly developed sophisticated means to extract rents in the form of local taxes, in exchange for which they offered protection from other militias in the area.[44] Unlike the Mobutu era, however, these taxes were not funnelled to Kinshasa but became part of a separate, regionally aligned economy. During a period of extreme insecurity, these forms of local protection in return for taxes became a widely accepted practice of governance across much of eastern Congo, further stripping the central government of any direct role in administering its peripheral populations.

In this way, a form of symbiosis emerged between the various armed factions and the communities of eastern Congo. Communities needed armed groups to secure their land, protect them from attack, and guarantee the export of locally produced resources to foreign markets. In return, armed groups required day-to-day support from communities, and a source of legitimacy to pursue their claims of territorial control. In some cases the symbiosis was clearly mutualistic—a win/win for both sides—whereas in others armed groups operated in a more predatory way on their surrounding communities.[45]

The dependence upon violence-based forms of governance was deepened as foreign support gradually shifted away from Kinshasa. For decades, Mobutu had enjoyed significant (if somewhat erratic) foreign support, including from Congo's neighbours, which had allowed him to maintain partial control of his patronage network via steady payments. However, the war triggered a near total loss of foreign support to Kinshasa, while Congo's neighbours plundered the resource-rich eastern territories for their own gain. The proliferation of ethnically based armed

[44] Hoffmann, Vlassenroot, and Marchais, 'Taxation, Stateness and Armed Groups', 1434–1456.

[45] For a description of different forms of symbiosis in the DRC, see Adam Day and Charles T. Hunt, 'UN Stabilisation Operations and the Problem of Non-Linear Change: A Relational Approach to Intervening in Governance Ecosystems', *Stability: International Journal of Security & Development* (2020): 1–23.

groups grew out of this need for local protection in a system where the state could not offer any itself, and where the best course for security was alignment with a foreign power. What Vlassenroot and Raeymaekers call an 'oligopoly of violent means'—where multiple national forces competed over Congo's resources—became an ideal breeding ground for locally based armed groups capable of protecting the immediate interests of their communities.[46]

Wartime governance in eastern Congo thus became contingent upon a local-transborder complex of relations, where Congolese militias, traditional authorities, local businesspeople, and elites competed and collaborated to move resources beyond Congo's borders into the hands of regional power-brokers. Lacking the means to organize their own local production, rebel forces and foreign armies looked to systematically exploit and control transborder trade to generate income. In turn, and lacking the ability to protect their resources from extraction to market, local businesses and community leaders accepted the often predatory practices of militias in exchange for safety.[47] This symbiotic relationship meant that the most expedient path to resources was through armed activity, rather than through affiliation with the central state. And as such, it meant that violence became a dominant modality for contesting control over transborder trade.

By the end of the Second Congolese War in 2002, a profound militarization of Congo's political system had taken place. No longer was Mobutu's network the principle way to achieve influence in the DRC; instead, militarized networks had established themselves in eastern Congo, secured themselves in communities, and established highly effective means of marketing resources beyond the country's borders.[48] Localized disputes over resources, land, and administrative authority were thus linked to broader regional agendas, as power-brokers in Kigali, Kampala, and Luanda jostled for control, each relying on their own set of armed groups.[49]

The result was what in other contexts Peter Coleman has termed a 'strong attractor' to violence, where gradually the possibilities for non-violent governance had shrunk close to zero.[50] In a 2016 interview, a Congolese politician in Kabila's inner circle candidly told me, 'The right to behave like the state in the East has everything to do with a gun and nothing to do with whatever title you have.'[51] Moreover, the wars created a heavy dependency on networks to move resources to the international markets, often through corridors secured by the dozens of militias that roamed in the border areas between the DRC and Uganda/Rwanda. These formed the initial conditions of the Congolese governance system in the post-war period.

[46] Vlassenroot and Raeymaekers, 'New Political Order in the DR Congo?', 39–52.
[47] Vlassenroot and Raeymaekers, 'New Political Order in the DR Congo?'.
[48] Vlassenroot, 'Reading the Congolese Crisis'.
[49] Vlassenroot, 'Reading the Congolese Crisis'.
[50] Peter Coleman et al., 'Intractable Conflict as an Attractor: A Dynamical Systems Approach to Conflict Escalation and Intractability', *American Behavioral Scientist* 50, No. 11 (2007): 1454–1475.
[51] Interview with senior member of Kabila's cabinet, 12 October 2016.

The *parapluie*—militarized protection rackets in Congo's post-war system

On its surface, the 2002 peace accord that ended the Second Congolese War advanced a Western model for Congolese statehood: national elections were held in 2006 resulting in Joseph Kabila rising to the head of state; a government-run process offered a pathway for the integration of armed groups into the newly reformed national army; and a regional peace and security framework reasserted the DRC's statehood after years of foreign army intrusion and meddling. But these state-like developments masked a continuation of the Congolese governance system, which adapted to the re-emergence of a centralized authority by resuming many of the same dynamics that had existed under Mobutu, including the return of a sprawling patronage network that linked Kinshasa to the peripheries of Congo and beyond. As Timothy Raeymaekers notes, Kabila was fundamentally unable to change the deeper patterns of the Mobutu system (indeed, there is little evidence he wanted to).[52]

The result was that the DRC's governance system partially reverted to the Mobutu-era characteristics of a protective relationship between centre and periphery in which elites in Kinshasa were able to offer influential administrative roles in return for resources. The use of informal networks rather than state institutions in turn contributed to continued underdevelopment of state capacity and a deepening reliance on Kabila's patronage network to secure the centre. However, the indispensable role of armed groups in governing eastern Congo did not dissipate after the war; instead, they evolved into crucial nodes in the system, particularly for marketing resources beyond Congo's borders.

The post-war period established the sovereign state in important and visible ways that affected the production of governance across the country. Perhaps most importantly, the resuscitation of the Armed Forces of the Democratic Republic of the Congo (FARDC) and development of a large security service across the country created a symbol of state power and an important tool for Kinshasa to influence the peripheries. Reflecting the newfound importance of the central state, soon after the 2002 peace accord many rebel movements transformed into political parties, attempting to gain influence in Kinshasa while maintaining the threat of force if their demands were not met.[53] At the same time, large-scale military integration of former armed groups into the FARDC offered a path for armed factions to be co-opted into the state.

However, the introduction of formal state institutions and nationally run integration processes quickly fell into the same patterns of patronage and protection that had characterized the Mobutu era. Beneath the veneer of formal government

[52] Raeymaekers, *Violent Capitalism*, 98.
[53] Verweijen, 'Stable Instability'.

institutions, Kabila and his elite cadre formed what Judith Verweijen has called a 'parallel government', a network of personal connections in which loyalty was exchanged for access to power and revenue-generating possibilities.[54] This network instrumentalized the state where necessary for its own gain—for example, targeting armed groups that posed a direct threat to Kabila's power—but made little effort to exert control or provide services throughout the country.[55] Moreover, Kinshasa consistently failed to transfer its required portions of tax revenues to the provinces[56] and never established effective public service provisions outside of the capital.[57] Kabila's overriding orientation towards shoring up his own cadre resulted in a failure of state administrative and regulatory capacities to develop.[58]

As had happened during the Mobutu era, one outcome of intentionally weak state governance was the co-optation of many state functions within a system commonly known as *rapportage* ('returning' or 'reporting back'). Under *rapportage*, state actors—from civil administrators to police and soldiers—were paid far less than what was necessary to sustain themselves, and salaries were often months late or not paid at all. At the same time, state positions were wholly within the gift of the presidency and the elite circle around Kabila, rendering it a conduit to the patronage network and a licence to predate. For example, a local police officer would be paid nearly nothing (sometimes as little as $15 per month) but would be expected to pay upwards into his/her chain of command in return for maintaining the job.[59] The expectation was clear: civil servants were to extract from the population.

This *parapluie* (or 'umbrella'), describes the protection received from the state, in return for which local state actors are expected to generate revenue. The Congolese administrative system was composed of a sprawling structure of these umbrellas, meaning that basic state services were constantly negotiated through small bribes, daily rents, and a myriad extractions of small sums from the population.[60] While I was living in Kinshasa, I was once detained by three police officers who threatened me with imprisonment unless I paid a bribe; not knowing the going rate, I offered them a $100 bill, which they took, laughingly telling me 'This is more than I make in three months.' I later discovered that $2 or $3 would have sufficed.

[54] Verweijen, 'Stable Instability'.

[55] Verweijen, 'Stable Instability'.

[56] Pierre Englebert and Emmanuel Kasongo Mungongo, 'Misguided and Misdiagnosed: The Failure of Decentralization Reforms in the DR Congo', *African Studies Review* 59, No. 1 (2016).

[57] Pierre Englebert, 'Congo Blues: Scoring Kabila's Rule', Atlantic Council, Africa Center, Issue Brief, May 2016.

[58] Schatzberg, *The Dialectics of Oppression in Zaire*.

[59] See Maria Eriksson Baaz and Ola Olsson, 'Feeding the Horse: Unofficial Economic Activities within the Police Force in the DR Congo', *African Security* 4, No. 4 (2011); Henri Boshoff et al., *Supporting SSR in the DRC: Between a Rock and a Hard Place* (The Hague: Netherlands Institute of International Relations, 2010); see also Carayannis, Vlassenroot, Hoffmann, and Pangburn, *Competing Networks and Political Order*.

[60] Trefon, 'Public Service Provision in a Failed State', 9–21.

The *rapportage* system, however, had to adapt to a post-war landscape in eastern Congo, where dozens of armed groups and their patrons had built a complex set of wartime accumulation networks stretching from artisanal mining hubs in isolated rural locales out to international markets. As Timothy Raeymaekers notes, the post-war transition did not destroy these networks; rather, they became partially integrated into the state reconfiguration process.[61] Businesses needed to find ways to reconnect their operations to state enterprise and benefit from the new centre of gravity and protection opportunities emanating from Kinshasa. Militias too saw the need to affiliate in one way or another with the power-brokers within the patronage system, particularly to secure their lines of trade beyond Congo's borders.[62] This often took the form of partnership with elements of the FARDC to traffic natural resources across the eastern border into Rwanda and Uganda, a relationship that allowed the militias to benefit from military protection while also providing resources for the FARDC to funnel up their *rapportage* chains of command.

Post-war governance thus took the form of relationships of reciprocal protection. Armed groups competed over the right to protect communities and their associated natural resources, while also competing to receive protection from the state. As Tatiana Carayannis et al. write, armed groups needed a *parapluie* (protection from an influential elite) to attain power in a given setting—a widespread technique of governing known as *trafic d'influence* ('influence peddling').[63] Reciprocally, elite politicians in Kinshasa required armed groups to provide them with resources and leverage in the peripheries, given that armed groups controlled the bulk of resource extraction points and routes throughout and beyond eastern Congo. While highly asymmetric, the relationship between the elite in Kinshasa and a wide variety of armed groups was thus one of often conflictual symbiosis, a violent negotiation over the right to govern where both sides required the presence of the other to survive.[64] Other authors have referred to this dynamic as 'political unsettlement', reflecting the unstable relationships born out of competition over access to the state but which also created systemic stability over time.[65]

This reciprocal relationship between armed groups and state actors has been fairly typical across eastern Congo, forging post-war networks that stretch to the elite in Kinshasa and well beyond the DRC's borders. 'Every politician has an armed group in the East', a Congolese parliamentarian told me in 2017. 'It is how to get influence in Kinshasa.'[66] In many cases, the link was along ethnic lines: elite

[61] Raeymaekers, *Violent Capitalism*, 119.
[62] Raeymaekers, *Violent Capitalism*, 170.
[63] Carayannis, Vlassenroot, Hoffmann, and Pangburn, *Competing Networks and Political Order*.
[64] Vlassenroot and Raeymaekers, 'New Political Order in the DR Congo?', 39–52.
[65] Verweijen, 'Stable Instability'; see also Christine Bell and Jan Pospisil, 'Navigating Inclusion in Transitions from Conflict: The Formalised Political *Un*settlement', *Journal of International Development* 29, No. 5 (2017): 576–593.
[66] Interview with a member of Nande parliamentary caucus, March 2016.

members of a particular ethnic group would retain ties to community protection militias, giving themselves greater influence in Kinshasa and also securing their lines of patronage. For example, a prominent Hutu leader and former governor, Eugene Serufuli, rose to power largely on the strength of the local defence forces he controlled in the Kivus in eastern Congo, which at one point numbered around 20,000.[67] His role as state governor of the Kivus was indistinguishable from his role as the puppeteer of a massive Hutu-based militia in the state. That militia, with strong ties to other groups in Rwanda, not only secured Serufuli's political interests among elite circles, but also ensured the livelihoods of Hutu communities across much of the Kivus. As a Hutu parliamentarian in Kinshasa told me, 'Serufuli protects us from attacks and feeds our families. In return, we feed him.'[68]

For ten years following the war, Kabila's government appeared to entrench itself further, winning elections in 2006 and 2011 and building a patronage network that stretched across the major resources of the country. As Judith Verweijen notes, this consolidation in the centre relied on a certain level of instability in eastern Congo, as elites derived much of their influence and resources from informal constellations of armed groups and business interests.[69] In one sense, stability moved like a pendulum across the country, with Kinshasa relying on apparent chaos in the East to ensure the elite needs were met. Kabila's security forces would occasionally step in to resolve an escalating crisis and secure national interests but would generally remain disengaged to allow the network to run its course.[70]

Over time this meant that the security of Kabila's position at the helm of the country became contingent upon the state *not* governing eastern Congo. Instead, the protection scheme at the heart of the Congolese system required that the network of brokers, middlemen, armed groups, and traders operated informally to accumulate wealth and pass it through the system like capillaries in a body.[71] Hugo de Vries has suggested that this lack of direct control by the state gave Congo a sort of 'archipelago statehood', with central authority only exercised in high-value economic enclaves.[72] Even this archipelago, however, was embedded in the protection system, as the combination of armed groups and transnational business interests evolved into the major source of influence and resources across eastern Congo.

As a result, in many settings armed groups became *de facto* administrative authorities, taxing the local population while also helping to bring in resources from

[67] For an in-depth description of Serufuli's ascent to power, see Luca Jourdan, 'New Forms of Political Order in North Kivu: The Case of the Governor Eugene Serufuli', Paper presented at the conference 'Beside the State: New Forms of Political Power in Post-1990's Africa', Milan, December 2005.

[68] Meeting note, Kinshasa, October 2016.

[69] Verweijen, 'Stable Instability'.

[70] Hugo de Vries, *Going Around in Circles: The Challenges of Peacekeeping and Stabilisation in the Democratic Republic of the Congo* (The Hague: Clingendael, 2015).

[71] Carayannis, Vlassenroot, Hoffmann, and Pangburn, *Competing Networks and Political Order*.

[72] De Vries, *Going Around in Circles*.

the international markets.[73] And in a system where politicians and businesspeople were never held accountable for their direct links to armed groups, the protection system quickly became normalized across Congo.[74] Timothy Raeymaekers has referred to this as an 'inverted power relationship between the supposed gatekeepers and the brokers of this regional political economy', where a cluster of non-state actors took on the day-to-day task of 'making the law'.[75]

The state's abrogation of its responsibility to govern does not mean the Congolese remained bereft of a sense of statehood in their country. In fact, the Congolese people have maintained a strong sense of *citoyenneté*—'moral obligation to the country'—from Mobutu's time to present.[76] Invented in the Mobutu era to stoke nationalist pride and shore up his single party regime, *citoyenneté* has been a basis for the kind of predatory fend-for-yourself lifestyles exemplified in much of the country, but also to encourage people to feel an obligation to provide public goods to their communities. In a system where the state has rarely been seen performing state-like activities, groups as diverse as militias, businesses, and community leaders have invoked a 'language of stateness', including the right to provide services, offer protection, and administer taxes to describe their day-to-day practices.[77]

I repeatedly found this notion of *citoyenneté* at the centre of my discussions with people in eastern Congo. In one encounter, I was speaking with a resident of Bukavo, a town on the southernmost tip of Lake Kivu. The area had been strongly affected by the presence of the Democratic Forces for the Liberation of Rwanda (FDLR), a Rwandaphone group formed largely out of those fleeing the 1994 genocide in Rwanda. In addition to posing a serious threat to civilians and being targeted by the Congolese army on many occasions, the FDLR had over time become an essential actor in the Congolese fabric, intermarrying its members into Congolese communities and gradually taking on a host of other roles, including community protection, delivery of charcoal, and a range of socio-economic activities.

'You see', the man said to me,

> even the FDLR has *citoneyenneté*, even though they are from Rwanda. They come here, they become part of our communities, and they start to feel like they belong, like they need to offer something as part of this country. The FDLR has become part of our Congo, whether we like it or not.

[73] Timothy Raeymaekers, 'Post-war Conflict and the Market for Protection: The Challenges to Congo's Hybrid Peace', *International Peacekeeping* 20, No. 5 (2013): 600–617.
[74] Verweijen, 'Stable Instability'.
[75] Raeymaekers, *Violent Capitalism*.
[76] Carayannis, Vlassenroot, Hoffmann, and Pangburn, *Competing Networks and Political Order*.
[77] Carayannis, Vlassenroot, Hoffmann, and Pangburn, *Competing Networks and Political Order*.

This notion of all citizens in one way or another acting 'as the state' was one of several key underlying rules that influenced the evolution of Congo's governance system during the post-war period.

Taken together, the most salient aspects of the post-war system were (1) the *parapluie* relationship between the centre and the periphery, where elites in Kinshasa were able to protect key state positions in return for influence and resources in eastern Congo; (2) the resulting underdevelopment of formal state institutions beyond the major cities, allowing for informal networks to flourish and feed the centre, creating a feedback loop that prevented state institutional development; (3) the role of violence in securing these relationships, and in maintaining sufficient threats on elite interests to connect community interests to power-brokers in Kinshasa; and (4) the brokering role of businesses in connecting the natural resources to foreign markets, thus completing the circuit by which influence and resources flowed around the DRC. Taken together, these characteristics acted as strong attractors, drawing resources and political influence towards the informal network rather than state institutions.

In conclusion, Congo displayed a form of 'punctuated equilibrium' through its post-colonial existence, where relatively long periods of stability were interrupted by moments of severe rupture.[78] The three most salient of these ruptures were Mobutu's ascent to the presidency, the outbreak of war in 1996, and the end of the Second Congolese War in 2002. In each, the visible character of Congo's governance system shifted significantly. However, through the lens of complexity theory, I have argued that the underlying rules proved remarkably resilient to more fundamental change, exerting strong path dependency over the course of the country. These underlying rules can be reduced to three types of relationships explored in this chapter: (1) the exchange of protection for resources (seen most clearly in the *parapluie* section above); (2) the symbiotic relationship among armed groups, businesses, and communities; and (3) a positive feedback loop in which the right to govern moves increasingly outside of formal state institutions, thus stripping them of authority and generating even greater reliance on informal networks to supply security and basic services.

As the next chapter explores, these underlying rules rendered the Congolese system extraordinarily resilient against attempts to reinvigorate state institutions. Instead, they created a set of steep valleys in the governance landscape of the country, ineluctably drawing in the enormous state-building resources provided in the post-war period. Much of the UN's twenty-year effort to bolster the Congolese state and help it govern the country found its way into these valleys.

[78] For a good description of punctuated equilibrium theory, see James L. True, Bryan D. Jones, and Frank R. Baumgartner, 'Punctuated-Equilibrium Theory: Explaining Stability and Change in Public Policymaking', in Paul A. Sabatier, ed., *Theories of the Political Process* (Cambridge, MA: Westview Press, 2017), 155–189.

6

Sisyphean statebuilding in the Congo

Why the UN's efforts failed

In 2016, I sat across from Congolese Minister of Foreign Affairs, Raymond Tshibanda, an elegantly dressed man in a bespoke suit speaking impeccable Parisian French. Along with the United Nations (UN)'s deputy head of mission, we were discussing the exit strategy for United Nations Organization Stabilization Mission in the Democratic Republic of Congo (MONUSCO), the UN's twenty-year old peacekeeping operation in the Democratic Republic of Congo (DRC). The paper we had drafted for Minister Tshibanda's consideration articulated the UN's vision of the Congolese state:

> MONUSCO's exit from the DRC will be contingent upon ... a sustained improvement of the security situation, institutional stability and democratic practices that will pave the way for the Congolese people to enjoy peace and prosperity in accordance with the human rights, fundamental liberties and the duties of the citizen and the State ... [including] the existence of functional State institutions in conflict-affected areas and a functioning democratic order that reduces the risk of instability, including adequate political space, observance of human rights and credible elections on a regular basis.[1]

Minister Tshibanda, in contrast, had sketched out a far different exit process: as soon as major armed groups had been reduced to a level that could be handled by the Congolese army alone, he said, MONUSCO was no longer needed. Issues of transformation of the security sector, free and fair elections, and institutional capacity to guarantee human rights protections were all well and good, but MONUSCO was not needed (or indeed welcome, according to many of my contacts close to President Kabila). Our conversation—polite and agreeable on its surface—presaged what would become a very difficult set of negotiations that ultimately would fail to produce a joint exit strategy for the mission. Towards the end

[1] Draft Non-Paper on MONUSCO's Exit Strategy, 9 December 2016 (on file with author).

States of Disorder, Ecosystems of Governance. Adam Day, Oxford University Press.
 DOI: 10.1093/oso/9780192863898.003.0007

of the meeting, Tshibanda picked up our draft strategy and said, 'If we follow this, MONUSCO will never leave, you will have set an impossible mission.'[2]

In this chapter, I explore why Minister Tshibanda was right: the UN had set itself an impossible task in asking a mission to transform Congo into a liberal state. This in itself is not a new revelation; a range of scholars have criticized the UN's intervention as being an unwitting replica of colonial rule,[3] a misguided effort that incentivized violence,[4] a poorly planned venture subject to elite capture,[5] a disconnected enterprise that failed to account for local conflict dynamics,[6] or a myopic effort unable to account for different scales of violence at local, national, and international levels.[7] Across this literature, the UN is typically described as an out-of-touch external actor pursuing a 'top-down' strategy to transform Congo into a liberal state, ignoring or incapable of addressing the many countervailing forces operating in the country.[8]

However, this chapter goes beyond the mainstream critiques of the UN to explore what Carayannis et al. have termed 'power networks' stretching across actors and communities in the DRC.[9] It is the central contention of this book that such networks operate as a complex system, self-regulating according to feedback loops and strong attractors which generate tendencies towards particular courses of action and behaviour. Unlike other studies, I do not argue that the UN's failure to achieve its statebuilding goals was due to any kind of shortcoming in the way the mission implemented its mandate (though there were certainly many), or faulty understanding of local realities (though it often did).[10] Instead, the interconnected network of governance in Congo self-organized around and with the UN mission, displaying the kind of emergent behaviour expected of complex systems. In this, the UN was not an external actor but rather became part of the Congolese system

[2] Author's meeting notes, on file.

[3] Alex Veit, *Intervention as Indirect Rule: Civil War and Statebuilding in the Democratic Republic of Congo* (New York: Campus Verlag, 2011).

[4] Andreas Mehler and Denis Tull, 'The Hidden Costs of Power-sharing: Reproducing Insurgent Violence in Africa', *African Affairs* 104, No. 416 (2006): 375–398; Maria Eriksson Baaz and Judith Verweijen, 'The Volatility of a Half-cooked Bouillabaisse: Rebel-Military Integration and Conflict Dynamics in the Eastern DRC', *African Affairs* 112, No. 449 (2013): 563–582.

[5] See, e.g., Hugo de Vries, *Going around in Circles: The Challenges of Peacekeeping and Stabilisation in the Democratic Republic of the Congo* (The Hague: Clingendael, 2015).

[6] Séverine Autesserre, *The Trouble with the Congo: Local Violence and the Failure of International Peacebuilding* (New York: Cambridge University Press, 2010).

[7] Jason K. Stearns, 'The Democratic Republic of the Congo: An Elusive Peace', in Gilbert Khadiagala, ed., *War and Peace in Africa's Great Lakes Region* (London: Palgrave MacMillan, 2017).

[8] See, e.g., Stein Sundstol Eriksen, 'The Liberal Peace Is Neither: Peacebuilding, Statebuilding and the Reproduction of Conflict in the Democratic Republic of Congo', *International Peacekeeping* 16, No. 5 (2009): 652–666.

[9] Tatiana Carayannis, Koen Vlassenroot, Kasper Hoffmann and Aaron Pangburn, *Competing Networks and Political Order in the Democratic Republic of Congo: A Literature Review on the Logics of Public Authority and International Intervention* (London: London School of Economics 2018).

[10] See, e.g., Eriksen, 'The Liberal Peace Is Neither', 652–666; Autesserre, *The Trouble with the Congo*.

itself, subject to the strong attractors that allowed the system to self-organize.[11] Over time, this meant the mission was not only unable to achieve many of the kinds of transformational change it had hoped for, but in fact unwittingly bolstered some of Congo's tendencies towards authoritarianism, predatory state practices, and violent forms of governance.[12]

Building on the description of Congo's governance system in Chapter 5, I briefly outline the UN's statebuilding logic in Congo and then focus on three interrelated areas where United Nations Mission in the Democratic Republic of Congo (MONUC) / MONUSCO most directly attempted to implement its statebuilding mandate: (1) ensuring the state's monopoly of violence; (2) extending state authority via stabilization; and (3) supporting an ambitious national security sector reform (SSR) agenda. In each, I consider how the UN's hopes for linear, gradual progress towards a more liberal state in Congo were thwarted by a highly adaptive complex system.

The UN's statebuilding logic

From the outset, MONUC described its role as 'assist[ing] a country ruined by war and civil strife to become once again a functioning State able to protect its citizens from war, hunger and abuse, and to give them opportunity for a better life.'[13] The Security Council, too, was clear: the UN's central goal was 'to provide assistance for the re-establishment of a State based on the rule of law.'[14] The fact that the DRC had been a functioning democratic system in the terms described by the Council was apparently irrelevant. Initially deployed to support the 1999 ceasefire agreement that ended the Second Congolese War,[15] the mission's statebuilding mandate grew significantly in the early 2000s to include support to the state-led disarmament, reintegration, and resettlement processes;[16] helping the national army address major escalations of violence in eastern Congo;[17] and support to national reforms to the legislature, elections, and security sector.[18] The mission again bolstered its support to the state in 2010, shifting to a stabilization mission (and its name from MONUC to MONUSCO) which expanded the resources dedicated to building state institutional capacity and extending state authority

[11] For a good description of endogeneity in UN peace operations, see Charles T. Hunt, 'Complexity Theory', in K. Oksamytna and J. Karlsrud, eds., *United Nations Peace Operations and International Relations Theory* (Manchester: Manchester University Press, 2020).

[12] During the crucial period of MONUSCO's stabilization mandate, the DRC's ranking on the Fragile States Index moved from seventh to second worst in the world.

[13] MONUC website (since taken down).

[14] United Nations Security Council Resolution, SC/Res/1493 (2003).

[15] United Nations Security Council resolution, SC/RES/1279 (1999).

[16] United Nations Security Council Resolution, SC/Res/1493 (2003).

[17] United Nations Security Council Resolution, SC/Res/1493 (2003).

[18] United Nations Security Council Resolution, S/RES/1565 (2004).

across the country. In 2013, following the fall of the eastern capital of Goma to the March 23 rebel group, MONUSCO was provided with an offensive military mandate, again to ensure the state's monopoly on violence by neutralizing armed groups.[19]

Throughout the mission's evolution, its statebuilding logic has always been to try to control the DRC's territory from the centre outwards.[20] The 'extension of state authority' is perhaps the most repeated phrase across the mission's various stabilization concepts and has been mirrored in Congolese government plans as well.[21] To achieve this, MONUSCO needed to help the Congolese authorities eradicate armed groups, build a legitimate set of state institutions, and then extend them geographically across the territory of eastern Congo. This linear, progressive concept of how change would take place in the DRC is common across peacekeeping,[22] but achieved a sort of apotheosis in the case of MONUSCO as the mission's mandate gradually swelled to include nearly every aspect of statebuilding, from ensuring the state's monopoly of force to securing the vast territory of eastern Congo from armed groups, building the infrastructure and institutions of the state, and pushing for what the mission's chief of political affairs told me was the ultimate goal, 'the democratic transformation of Congo into a viable state, like one of ours'.[23] As I describe below, the mission's linear logic sought to change Congo's complex system of governance but instead was quickly absorbed by it.

Armed groups

In the immediate aftermath of the war, armed groups were rife in eastern Congo, including several large militias backed by Rwanda and Uganda (indeed in some areas their national armies retained a presence on Congolese territory for years). In 2003, the UN estimated that roughly 330,000 combatants needed to be integrated into the army, while dozens of smaller militias rendered the total number of non-state armed groups essentially uncountable.[24] The core goal of the post-war transition therefore was to establish the state's monopoly on legitimate violence by integrating the former rebel forces into the newly formed national army and

[19] United Nations Security Council Resolution, S/RES/2098 (2013).

[20] See Stephen Jackson, 'Borderlands and the Transformation of War Economies: Lessons from the DR Congo', *Conflict, Security & Development* 6, No. 3 (2006): 425–447.

[21] See, e.g., Congolese Prime Minister Muzito's 2009 statement on the government's stabilization plan, 'A durable peace … is only possible if supported by a complete extension of state authority.' Adolphe Muzito, 'Allocution à l'occasion du lancement des travaux sur le "Plan de Stabilisation et de reconstruction de l'Est de la République Démocratique du Congo"', Office of the Prime Minister (on file with author).

[22] E.g. in Mali and Central African Republic, the acronym RESA (Re-establish and Extend State Authority) has become widely used in defining mandates.

[23] I was regularly in meetings with the heads of sections of MONUSCO in 2016.

[24] Renner Onana and Hannah Taylor, 'MONUC and SSR in the Democratic Republic of the Congo', *International Peacekeeping* 15, No. 4 (2008): 501–516.

helping the state reduce the threat from the remaining militias. From the outset, this was a confusing process marked by spontaneous calls for integration by armed groups, a highly dysfunctional nationally led process, and deeply politicized decisions about eligibility and chains of command. This section traces the UN mission's role in addressing the threats posed by armed groups, arguing that its efforts to guarantee a state monopoly of force became tangled in the complex system of governance in eastern Congo, perversely resulting in even greater reliance on violence.

From the outset, MONUC's support to disarmament, demobilization, and reintegration (DDR) in Congo placed it in the role of gatekeeper for armed groups to access the state, demanding that combatants disarm and demobilize as a condition for joining the ranks of the national army. Alex Veit's in-depth study of MONUC's intervention in Ituri highlights this gatekeeper role, in particular the ways in which it attempted to guide the actions of armed groups away from patterns of violence.[25] However, MONUC often proved a poor interlocutor, unable to broker sustainable deals for armed groups to lay down arms and join the army. Politicians in Kinshasa regularly reneged on promises of integration, while armed groups refused to integrate fully, often returning to the bush to continue fighting in order to gain greater leverage for the next round of integration negotiations. Cycles of demobilization, integration, desertion, and remobilization meant that, by 2016 the major armed groups remained largely intact, while dozens of smaller groups had formed across eastern Congo.[26]

Several reasons have been given for the failure to sustainably demobilize groups like the Patriotic Resistance Force in Ituri (FRPI) or the Democratic Forces for the Liberation of Rwanda (FDLR) in the Kivus. Some, like Séverine Autesserre, have correctly argued that underlying local disputes over land and resources were overlooked by a detached and isolated UN, meaning that cycles of violence and the need for armed groups to protect local interests continually overrode any efforts at peacemaking.[27] Alex Veit suggests that the problem was one of asymmetric power at the national and local levels, where armed groups had diminishing authority as they left their local setting and could only access the state by retaining the threat of violence.[28] Others have placed blame on the government, which often failed to honour integration agreements, chronically underpaid its soldiers, and attempted to break up armed groups to weaken them and remove them from their power base, even during negotiations.[29] These findings help to identify some of the most important pieces of the integration puzzle, but do not offer a holistic picture, in part

[25] Veit, *Intervention as Indirect Rule.*
[26] Judith Verweijen and Claude Iguma Wakenge, 'Understanding Armed Group Proliferation in Eastern Congo', Rift Valley Institute PSRP Briefing Paper 7, December 2015.
[27] Autesserre, *The Trouble with the Congo.*
[28] Veit, *Intervention as Indirect Rule*, 170.
[29] Baaz and Verweijen, 'The Volatility of a Half-cooked Bouillabaisse', 563–582.

because they tend to consider armed groups solely through the lens of non-state actors.

In contrast, and as described in Chapter 5, the post-war period witnessed the growth of armed groups as essential to a form of networked governance that emerged in eastern Congo. While they challenged the state directly, they also performed the role of public authorities in a form of symbiotic relationship with communities, businesses, and elements of the state. Collecting taxes, protecting community interests, participating in the transfer of natural resources out of Congo, and executing the demands of power-brokers in Kinshasa, armed group members were not merely individuals hoping for a position within the state but were already the *de facto* governing authority in many places. In fact, the state had never attempted to govern the peripheries of the country, and in this Kabila displayed little difference to Mobutu in his lack of interest in building a coherent national security service that would control the territory of Congo. Instead, and following the previous patterns of governance established for decades, the political elite in Kinshasa looked to manipulate uncertainty in the integration process to control armed groups, limit their access to power, or leverage them against rivals. A chaotic, dysfunctional, and continually incomplete integration process served these purposes well, though it tended to frustrate the UN's objectives.

Congo's integration process operated in this context as a negative feedback loop in the broader governance system of the country, working to return the system back to its original state whenever it became unsettled.[30] When a given setting became overly violent—such as Ituri in the early 2000s—armed groups would be offered integration as a way to regulate the situation back to stability and assure Kabila's role at the centre. But that stability also required the continued presence of at least some armed groups to control access to resources and guarantee that community interests were balanced; after a period of time the integration would be abandoned by all sides and many ex-combatants would return to their former armed groups.

The role of armed groups as essential actors in the local governance scheme meant they were constantly pulled between a desire to pressure Kinshasa in order to gain political traction for their communities, and the equally strong pull of needing to subsist off local resources. After a period of neglect or punishment from the centre, these groups would again attempt to leverage their power through localized violence, once again generating a demobilization and a temporary integration process. As a result, over three national DDR plans and nearly twenty years of the mission's efforts to support demobilization, nearly none of the hoped-for dismantling of armed groups took place in a sustained fashion.[31]

[30] As described in the initial chapters, a negative feedback loop operates as a corrective, preventing further change and returning the system to its original condition.

[31] See Evert Kets and Hugo de Vries, 'Limits to Supporting Security Sector Interventions in the DRC', Institute for Security Studies Paper No. 257, July 2014; Maria Eriksson Baaz and Judith Verweijen,

From MONUC/MONUSCO's perspective, this was experienced as a frustrating failure. Each time the mission stepped in to support another demobilization process, it would appear to peter out as internal squabbling within the government led to broken promises of integration levels, while fickle armed group leaders would renege and disappear back into the bush. In some instances, intervention would result in a fracturing of the armed group, or an integration where only a small subset of the group was brought into the national army while the remaining militia members reconstituted themselves (what Alex Veit has cleverly described as a 'Matryushka doll' effect of armed groups).[32] However, when understood in terms of the symbiotic relationship between the armed groups and their communities—and indeed a form of symbiosis between the political elite and the armed groups that secured their interests in the periphery—the failure of sustained demobilization appears inevitable. Full disarmament would strip local communities of protection, access to international markets, and continued leverage over Kinshasa. Equally, it would strip power-brokers in Kinshasa of their base in the peripheries. As one senior politician with clear ties to an eastern militia told me in confidence, 'My people keep arms to stay in the game, to participate in the market for influence.'[33]

In Ituri, for example, dozens of attempts to broker a demobilization deal with the locally recruited FRPI never finished off the group, which continues to this day. In my conversations with MONUSCO's leadership in 2016, this was consistently described as a lack of political will by the government to meaningfully deliver development gains to the communities of Ituri, which meant the FRPI had to resort to violence to maintain pressure on the state and protect their interests against local encroachment.[34] A former member of the FRPI told me, 'the government can never offer us more than what we can get by going back into the bush and fighting them.'[35] Here, the system displayed a limited phase space—the range of possible outcomes given its underlying rules—allowing for partial demobilization and integration of the FRPI, but never an all-out end to the incentive structure driving the conflict. The FRPI was a necessary node in the governance system of Ituri, meaning that efforts to dismantle and integrate it into the state continually confronted the gravitational pull of its role in local conflict dynamics and communal protection.

This push and pull feature of armed group demobilization persisted even as the UN's approach became increasingly robust and militarized. In 2013, following the M23's attack on Goma, the Security Council gave the mission an offensive

'Between Integration and Disintegration: The Erratic Trajectory of the Congolese Army', Social Science Research Council, Conflict Prevention and Peace Forum, 2013.

[32] Veit, *Intervention as Indirect Rule*, 176.

[33] Interview with senior member of Hutu parliamentary caucus, Kinshasa, July 2016 (translation mine).

[34] Interview with MONUSCO staff member, Goma, February 2016.

[35] Interview with former FRPI member, Goma, February 2016.

force mandate, equipping it with a Force Intervention Brigade (FIB) of attack helicopters and greater military capabilities.[36] The core purpose of this mandate was to allow the UN to help the state 'neutralize' armed groups, especially those that posed a particular threat to the state or civilians. MONUSCO's neutralization mandate came to dominate much of the discourse on the UN in the DRC, and certainly raised expectations that the UN would be better placed to ensure the state's monopoly over violence.[37]

However, MONUSCO's offensive use of force did not deliver the expected sustained neutralization of armed groups in eastern Congo. There were moments where the mission's operations contributed to a temporary weakening of an armed group—such as a 2014 military operation against the FRPI, which reportedly killed 700 militia members—but these gains soon evaporated. By 2016, the FRPI had reconstituted itself in Ituri and was again carrying out attacks against the civilian population while simultaneously running illicit trade across Congo's borders. Similarly, between 2013 and 2016 in the Beni area of North Kivu, MONUSCO carried out a series of offensive operations jointly with the Armed Forces of the Democratic Republic of the Congo (FARDC) against the Allied Democratic Forces (ADF), a ruthless armed group responsible for thousands of civilian deaths. Not only did these fail to neutralize the group or create a more protective atmosphere for the surrounding communities, evidence suggests that the risks increased following MONUSCO's operations.[38] Higher rates of kidnappings pointed to the ADF resupplying its forces in the aftermath of a confrontation, while reprisal attacks in the days and weeks following MONUSCO's interventions were regular and predictable.[39]

While serving as the Senior Political Adviser to MONUSCO in 2016, I was tasked to develop tailored strategies for the priority armed groups, including the FDLR, ADF, FRPI, and the remnants of the Lords Resistance Army (LRA). In working with the mission to develop these strategies, I noticed a common thread across the UN leadership: armed groups were only spoken of in terms of their risks to civilians, not any of the other roles that they played in society. In a senior leadership retreat in mid-2016, hours were spent discussing how joint operations would proceed against the armed groups, but no mention was made of the role these groups played in eastern Congolese communities or the broader Congolese political sphere. This viewpoint was reflected in countless reports of the secretary-general to the Security Council, which consistently counted the number

[36] United Nations Security Council Resolution, S/RES/2098 (2013).

[37] It is beyond the scope of this book to elaborate the protection of civilians functions of the FIB, which grew in importance over time.

[38] Adam Day, 'Neutralization of the ADF as Part of a Mission-wide Approach to Protect Civilians and Stabilize the Beni/Northern Lubero Area', 5 September 2016 (confidential MONUSCO document, on file with author). I was told the same by numerous residents of Beni during my visits there in 2016.

[39] Interviews with MONUSCO staff members, Beni, 2016.

of civilians killed by armed groups, but never detailed their other functions or motivations in eastern Congo. Internal reports by the mission's Joint Mission Analysis Centre (JMAC) often had detailed descriptions of the underlying inter-communal disputes that contributed to armed activity in a given area—such as the Hema/Lendu tensions in the FRPI areas of Ituri—but I rarely saw an analysis that acknowledged the governance roles of these groups, certainly not in the public domain. This meant that, while individuals in the mission often had nuanced understandings of these groups, the scope for the groups to be described in anything other than security terms in our strategic documents was close to zero.

Here, MONUSCO's model simply failed to reflect the reality of eastern Congo. Considering the groups as security threats, the mission leadership believed that military pressure would weaken armed groups, force them to the negotiating table, and eventually lead to a brokered demobilization and integration deal. In the case of so-called 'foreign' armed groups, there was an additional misperception that groups like the ADF or FDLR might be driven to abandon eastern Congo altogether. However, these groups were simultaneously performing important other functions in the governance system of the East, often providing community security, basic services, and connecting communities to the international markets for natural resources. UN/FARDC military operations in places like Ituri and Beni did not result in greater security but instead sowed confusion, creating greater demand for physical protection within the surrounding communities, for which they often turned to armed groups.[40] Absent a viable or trusted state security presence, the demand for protection from armed groups increased, driving militia mobilization rather than reducing the strength of the group. As Raeymaekers and Verweijen have demonstrated, the ironic outcome of efforts to quash armed groups in eastern Congo has been the incentivization of violence and a proliferation of militias.[41] By the end of 2016, the UN estimated that the number of armed groups had grown to well over seventy, a 400 per cent increase over the number in the mid-2000s.[42]

The use of force against armed groups also obscured the important role they played in local governance. Here, another example illustrates the system at work. In North Kivu, the FDLR had formed in 2000 as an amalgam of Hutu armed groups with aspirations of changing the Tutsi-led government in Kigali. Its armed wing boasted a fighting force of 12,000 combatants by 2002, while its capacity to hold

[40] For a good critique of the FIB, see Denis M. Tull, 'The Limits and Unintended Consequences of UN Peace Enforcement: The Force Intervention Brigade in the Dr Congo', *International Peacekeeping* (2017): 1–24; see more generally, Charles T. Hunt, 'All Necessary Means to What Ends? The Unintended Consequences of the "Robust Turn" in Un Peace Operations', *International Peacekeeping* 24, (1) (2017/01/01 2017): 108–131.

[41] Judith Verweijen, 'Stable Instability: Political Settlements and Armed Groups in the Congo' (London: Rift Valley Institute, 2016); Timothy Raeymaekers, 'Post-war Conflict and the Market for Protection: The Challenges to Congo's Hybrid Peace', *International Peacekeeping* 20, No. 5 (2013): 600–617.

[42] United Nations, 'Report of the United Nations Secretary General on the Situation in Eastern Congo', S/2016/1130, December 2016.

and defend territory gained it the title of 'a state within a state' in eastern Congo.[43] A series of FDLR incursions into Rwanda in the early 2000s, along with suspicions in Kinshasa that Kigali was supporting anti-Kabila elements in eastern Congo, meant that the FDLR was at the centre of regional dynamics and a major risk factor for stability in the region. For much of MONUC/MONUSCO's lifespan, the FDLR has been considered the top priority armed group, due to its fighting strength, threat to civilians, and unwillingness to demobilize.

Frequent joint military operations by the Congolese army and the UN attempted to 'neutralize' the FDLR, and periodically the UN and the government would claim a major gain. The assumption was that sufficient military pressure would cause the FDLR leadership to relent, allowing for a full demobilization process and the eventual return of the ex-combatants to Rwanda. Periodic overtures by the FDLR leadership—including a temporary announcement in 2013 that it would lay down arms—kept hopes alive that a strategy based on the use of force would deliver results.[44] In 2015, an optimistic FARDC chief of staff announced that the fighting capacities of the FDLR had been reduced from 7,500 combatants to a mere 1,400, arguably rendering it a minor group that could be met by Congolese security forces alone.[45]

However, this optimism was misplaced as the FDLR appeared to fracture, spread, and persist across North Kivu, attacking civilians throughout much of 2016.[46] The FDLR's resilience in the face of sustained military pressure by the state and the UN ran against the prevailing wisdom of the international community that force would effectively neutralize armed groups. But seen through the lens of a complex, networked system, it makes sense that this strategy would ultimately fail. Over a twenty-year period, the FDLR had evolved from a foreign armed group focused on Hutu rights in Rwanda into a crucial aspect of the Congolese governance system. High rates of intermarriage and constant trade across eastern Congo meant the group was deeply embedded in the social fabric of the region, and relied upon to defend local Congolese Hutu interests concerning land, natural resources, and access to foreign markets. Heightened interethnic tensions in the 2014–16 period meant the FDLR could easily recruit from the Congolese Hutu population, deepening its connections within the DRC.

In fact, over time, the FDLR had become a crucial provider of key goods to the eastern capital city of Goma, operating closely (if illicitly) with the state and local businesses. For example, the FDLR maintained an elaborate operation in which

[43] Anna Gyorgy, 'Guerillas in the Mist: The Congolese Experience of the FDLR War in Eastern Congo and the Role of the International Community', Pole Institute, February 2010.

[44] Interviews with MONUSCO JMAC, Office of the SRSG, Office of the DSRSG Rule of Law, and Force, Goma/Kinshasa, 13–17 September 2017.

[45] MONUSCO website, https://monusco.unmissions.org/node/100043805.

[46] United Nations Security Council, 'Report of the Secretary-General on the United Nations Organization Stabilization Mission in the Democratic Republic of the Congo', S/2016/233, 9 March 2016, para 25, available at https://undocs.org/pdf?symbol=en/S/2016/233

it illegally obtained charcoal from the nearby Virunga National Park, transported the charcoal via a series of checkpoints manned by the corrupt army officials, and then marketed it in Goma with local businesses.[47] MONUSCO's 2017 attempts to disrupt this operation by attacking the FDLR and arresting the complicit army commanders meant that Goma's residents needed to be provided new sources of charcoal for their daily cooking. Similar arrangements across much of North Kivu—in which the FDLR worked closely with local officials and businesses to protect populations and/or provide essential services to communities—meant that the group was both a serious threat to civilians and a state-like governance actor.

The UN's efforts to neutralize armed groups thus encountered, and were absorbed by, the complex system of governance in eastern Congo. As described in Chapter 5, armed groups were integral aspects of an interdependent system of governance that secured and marketed natural resources, provided protections for communities, participated indirectly in national-level political jockeying, and entered into longstanding disputes over land and local authorities. A joint UN/FARDC attack on an FRPI unit in Ituri meant that the other nodes in the system readjusted: Lendu communities (from which the FRPI arose) would demand greater protection against their Hema counterparts, while temporary disruptions in the mineral trade affected business interests stretching from Ituri to Kinshasa and beyond.[48] Military operations against the other major groups—particularly the FDLR and ADF—tended to have similar results: the groups might scatter and appear to weaken, but their deeper roles within the social and political system would allow them to again build up and regroup. While the minutiae of these effects locally within the system are too detailed to parse here, the broad impact was that over time the system adapted to efforts to militarily disrupt/degrade these groups, and patterns persisted without changing the underlying rules. Armed groups remained (and remain) integral to the way in which eastern Congo self-organizes.

MONUSCO's operations in fact appear to have contributed to a positive feedback loop that drove the Congolese system towards violent forms of governance. By gradually increasing its own military strength and willingness to take offensive action, MONUSCO was more disruptive to the armed groups. But this disruption only drove a need for the system to re-establish equilibrium, which in turn demanded greater reliance on armed groups (not the state). Over time, one outcome appears to have been the proliferation of smaller militias which eluded the focus of the FARDC and MONUSCO, but which were still able to participate in the networks of power at the local level.[49] These smaller groups may pose less of a direct threat to the state when considered individually, but collectively they directly

[47] Author's internal analysis from time as Senior Political Adviser to MONUSCO (on file).
[48] International Crisis Group, 'Congo: Quatre priorités pour un paix durable en Ituri', Nairobi, 2008.
[49] See Verweijen and Wakenge, 'Understanding Armed Group Proliferation in Eastern Congo'.

undermine the overarching goal of the UN, which has always been to help guarantee the state's monopoly of violence across Congo's territory. The deep irony is that the UN's attempts to end the patterns of violence in eastern Congo have had the unintended consequence of entrenching them still further.[50] A complexity-driven analysis, however, has revealed that these dynamics should have been expected.

Stabilization

I once asked a Canadian officer in MONUSCO what the mission's stabilization mandate meant, given that it had been a top priority for the mission since 2010. 'It means shape, clear, hold, build', he told me, 'just like Afghanistan'. This formula, drawn from counterinsurgency doctrine, suggests that insecurity can be addressed by controlling the battlefield, clearing it of non-state armed actors, protecting the territory from incursions, and developing state capacities on that newly taken soil. When Martin Kobler, a former special representative of the secretary-general (SRSG) of MONUSCO, presented his 2013 stabilization strategy to the Security Council, he employed this concept, describing the 'islands of stability' which would extend state authority into key areas of eastern Congo, creating a positive 'ripple effect' across the entire territory.[51]

However, as described in Chapter 5, the DRC was not a chaotic sea of instability dotted with islands of state capacity; instead it presented a complex and interdependent network of actors which together generated a highly resilient governance system involving state and non-state actors. Attempts to superimpose new state security and rule of law institutions onto this system did not result in the kind of archipelago of stability envisioned by the UN; rather MONUSCO found itself caught up in and unwittingly bolstering a system with strong attractors towards violent, predatory forms of governance. This section focuses on MONUC/MONUSCO's stabilization efforts between 2008 and 2016, demonstrating how the symbiotic relationships among state, armed groups, and other actors worked against the goal of 'bringing the state back in'.

The International Security and Stabilisation Support Strategy (I4S)[52] was developed in the context of the 2008 Goma accords, when some of the largest armed groups in eastern Congo agreed to lay down arms and either integrate into the army or reintegrate into their communities. The UN saw this as an opportunity to make serious progress towards ending armed group activity in eastern Congo

[50] Tull, 'The Limits and Unintended Consequences of UN Peace Enforcement', 167–190.

[51] Alberto Barrera, 'The Congo Trap: Islands of Stability in a Sea of Instability', *Stability: International Journal of Security and Development* 4, No. 1 (2015): 1–16.

[52] Initially, the stabilization strategy was called the 'ISSSS' but became 'I4S' when the government adopted its own strategy, the STAREC. Acknowledging the distinction, I nonetheless use 'I4S' throughout for ease of reference.

and accordingly put the full weight of the mission behind stabilization. In North and South Kivu, six areas were identified where armed groups posed a significant risk of a return to open conflict; here, MONUC supported the Congolese military operations to 'clear out' the groups.[53] Into the void created by these operations, the UN and bilateral donors would support the government in building new roads, constructing rule of law institutions (courts, police stations), and ramping up socio-economic projects such as hospitals and schools. Between 2008 and 2012, sixty projects worth nearly $400 million were implemented, tens of thousands of former combatants were disarmed and demobilized, and hundreds of kilometres of road were rehabilitated.[54] Throughout, the I4S was developed as a direct support plan to the government's national stabilization strategy (STAREC), meaning the state led on prioritizing areas for stabilization in eastern Congo.[55]

In 2011, however, it became evident that the stabilization effort had produced very little impact on the ground. According to an I4S internal assessment, only two of the six priority areas had shown any improvement, two had remained the same, and two had in fact worsened.[56] Major armed groups continued to operate in all of the six priority areas, and some had increased their levels of violence during this period, causing a spike in displacements.[57] In areas where roads had been rehabilitated and ostensibly brought under state control, barriers for illegal taxation multiplied, usually manned by off-book state security agents.[58] Newly installed courts and prisons were often left empty, or side-lined by traditional authorities who saw them as a threat to customary rule.[59] Predation emerged in areas where unpaid state officials had been deployed, while many of the newly hired security agents retained their affiliation to armed groups.[60] Capturing the view of many non-governmental organizations (NGOs), Oxfam suggested that the UN's stabilization efforts had caused more harm than good, diverting resources

[53] De Vries, *Going around in Circles*.

[54] MONUSCO, 'International Security and Stabilisation Support Strategy Quarterly Report, 2009–2012'.

[55] For a good comparison of I4S and STAREC, see Sarah Bailey, 'Humanitarian Action, Early Recovery and Stabilisation in the Democratic Republic of Congo', Overseas Development Institute Humanitarian Policy Working Group Paper, July 2011, 4.

[56] MONUSCO, 'International Security and Stabilisation Support Strategy Situation Assessment 2011'.

[57] Emily Paddon and Guillaume Lacaille, 'Stabilising the Congo: Forced Migration', Policy Briefing 8, Refugee Studies Centre. Oxford Department of International Development (noting a resurgence of the FDLR during this period).

[58] According to MONUSCO, 'International Security and Stabilisation Support Strategy Situation Assessment 2011' report, 55 per cent of 'police' deployed along the roads in North Kivu were not on the government payroll. See also Sam Dixon, 'Why Efforts to Stabilise the DR Congo Are Not Working', Oxfam Horn, East and Central Africa Blog, 4 July 2012, available at https://www.oxfamblogs.org/eastafrica/?p=4484

[59] De Vries, *Going around in Circles*, 50.

[60] Bailey, 'Humanitarian Action, Early Recovery and Stabilisation in the Democratic Republic of Congo'.

away from the neediest populations and instead politicizing funding by supporting government priority areas.[61]

These failings did not go unnoticed, and in 2012 the Security Council demanded that MONUSCO revise the I4S. The subsequent 2013–17 strategy maintained MONUSCO's supporting role to the government, but placed greater focus on local drivers of power, issues of land and identity, and improving relations between the state and local communities.[62] Here, stabilization was defined as 'a process where state and society build reciprocal accountability and address locally specific causes of violent conflict.'[63] This placed stabilization squarely in the centre of MONUSCO's work, linking it to the military operations to clear areas, the DDR processes to hold them, the SSR work to build strong, viable state institutions, and the local conflict resolution work of civil affairs. The more local focus was meant to empower provincial government actors to help set priorities in development programming and avoid elite capture from Kinshasa. New zones for stabilization programming were selected with the government, and a greater number of civil society groups were involved in shaping stabilization projects.[64]

As with the first wave of stabilization, however, MONUSCO's efforts to extend state authority and broker improved state-society relations in eastern Congo in the 2012–16 period largely failed to achieve their objectives. While pointing to incremental, short-term achievements in project areas, even the I4S promotional material acknowledged that it was unclear whether the work 'has impacted the cycles of violence and instability in the long term'.[65] In fact, by 2016, armed groups had proliferated still further in priority areas, threatening state security services in many of the areas where the I4S had spent its largest sums of money.

Explanations for the failure of stabilization in eastern Congo vary, but tend to argue that the 'top-down' approach of MONUSCO rendered it too close to the government, out of touch with local and regional realities, and tending to increase the predatory practices of the state.[66] The concept of 'islands of stability' appears almost comical in some of the critiques of MONUSCO, seen as a simplistic slogan drawn from counterinsurgency doctrine without meaningful application to the

[61] Hannah Cooper, 'More Harm than Good? UN's Islands of Stability in DRC', Oxfam Policy and Practice Blog, 8 May 2014, available at https://views-voices.oxfam.org.uk/2014/05/islands-of-stability-in-drc/

[62] MONUSCO, 'International Security and Stabilisation Support Strategy 2013–2017' (on file with author).

[63] Hugo de Vries, 'The Ebb and Flow of Stabilisation in the Congo', Political Settlements Research Programme Briefing Papers No. 8, Political Settlements Research Programme, 2014.

[64] Randi Solhjell and Madel Rosland, 'Stabilisation in the Congo: Opportunities and Challenges', *Stability: International Journal of Security & Development* 6, No. 1 (2017): 1–13.

[65] MONUSCO, 'International Security and Stabilization Support Strategy, Annual Report, 2016'.

[66] See David Curran and Charles T. Hunt, 'Stabilization at the Expense of Peacebuilding in UN Peacekeeping Operations: More than Just a Phase?', *Global Governance: A Review of Multilateralism and International Organizations* 26, No. 1 (2020): 1–23; de Vries, *Going around in Circles*; International Crisis Group, 'Eastern Congo: Why Stabilisation Failed', Briefing 91, 4 October 2012.

Congolese context.[67] Even the more nuanced approach to stabilization from 2012 onwards appears to have been thwarted by a government unwilling to meaningfully invest in its own national plan, instead treating the I4S as a way to convince donors to pay for a wish-list of state-run projects. In my interviews with UN and NGO officials, the most common lament was the lack of political will of the government. While some scholars lauded the potential for I4S to truly develop a 'bottom-up' approach to stabilization, they suggested that MONUSCO tended to work against itself, drawn ineluctably back to old models involving use of force, technical solutions to political problems, and poor community engagement.[68]

I here argue that the UN's inability to deliver on stabilization can be more convincingly explained in complexity terms. As described in Chapter 5, the strength of the Congolese system is in its reciprocal relationships of protection: powerful political actors at the centre rely upon state officials, armed groups, and businesspeople to generate resources and secure authority in the periphery. In turn, local actors are often able to guarantee their survival via a combination of patronage, involvement in marketing natural resources, and reliance on armed groups. The UN's stabilization programming offered new opportunities within this system. Government officials, particularly those with influence over national stabilization planning, saw stabilization funding as a way to secure greater leverage in the periphery, extending their lines of influence deeper into communities without having to expend their own funds. As evidence of this, by 2012, three years after stabilization programming had started, the government had only spent $320,000 of its own money on any of its national plan.[69] During the same period, the government directly requested the Security Council for equipment for twenty-three police battalions and vehicles for 145 territorial administrators, while the army's plan was a nearly $700 million list of equipment requested from donors.[70] The signal was fairly obvious: Kinshasa was happy to receive stabilization resources, but unwilling to distribute its own funds to the provinces.

In fact, President Kabila made his intentions clear from the outset: in 2009 he declared that stabilization was 'first of all, [to] consolidate the authority of a state that has only just been restored, in a context where centrifugal tensions could

[67] See, e.g. Christopher Vogel, 'Islands of Stability or Swamps of Insecurity? MONUSCO's Intervention Brigade and the Danger of Emerging Security Voids in eastern Congo', *Africa Policy Brief*, February 2014, 7.

[68] Solhjell and Rosland, 'Stabilisation in the Congo', 1–13; Randi Sohhjell and Madel Rosland, 'New Strategies for Old Conflicts? Lessons in Stabilisation from the Democratic Republic of the Congo', Norwegian Centre for Human Rights, Thematic Paper Series, June 2016.

[69] MONUSCO, 'International Security and Stabilisation Support Strategy Quarterly Report, January to March 2012'; also cited in Ian D. Quick, *Follies in Fragile States: How international stabilisation failed in the Congo* (London: Double Loop Press, 2015), 151.

[70] United Nations, 'Thirty-first Report of the Secretary-General on MONUC', 30 March 2010, UN Doc S/2010/164, paras 98–108.

yet reassert themselves.'[71] Here, however, 'consolidation of state authority' meant maintaining the relationships of protection between the centre and the periphery, a relationship that relied on resources to flow from the provinces to the capital. What Kabila astutely termed 'centrifugal tensions' describes the risk that these relationships might be disrupted before his network was in place. Keeping the peripheries dependent on the centre was thus crucial to his own survival. As evidence of this, contrary to the Constitution, the government refused to allocate 40 per cent of national revenues to the provinces, prompting some governors to speak of being 'asphyxiated' by Kinshasa.[72] The system simply was not set up for resources to flow outward from the centre.

At the same time, the government readily agreed to the UN's plans to focus stabilization on rule of law institutions and infrastructure (roads), both of which required significant funds to be channelled into extending state presence further into the eastern countryside. These projects gave the government greater reach and thus more capacity to extract from local communities without needing to fundamentally shift the way in which resources flowed towards the centre. One particularly incisive criticism of MONUSCO pointed out that state institutions and infrastructure were conceived purely as tools, with no deeper analysis of what they were being used for; as such, the UN's stabilization planning fundamentally overlooked the primary function of institutions, to assist the informal *trafic d'influence*.[73]

A 2014 survey conducted by Harvard Humanitarian Initiative of 5,200 Congolese revealed the comprehensive lack of reliance on formal state institutions, pointing to a serious mismatch between the UN's approach and Congolese perspectives. In response to the question 'What should be the government's top priority?' fewer than 2 per cent of respondents listed 'justice' or 'roads', while 'peace, security, and payment of salaries', combined for nearly 70 per cent of responses. When asked how security could be achieved, respondents overwhelmingly pointed to payment of the army and the police, whereas constructing new institutions and infrastructure did not even feature in their responses.[74] These views directly contrasted with the joint UN/government/donor approach to stabilization, which was

[71] Joseph Kabila, 'Discours du Prèsident de la République sur l'état de la nation', Kinshasa, 7 December 2009, English version quoted in International Crisis Group, 'Congo: A Stalled Democratic Agenda', Africa Briefing 73, 2010.

[72] Pierre Englebert, 'Décentralisation, incertitude, et despotism de proximité en République Démocratique du Congo', Papier préparé pour le Projet RDC—Provinces-Décentralisation du Musée Royal de Tervuren, Belgique, 2011; DigitalCongo, 'Rétrocession de 40% des recettes aux provinces: Gouverneurs et deputés provinciaux prêts à traduire le gouvernement devant la justice', 17 June 2009; Muriel Devey, 'Moïse Katumbi: Je gère le Katanga comme un entreprise', *Jeune Afrique*, 24 May 2011.

[73] Quick, *Follies in Fragile States*, 57.

[74] Patrick Vinck and Phuong Pham, 'Searching for Lasting Peace: Population-Based Survey on Perceptions and Attitudes about Peace, Security and Justice in Eastern Democratic Republic of the Congo', Harvard Humanitarian Initiative, UN Development Programme, July 2014.

rolling out new police stations, paving new roads, and expanding the number of officials on the security services payroll. The Congolese interviewees understood that the underfed protection racket that underpinned governance in eastern Congo meant greater numbers of unpaid security officials would create new risks of predation, new demands for bribery and rent extraction, and new nodes in the network feeding upwards to Kinshasa. As a Congolese participant in one of the stabilization planning meetings in 2011 adeptly summarized, 'What's the point of more officials? You'll dump them there and then they'll have to get by any way they can.'[75]

The UN's problem can be stated in simple terms: in much of eastern Congo, basic security and rule of law was not provided by the state security services and there was no quick way to transform this part of the system. In a 2008 survey in North Kivu, only 8 per cent of respondents answered, 'the police' when asked 'Who protects you?'[76] The formal justice system was essentially unknown beyond the major cities of eastern Congo, with fewer than fifty courts ostensibly servicing a rural population of forty-two million people. Even where state courts were in place, polling indicated extraordinarily low public confidence in these institutions.[77] By 2012, several years into the UN's stabilization efforts, community research found the Congolese overwhelmingly preferred to resolve their conflicts through unofficial, non-state channels, due to 'the propensity of [state security officials] to extort money and goods.'[78] This resonated with my own work and research in eastern Congo, where I witnessed deep suspicion of state-led initiatives to resolve conflicts and deliver security. 'The government is more of an enemy than a friend', one resident of Beni told me. 'We have to build our own protection from the government, not with it.'[79]

A major external review of the 'islands of stability' approach captured part of the issue, though this did little to solve it in the longer term:

> It is unacceptable to pretend that state authority is appropriately restored by facilitating the deployment of underequipped, underpaid, poorly supported Congolese officials ... Given the extreme difficulties that the Congolese Government

[75] Quoted in Quick, *Follies in Fragile States*, 37.

[76] Patrick Vinck and Phuong Pham, 'Living with Fear: A Population-based Survey on Attitudes about Peace, Justice, and Social Reconstruction in Eastern Democratic Republic of the Congo', Berkeley-Tulane Initiative on Vulnerable Populations, 2008.

[77] Gallup Poll, 'Few Urban Congolese Have Confidence in Institutions', 2008, available at https://www.congoforum.be/en/2008/05/05-23-08-gallup-few-urban-congolese-have-confidence-in-institutions/.

[78] Oxfam, '"For Me, but without Me, Is against Me": Why Efforts to Stabilize the Democratic Republic of the Congo Are Not Working', Oxfam Lobby Briefing, 2012 (NB: internal polling conducted by MONUSCO during this period revealed similarly low confidence in the institutions that were being created under the I4S).

[79] Notes from July 2016 visit to Beni (on file with author).

> continues to have in providing adequate resources, the international community will need to carefully think through its role in this area.[80]

While the underfed nature of the security services certainly contributed to their predatory behaviour, that report failed to capture the central function of such services in the broader system. Police officers may have been underpaid, but this was because they performed a crucial mediation between the state and society, extracting resources in return for the promise of access to Kinshasa's elite. 'Poorly supported Congolese officials' were not an aberration in the system that needed solving by transforming the salary system in Kinshasa, they were the result of decades of rule in which local-level state officials were expected to feed resources upwards in return for access to the protection of the state: Mobutu's paraplui in action.

Overly focused on state institutional capacity, stabilization thus created perverse incentives within the eastern communities. Local leaders, including those of armed groups, quickly recognized that stabilization funding would be generated in response to violence, meaning areas experiencing instability were more likely to be targeted for money. For example, between 2014 and 2016, a wave of attacks by the FRPI in Ituri presaged a significant stabilization effort there, with MONUSCO subsequently offering over $6 million in programming to help resolve the conflict.[81] 'Our funding follows the conflicts', one member of MONUSCO told me in 2016, explaining that higher rates of violence would affect how MONUSCO prioritized stabilization funding. Similar to the efforts to integrate armed groups described above, MONUSCO's stabilization thus appeared to contribute to a strong attractor for violence in eastern Congo, incentivizing groups to cause sufficient violence to be 'rewarded' with funds.

In this sense, MONUSCO acted as a weak intermediary in the Congolese governance system. The mission was able to channel resources, but only in a way that either reinforced the existing protection-driven system (by providing state officials more largesse) or incentivized armed groups towards violence. Unable to fundamentally shift the underlying relationships among the range of actors competing over governance in eastern Congo, the mission's energy appeared to amplify the tendencies towards violent forms of governance and predatory

[80] Tamagnini et al., 'Strategic Review of the International Security and Stabilisation Support Strategy for Eastern DR Congo', July 2010.

[81] United Nations, 'Report of the Secretary-General on the United Nations Organization Stabilization Mission in the Democratic Republic of the Congo', S/2014/698, para. 34; United Nations, 'Report of the Secretary-General on the United Nations Organization Stabilization Mission in the Democratic Republic of the Congo', S/2014/157; United Nations, 'Report of the Secretary-General on the United Nations Organization Stabilization Mission in the Democratic Republic of the Congo', S/2013/757, para. 28.

practices. Here, too, MONUSCO's efforts to create and bolster new state institutions had an unintended outcome: lacking support from the central government, these institutions tended to be underfunded, staffed by newly appointed state officials without salaries, whose only recourse for livelihoods often was to follow the same path of local rent seeking, tolls at road blocks, bribery, and extortion.

The increasing tendencies towards violence were not isolated to the communities of eastern Congo but were also displayed by MONUSCO itself. Over its near twenty-year history, the mission became increasingly dependent upon the use of force to take forward its mandated tasks, most obviously in the 2013 creation of the FIB. Formed to drive the rebel M23 group out of Goma, the FIB became the defining aspect of MONUSCO, the most frequently cited reason the mission should be able to drive armed groups from the territory of eastern Congo and help secure it for the state. Unfortunately, this overriding focus on use of force appears to have made MONUSCO's blind spot to the governance functions of armed groups even larger: in wide ranging interviews between 2016 and 2017, I encountered a recurrent mindset that saw use of military force as the sole tool for addressing armed groups and stabilizing the East. 'Stabilisation means we drive out the armed groups so the army can come in and secure the area, then we can start development', one MONUSCO military planner told me. But instead of islands of stability rising up in the ungoverned seas, the UN found itself pulled by the strong undercurrents of eastern Congo's governance system towards endless waves of violence.

Security sector reform

Emerging from years of war and decades of kleptocratic rule, Congo's defence, police, and justice institutions have been consistently ranked as some of the poorest in the world.[82] From the outset of the UN mission, reforming the sprawling security apparatus of the Congolese state was a core task, one tied directly to its broader statebuilding project and the goal of liberal, effective state institutions.[83] As this section explores, however, nearly twenty years of SSR and hundreds of millions of dollars in international funding resulted in essentially none of the hoped-for transformations. By 2017, Congo's formal security sector remained more of a patronage network than ever, and more of a risk to civilians than the armed militias roaming eastern Congo.[84]

[82] See, e.g., Transparency International, 'Corruption Perceptions Index: The Democratic Republic of the Congo', available at https://www.transparency.org/country/COD.

[83] United Nations Security Council Resolution, S/Res/1484 (2003), para. 5.

[84] See Henri Boshoff, Dylan Hendrickson, Sylvie More et al., *Supporting SSR in the DRC: Between a Rock and a Hard Place* (The Hague: Netherlands Institute of International Relations, 2010).

My central argument is that previous efforts to explain this failure only provide part of the picture. Individual greed and corruption within the Congolese system, along with chronic shortcomings in command and control of the security forces, are important factors in limiting the impact of SSR.[85] Deeply deficient salaries among the security services also may explain some of the patterns of predatory behaviour.[86] There is merit to the scholarship that has pointed to the overly technical approach by the UN and its partners, which may have overlooked the political motivations of the country's leadership in keeping the security services weak and dependent upon the centre.[87]

However, even taken together this scholarship is unable to fully account for the comprehensive failure of SSR to meaningfully shift the way in which the Congolese security system operates. For example, increases in salaries for the police and army, which more than doubled in the 2006–9 period, had essentially no impact on the kinds of predatory behaviour supposedly emanating from underpayment.[88] Far from being ad hoc personal acts of corruption and abuse, the Congolese security system has displayed a highly organized set of interrelated behaviours in which resources flow upward through the hierarchy.[89] Here, I argue, the system demonstrates a strong attractor towards relationships of protection and symbiosis between the centre and periphery, where networks of political, military, and private actors collectively adapt to SSR efforts by co-opting them. By locating SSR efforts within the complex system of governance described in Chapter 5, I here explore how the UN's interventions fed back into the system in ways that have entrenched existing patterns of authoritarianism and violent forms of governance.

In the immediate post-war context, MONUC's SSR work was predominantly focused on the newly formed national army and police. This included training units in human rights and international humanitarian law; coordinating donor support to the Congolese state; and advice to the ministries on establishing basic structures and institutional chains of command in line with international standards.[90] MONUC also supported the nationally led *brassage* process, which created integrated brigades designed to break up former militias and separate them from their former community support bases. Between 2003 and 2006, MONUC's efforts were welcomed by the government, which saw a need to bolster the integration of armed groups and reduce the risks of spoilers ahead of the national elections.[91] New flows

[85] See, e.g., Eirin Mobekk, 'Security Sector Reform and the UN Mission in the Democratic Republic of the Congo: Protecting Civilians in the East', *International Peacekeeping* 16, No. 2 (2009): 273–286.

[86] See Maria Eriksson Baaz and Ola Olsson, 'Feeding the Horse: Unofficial Economic Activities within the Police Force in the Democratic Republic of the Congo', *African Security* 4 (2011): 223–241.

[87] See Kets and de Vries, 'Limits to Supporting Security Sector Interventions in the DRC'.

[88] Baaz and Olsson, 'Feeding the Horse'.

[89] Baaz and Olsson, 'Feeding the Horse'; see also Raeymaekers, 'Post-war Conflict', 600–617.

[90] Mobekk, 'Security Sector Reform and the UN Mission in the Democratic Republic of the Congo', 273–286.

[91] Kets and de Vries, 'Limits to Supporting Security Sector Interventions in the DRC'.

of donor funding allowed the presidency to incentivize integration, buy off rebel groups, and shore up its position ahead of the country's first presidential election.

Over the life of the mission, the UN increasingly saw SSR as its raison d'être and by 2009 the mission's mandate centred on 'comprehensive reform of the security sector'.[92] However, between 2006 and 2017, the mission's support to SSR appeared to founder on endless obstacles and invisible resistance. Coordinated SSR in fact appeared to run directly counter to the government's efforts, which appeared designed to break up international donors into separate bilateral programmes supporting isolated branches of the security services.[93] By *disorganizing* the donor effort, Kabila could secure international funding without risking transformational changes in the system; importantly, it meant that improvements to the command and control structures of the military—which would have potentially limited the presidency's ability to bypass the hierarchy and instrumentalize local commanders—were never the subject of serious reforms.[94] A coordinated international effort might have exposed more clearly the lack of structural changes taking place across the security services, and may indeed have created a collective donor demand for greater accountability. Under an *uncoordinated* effort, however, the government could generate the appearance of reform on many fronts, while putting no tangible effort into change. In 2008, for example, a presidential decree was issued demanding accountability for FARDC crimes, but no state funds were allocated to pay for the military court that would implement the decree; the success of that reform depended solely upon the willingness of an external donor to pay for it.[95]

Strangely, the UN and bilateral donors managed to simultaneously recognize that the government had no interest in meaningful SSR, while also directing even greater effort and resources on a centralized national reform plan. Here, one of the most frequently repeated complaints by the UN and donors was that the Congolese leadership 'lacked the political will' to undertake serious reforms, preferring instead to profit from corrupt practices across its security services.[96] Despite this clear understanding of internal motivations, MONUC's SRSG declared in 2008 that all SSR efforts needed to be based upon a 'national management plan', and SSR staffing was concentrated almost exclusively at the Kinshasa level.[97] MONUC's budgets listed as SSR's core performance indicator 'adoption of a comprehensive

[92] United Nations, 'Report of the United Nations Secretary General on the Situation in the Democratic Republic of the Congo', S/2009/623, 28 December 2009, para. 101.

[93] Boshoff, Hendrickson, More et al., *Supporting SSR in the DRC.*

[94] Boshoff, Hendrickson, More et al., *Supporting SSR in the DRC.*

[95] Boshoff, Hendrickson, More et al., *Supporting SSR in the DRC.*

[96] See, e.g., Oxfam America, 'No Will, No Way: US-Funded Security Sector Reform in the Democratic Republic of the Congo', 2010; Sébastien Melmot, 'Candide au Congo: L'échec annoncé de la réforme du secteur de sécurité', *Focus Stratégique* 9, Institut Français des Relations Internationales (2009).

[97] Radio Okapi, 'DRC Security Sector Reform: Alan Doss Recommends Coherency in the Implementation of the Programme', 27 February 2008.

strategy and action plan' for reform of the security and defence sector by the state,[98] while year after year the mission had to report the disappointing (but entirely predictable) news that progress had been 'limited in this area'.[99]

At the more local level too, the UN's efforts to improve the behaviour of the security services through training did not appear to have a significant effect on their widespread predatory practices. This was partially the result of the underfed governance system where neglected soldiers had to live off the land, often employing the threat of violence to generate small sums of revenue to feed themselves and their superiors.[100] Soldiers actively participated in the illicit mining of minerals, the timber trade, and a wide variety of other illegal activities that allowed them to sustain themselves across eastern Congo.[101] Here, the UN's training sessions offered no real alternative to this system of protection; soldiers would exit a training session still needing to generate revenues for their superiors, and were offered no other means than to extract it from the population.[102] A Congolese national staff member in MONUSCO once explained to me, 'The police will always come to a training because of the food and the per diem, but that only lasts one day.' From the government's perspective, training thus functioned more as a box that needed to be ticked in order to receive additional donor support to the military than a tool of cultural and behavioural transformation for the Congolese National Police (PNC) / FARDC.

The result was that the UN became enmeshed in what DiMaggio and Powell have dubbed 'institutional isomorphism', the creation of the appearance of highly functional security services as a way to disguise their underlying shortcomings.[103] Examples of this were everywhere, but one of the most widely used with donors was a 2011 photo of the inauguration of a police commissariat in Rutshuru, North Kivu. In it, newly trained police stand to attention in front of a recently constructed station, holding rifles neatly over their shoulders and standing on a freshly whitewashed road. A brass band plays in the background and an officer stands before the troops holding a sword. On its surface, the photo depicts a freshly minted, professional police force, a success story for donors. Examining it more closely, however, Ian Quick (a former UN staffer) points out that fewer than half of the officers possess working firearms, the uniforms are mismatched and patchy, the sword is a fake, and the battalion has no identifying insignia.[104] While this vignette paints

[98] United Nations, 'Budget for the United Nations Organization Mission in the Democratic Republic of the Congo for the Period from 1 July 2008 to 30 June 2009', UN Doc A/62/755, 18 December 2009.

[99] See, e.g., United Nations, 'Report of the Secretary General on the Situation the Democratic Republic of the Congo', UN Doc S/2012/355, 23 May 2012, paras 57–58.

[100] Veit, *Intervention as Indirect Rule*, 233.

[101] See Baaz and Verweijen, 'Between Integration and Disintegration'.

[102] See S. Van Damme and Judith Verweijen, 'In Search of an Army: How the FARDC Can Improve Civilians' Safety', Oxfam International Policy Brief, 2012.

[103] Paul DiMaggio and Walter Powell, 'The Iron Cage Revisited: Institutional Isomorphism and Collective Rationality in Organizational Fields', *American Sociological Review* 48, No. 2 (1983): 147–160.

[104] This photo is reproduced in Quick, *Follies in Fragile*, 38.

a somewhat comical picture of the impoverished security services, the broader impacts of failed SSR were extremely serious, over time rendering the state by far the most dangerous force across the DRC.

The inability of the UN to generate either top-down or bottom-up results on SSR can be explained in systemic terms as two strong attractors in Congo's governance system. As laid out in Chapter 5, decades of kleptocratic rule and war had created a central government that relied upon informal networks of influence stretching through and beyond the security services. Thousands of individual Congolese men and women participated in this network daily, feeding small amounts of money upwards through the hierarchy, receiving various forms of protection and services in return. Armed groups and business interests were connected to this system via the marketing of natural resources beyond the DRC's borders, and their roles in local forms of governance. SSR was a potentially disruptive element to this system, given that it aimed at imposing new centralized chains of command and institutionally based payment schemes. Unable to fundamentally alter the underlying symbiotic relationships at the heart of the system, however, the proponents of SSR watched as their efforts evaporated.

In local communities, attempts to professionalize and train security actors ran into a different aspect of the same system: professional officers who solely participated in formal chains of command and were unable to feed themselves and their superiors off the local community were useless nodes in the system, disconnected from the networks of power that governed the country. As such, SSR was not only perceived as a foreign imposition that needed to be resisted,[105] but a potentially dangerous attempt to disrupt the immediate livelihoods of those involved. 'The government will never pay me', a police officer complained to me, 'because it is my job to pay my boss. If I pay him, then I can feed myself.'[106]

The result was that MONUSCO's SSR achieved essentially none of its intended impacts, but it did become instrumentalized by the power-brokers of the DRC. In the 2003–6 period, for example, SSR support was used by the FARDC to break up armed groups with political ambitions, detaching them from their support bases and constraining their leverage on President Kabila. Indeed, the incomplete integration and partial reconfiguration of the national army provided Kabila with a malleable tool with which to incentivize and punish armed groups, while keeping the reins of power firmly in his grasp. This instrumentalization of SSR became clear over time, as the government's willingness to engage with donors and the UN waxed and waned, depending on the risks it faced from armed groups in the peripheries. For instance, following the 2008 Goma

[105] Maria Eriksson Baaz and Maria Stern, 'Being Reformed: Subjectification and Security Sector Reform in the Congolese Armed Services', *Journal of Intervention and Statebuilding* 11, No. 2 (2017): 207–224.
[106] Discussion with a police officer, Kinshasa, March 2016.

agreements with several armed groups, the government briefly accepted coordinated SSR support, but quickly abandoned the process when the groups had been demobilized.[107]

Nearly twenty years after it first took on an SSR mandate in Congo, MONUSCO was confronted with the harsh reality that nothing much had changed. One of the most striking aspects of this, however, was the ability of the mission's staff to laugh this off as a sort of inevitable downside of doing business in a country like the DRC. In one of my first meetings with SSR colleagues in MONUSCO in 2016, I asked why there had been so little progress on SSR. One colleague replied, 'The problem is that they [the Congolese] are not serious about reform, so they never change how they do business. But that's not really our problem, we just need to implement this mandate.'

Conclusion

This chapter has examined three interrelated attempts by the UN to build up the Congolese state: (1) to guarantee its monopoly on the legitimate use of force; (2) to stabilize the eastern reaches of the country; and (3) to professionalize and reform the security sector. In each, I have argued that the UN's approach suffered from a sort of conceptual myopia—determined that the restoration and extension of state authority would resolve instability, the UN failed to account for the dynamic system of governance that existed across state/non-state, national/local, and institutional/personal spheres. The mission's interventions tended to favour the state and/or be instrumentalized by it, at times creating temporary imbalances in the system, but never fundamentally transforming the underlying rules and relationships. If anything, much of the UN's statebuilding work in the DRC appears to have reinforced the pre-existing tendencies for highly autocratic, predatory forms of governance.

This does not mean that MONUSCO itself should be considered a failure per se. The mission has participated in a twenty-year journey in which the DRC transitioned from a highly fractured post-war constellation of actors towards a consolidation of the country into a unified, if highly volatile entity. My central contention is that Congo's stability—its capacity to absorb shocks without a more fundamental reordering of the underlying rules of society—is far less dependent upon the institutions of state than is often assumed. In fact, the stability of the Congolese system may be largely contingent on its ability to move from high degrees of violence in the peripheries to high degrees of political uncertainty at the centre, each swing of the pendulum keeping the country more or less centred.

[107] Discussion with a police officer, Kinshasa, March 2016.

As Judith Verweijen notes, 'despite Congo's potential for flux, its instability is, for the most part, stable.'[108]

Here, complexity thinking offers an explanation for these recurrent failures that goes beyond the usual mantra of 'no political will'. UN parlance consistently blames national actors for failing to demonstrate sufficient personal and institutional motivation for the kinds of transformational change demanded. In MONUSCO, President Kabila's unwillingness to support the mission's mandate was one of the most frequent excuses I heard. It was true, President Kabila and his cadre were often more obstructionist than helpful, ready to accept more international funds but reluctant to disrupt a system that had kept them in power for decades. However, even Kabila's scope for action can be seen as deeply constrained when the broader governance system of the DRC is considered. The protection network that sustained millions of Congolese intersected with a lucrative artisanal mining production marketing hundreds of millions of dollars of precious metals annually, creating a web of symbiotic relations that could not easily be broken merely by *diktat* from above. Regardless of whether Kabila possessed the political will, the Congolese system did not exhibit the phase space that would have allowed for the kinds of change demanded by the UN's mandate, at least not via a linear progression of gradually increasing state capacity.

Finally, this chapter has shown that MONUC/MONUSCO was not merely an external actor attempting to implement a mandate but is better considered part of the system itself. Its attempts to engage armed groups, stabilize territory, and professionalize the security services all meant that the UN participated in the network that generated public authority, often with unintended consequences. Thinking of the UN as endogenous to the system, rather than as a detached actor attempting to influence change from the outside, is an important contribution of complexity thinking to this analysis.

[108] Verweijen, 'Stable Instability'.

PART III
END STATES

Part Two of this book traced the evolution of two very different systems of governance in South Sudan and the Democratic Republic of Congo (DRC), from their colonial periods to the near present. The principal argument was that each setting displayed complex, interdependent systems of governance with sets of underlying rules that tended to frustrate the United Nations (UN)'s statebuilding efforts. Here, the tools of complexity theory—in particular the notions of symbiotic relationship, feedback loops, and strong attractors—offered an explanation for the failure of the UN's work.

Part Three expands the analysis beyond the horizon of independent case studies, first by comparing the cases of South Sudan and the DRC, and then by making some broader generalizations regarding how complexity theory can help us understand statebuilding in a variety of other settings. Chapter 7 argues that the Congolese and South Sudanese systems, while different in many respects, share several characteristics that tend to work against UN-led statebuilding. Both possess highly interdependent systems of governance with strong attractors to violence as a stabilizing aspect of the system. Both have exhibited a very limited tendency to change in the kind of linear gradualist path expected by the UN, and thus both have arrived at similar outcomes: the UN was unable to generate a fundamental governance transformation.

This comparison in systemic terms adds significant findings to the political economy and political science research on statebuilding to date. While much of this scholarship has found the UN to be disconnected from local realities and pursuing ineffective top-down strategies, it has not explored the underlying patterns in different systems that generate resistance to change. Merely pointing to 'corruption', 'lack of political will', or 'local realities' tends to punt the question rather than address it. Complexity offers insights into the patterns at play across different systems, explaining the ways in which extremely disparate systems can frustrate statebuilding.

Chapter 8 suggests that the findings from South Sudan and the DRC are typical of UN statebuilding around the world, including in Libya, Afghanistan, Mali, Central African Republic, and Somalia. Across these settings, evidence of highly networked, interrelated systems of governance contrasts with the UN's boilerplate 'extension of state authority' mandates. Indeed, even in so-called 'success' stories of peacebuilding, such as Liberia, there is strong evidence that complex governance systems involving a range of non-state actors remain crucial to stability. Despite some advancement at the policy level towards concepts of systemic resilience that might allow for more nuanced approaches that align with these findings, they have not meaningfully filtered into statebuilding and peacebuilding practice. Drawing from complexity thinking, Chapter 8 offers several concrete policy implications for the future of statebuilding, demonstrating how a systems-based approach can transform the practice of conflict prevention and peacebuilding.

The book concludes that the insights from complexity thinking have application more broadly in the realm of global governance. Here, liberal institutionalists have relied upon statebuilding as a practice that reaffirms liberal world order, prevents the growth of competing models, and heads off perceived security threats from ungoverned states. Today, that order appears increasingly in disarray as major powers retreat from multilateral institutions in pursuit of narrow national interest, while non-state actors have assumed a far greater role in global dynamics. While these trends have caused handwringing among proponents of liberal rules-based international order, complexity thinking offers hope that new forms of order may emerge from these constellations of increasingly interconnected actors. Indeed, it suggests that if the UN is to play an influential role in global governance, it would best think in complex systems terms about how to become more connected to the nodes that matter.

7
Resilient systems of governance: Comparing South Sudan and Congo

South Sudan and the Democratic Republic of Congo (DRC) are very different places with distinct governance systems resulting from their unique histories. They underwent disparate forms of colonial rule, contrasting post-colonial periods (one dominated by its neglect by Khartoum, the other by the charismatic autocrat Mobutu), experienced their own civil wars, and have developed distinct post-war governance arrangements. Having lived in both countries, I found the day-to-day experiences very different as well; much of life in the DRC felt like a frenetic blur of activity, a constant marketplace, while South Sudan seemed to move at a slower, more rural pace. In some ways, I felt the character of the countries could be compared to their rivers: the calm, irresistible waters of the Nile versus the turbid, coursing flows of the Congo River—both contain crocodiles.

Despite their separate paths, both South Sudan and the DRC have arrived at a similar destination in their statebuilding experiences: after enormous amounts of international assistance based on analogous models of liberal governance, neither country has built effective state-run governance institutions. When I last arrived at the airport in Juba, I knew I needed to make an informal payment in a back office if I was to receive the correct stamp on my passport, money that fed a sprawling and largely invisible network of patronage and small-scale rent seeking. Similarly, in Kinshasa my visa request 'disappeared' until I was able to pay a middleman for its discovery, thus helping a gatekeeper maintain his position within the Congolese *parapluie* system. Travelling across both countries, I constantly found myself confronted with evidence of highly evolved forms of governance in which the state was but a marginal player, from the cooking charcoal that was delivered by armed groups in eastern Congo to the South Sudanese traditional chief who dispensed justice after an intercommunal clash.

While it may rankle outsiders to have to undergo minor forms of corruption on a daily basis, I here argue that the thriving informal sectors in both settings point to a common set of attributes in the Congolese and South Sudanese systems of governance. Both have developed highly relational systems in which protection, security, goods, and identity are exchanged in patterns that produce predictable—if often violent—forms of public authority, with state institutions only one of many

States of Disorder, Ecosystems of Governance. Adam Day, Oxford University Press.
 DOI: 10.1093/oso/9780192863898.003.0008

actors in the relationship. My principal argument in this chapter is that complexity theory offers a meaningful lens for comparing across the two cases, articulating systemic similarities even while taking into account significant differences in the trajectories of the two countries. In this respect, complexity thinking helps to address the issue of equifinality in the cases, explaining how two very different systems can arrive at similar statebuilding outcomes.

Drawing on the more in-depth studies in previous chapters, a cross-case comparison in these terms yields four broad conclusions: (1) both South Sudanese and Congolese systems rely upon a network of interconnected symbiotic relations stretching across state, traditional, and business actors (indeed rendering these labels largely meaningless in many settings); (2) both systems self-regulate via feedback loops that tend to deny the possibility of building governance capacity solely in the formal institutions of the state; (3) as a result of their respective civil wars, both systems evolved strong attractors to violent forms of governance; and (4) these systemic characteristics have meant that the phase space—the realm of possible outcomes at a given moment—did not allow for a direct, linear transition into liberal models of the state during the United Nations (UN) peacekeeping missions' tenure. Taken together, these systemic attributes have not only worked against the goals of UN-led statebuilding, I argue they incorporated the UN's efforts into their underlying patterns. Here, UN peace operations are better thought of as endogenous to the system, subject to its rules and tendencies, rather than as an external actor effectuating change from outside. In many instances, there is evidence that the UN's work has unwittingly contributed to precisely the kinds of predatory, authoritarian behaviour it was designed to end.

Initial conditions

In complex systems, initial conditions matter a great deal: they shape the phase space, the realm of possible activity at a given moment.[1] A difficulty in examining socio-political systems is the lack of a defined starting point; both the DRC and southern Sudan had well-developed systems of governance prior to colonial rule, some elements of which persist to this day. Hundreds of years before colonization, the Nuer and Dinka communities of southern Sudan lived under interlinked lineage-based governance arrangements without a centralized authority.[2] Likewise, the Kongo Kingdom's 400-year existence saw the existence

[1] Kurt A. Richardson, 'Complex Systems Thinking and Its Implications for Policy Analysis', in Göktug Morçöl, ed., *Handbook on Decisionmaking* (University Park, PA: Penn State University Press, 2006), 189–221.

[2] Edward Evans-Pritchard, *The Nuer: A Description of the Modes of Livelihood and Political Institutions of a Nilotic People* (Oxford: Oxford University Press 1940), 12; Luka Biong Deng Kuol and Sarah

of a highly sophisticated governance system linked by trade, intermarriage, and overlapping protection arrangements.[3] While these earlier forms of rule are largely beyond the scope of this book, they often reappear in different forms in colonial and post-colonial periods, acting as a sort of undercurrent to the systems of governance that later emerge.

A common aspect of the colonial periods of both the DRC and southern Sudan was the decision of the colonizing powers to rely on traditional or customary authorities as agents of the state. This meant that few formal administrative centres were established beyond major urban areas, which were used primarily for the extraction of natural resources from the countryside. In southern Sudan, slave trading routes created nodes of administrative authority that were subsequently used to move natural resources northwards to Khartoum and beyond.[4] The Anglo-Egyptian colonial powers relied on these nodes, appointing traditional leaders as local police and judiciaries to implement coercive economic policies such as forced labour and compulsory taxation of crops.[5] Similarly, the brutal Belgian colonial regime in Congo relied upon a network of small towns through which it extracted the country's natural resources, relying upon forced labour and compulsory taxation to profit as much as possible.[6]

This reliance on traditional forms of rule created a symbiotic relationship at the heart of both governance systems. Customary chiefs played a mediating role for the colonial powers, exercising the state's authority in the absence of formal state institutions; at the same time, they maintained traditional forms of rule, regulating local trade, marriage, justice, and services across communities. Citizens needing access to state resources had to pass through the gate kept by traditional leaders; their reliance on the state was mediated through customary rule. Similarly, the colonial powers relied upon traditional leaders to provide them with sufficient legitimacy to maintain their rule and extend state authority beyond the main urban areas.

This symbiosis was not a mutually beneficial one, but can be thought of more as a parasitic relationship: the state drew resources from the cashless hinterlands, extracting goods via quasi-state traditional authorities without providing much in

Logan, eds., The *Struggle for South Sudan: Challenges of Security and State Formation* (London: I.B. Tauris, 2019), 82–103; Edward Evans-Pritchard, 'The Ethnic Composition of the Azande of Central Africa', *Anthropological Quarterly* 31, No. 4 (1958): 95–119.

[3] See John K. Thornton, *The Kingdom of Congo. Civil War and Transition, 1641–1718* (Madison, WI: University of Wisconsin Press, 1983); William Graham Lister Randles, *L'ancien royaume du Congo des origins à la fin du XIXe siècle* (Paris: Éditions de l'École des hautes études en sciences sociales, 2002).

[4] Edward Thomas, *South Sudan: A Slow Liberation* (London: Zed Books, 2015), 58.

[5] Thomas, *A Slow Liberation*, 96.

[6] See Andreas Exenberger and Simon Hartmann, 'Extractive Institutions in the Congo: Checks and Balances in the Longue Durée', in Ewout Frankema and Frans Buelens, eds., *Colonial Exploitation and Economic Development: The Belgian Congo and the Netherlands Indies Compared* (London and New York: Routledge, 2013), 18–39.

return.[7] The relationship between the state and these authorities thus never created much institutional capacity beyond the most limited form in urban areas, though rural populations did rely upon traditional authorities to protect their interests vis-à-vis the colonial powers. Not only were there few state resources dedicated to governance institutions in the peripheries, the reliance on lineage-based leaders meant that the 'institution' of the state was passed from father to son, kept within ethnic communities in a way that reaffirmed pre-colonial ruling structures.

In some respects, this colonial pattern of indirect rule constitutes the initial conditions for the governance systems that evolved in both the DRC and southern Sudan, though of course earlier forms of rule should not be disregarded. As in any complex system, initial conditions do not dictate the course of history, but they do establish a set of patterns that can grow deeper over time. The mediated nature of governance (the ways in which public authority has been constantly negotiated as among a range of actors) has constituted one of the underlying patterns in both the DRC and South Sudan, influencing how later iterations of both systems evolved.

Symbiosis between the centre and periphery

Symbiotic relationships between state and society are not unique to the systems in the DRC and southern Sudan; in fact, even the most Weberian description of the state could be thought of as a symbiotic exchange of services for legitimacy, both sides needing the other to survive. What differentiates the DRC and southern Sudan is the nature of the relationships that evolved over time. In both systems, the right to exercise the role of the state was contested, the result of negotiations that treated governance as a resource for survival. And in both systems, the role of traditional authorities as middlemen and brokers helped to maintain the lineage-based ethnic basis for local self-rule.

While Mobutu appeared to run the paradigmatic controlling dictatorship, his form of rule is best described as a withdrawal of the state from the day-to-day administration of the country. Never building meaningful public institutions beyond the capital, Mobutu's system instead relied upon a continuation of the use of traditional leaders to generate revenues for the state, combined with a call on the population to fend for themselves.[8] Over time, a network of redistribution

[7] For a more thorough description of different forms of symbiosis, see Adam Day and Charles T. Hunt, 'UN Stabilisation Operations and the Problem of Non-Linear Change: A Relational Approach to Intervening in Governance Ecosystems', *Stability: International Journal of Security & Development* (2020): 1–23.

[8] Alex Veit, *Intervention as Indirect Rule: Civil War and Statebuilding in the Democratic Republic of Congo* (New York: Campus Verlag, 2011), 90.

formed, where the elite power-brokers were linked with traditional authorities and provincial politicians, all formally nominated as part of Mobutu's political party.[9] Unconstrained extraction of rents (by state actors as well as ordinary citizens) was the ordering principle of this system, what Luca Jourdan calls a 'social pact' where the state withdrew from any governance function in exchange for the right to act unlawfully.[10]

Instead of the state, communities turned to their own traditional authorities, not only because they were more legitimate and effective sources of governance, but also because traditional authorities proved capable of brokering protection and services from the state. The result was a form of symbiosis in which all parties—the elites in Mobutu's circle, local leaders, and ordinary citizens—fed together off what was called 'the state'. Rather than a Weberian exchange of services and protection for legitimacy, Mobutu's system treated the state as an object of negotiation, a conduit to Zaire's wealth. This notion of feeding off the state has persisted to this day: In dozens of interviews and conversations with Congolese citizens, I found that eating and feeding were two of the most common words used to describe their relationship with state authorities. This of course aligns with chronic malnutrition and the day-to-day challenges of acquiring food in the DRC, but also points to a different conceptualization of the state as a source of nutrition to be negotiated and fought over, rather than a formal set of governing institutions.[11]

Southern Sudan's governance system similarly evolved around symbiotic relationships spanning state, traditional, and private actors, though with some important differences to the Congolese system. Sudan's post-independence period was largely shaped by the two civil wars that arose out of Khartoum's attempts to impose assimilationist rule on southern Sudan. One of the most important modalities for controlling southern Sudan was Khartoum's manipulation of the southern economy: while southern leadership was granted significant *de jure* autonomy, it was never permitted any control of its budget.[12] This left the southern leadership with few incentives to generate revenue from taxation or natural resources (which would all be absorbed by Khartoum), but rather to see the state as a source of individual economic opportunity. A staggering 96 per cent of state expenditures in southern Sudan went to government salaries and wages, whereas nearly nothing went towards development, health, education, or infrastructure.[13] Moreover,

[9] Koen Vlassenroot and Timothy Raeymaekers, 'New Political Order in the DR Congo? The Transformation of Regulation', *Africa Focus* 21, No. 2 (2008): 39–52.

[10] Cited in Koen Vlassenroot and Timothy Raeymaekers, *Conflict and Social Transformation in Eastern DR Congo* (Gent: Academia Press Scientific Publishers, 2004), 226.

[11] This notion of eating also arises in Theodore Trefon, *Reinventing Order in the Congo: How People Respond to State Failure in Kinshasa* (London: Zed Books, 2005), 12.

[12] Thomas, *A Slow Liberation*, 67.

[13] Thomas, *A Slow Liberation*, 93.

positions within local government were distributed along traditional kinship lines, in keeping with the decision to allow traditional authorities to play a direct role in governing the South.

Within southern Sudan, a pattern of symbiosis also emerged, particularly around urban concentrations of people and wealth. Here, it is important to recall that many of the rural communities of southern Sudan have traditionally lived as cashless societies, utilizing a system of bridewealth, cattle, and barter as the major forms of economic exchange.[14] As towns grew into centres of power through the colonial and post-colonial periods, cashless rural societies were drawn towards urban areas where traditional authorities were able to resolve disputes, secure rights to resources, and participate in economic development. But rural communities also saw urban economies as a foreign imposition, a violent penetration of their moral and physical space.[15] Particularly around land rights, but also across a wide range of governance powers that had been customarily addressed within the kinship networks of communities, rural populations found themselves in the uncomfortable position of needing traditional authorities as mediator between their own everyday reality and the realm of the state.[16] Communities were drawn to urban centres for resources, but also saw themselves as morally and politically distinct from the towns. For example, when examining how rural communities related to urban centres and traditional authorities around land issues in southern Sudan, Naseem Badiey's research has demonstrated the communities' 'continuing desire to preserve a *distance* from the state' and protect their moral identity as the corrupting influences of the centre.[17]

Symbiotic relationships are often portrayed as win-win mechanisms, but many evolve more as a linked competition over the resources needed to survive. The post-colonial periods of both southern Sudan and Zaire exhibit an admixture of symbioses: in some instances the central government appears to act as a predator or a parasite, feeding off the population to their detriment; in others communities negotiate some benefits from the state via traditional authorities. Common across these relationships, however, is the fact that governance—the right to provide security and services to the southern population—is negotiated and contested, not merely residing in state institutions.

[14] Cherry Leonardi, 'Paying "Buckets of Blood" for the Land: Moral Debates over the Economy, War and State in Southern Sudan', *Journal of Modern African Studies* 49, No. 2 (2011).

[15] Leonardi, 'Paying "Buckets of Blood"', 216.

[16] For a comprehensive analysis of how centre-periphery dynamics played out in land disputes, see Nasseem Badiey, *The State of Post-conflict Reconstruction: Land, Urban Development and State-building in Juba Southern Sudan* (Oxford: James Currey, 2014), 110 ('land debates may mask concerns over the destabilizing processes unleashed by the expanding presence of the state').

[17] Badiey, *The State of Post-conflict Reconstruction*, 218 (emphasis added).

Feedback loops organize the system

Complex systems are organized by feedback loops, ways in which information and energy are directed into the system to either amplify change or correct it. Both the DRC and southern Sudan exhibit similar positive feedback loops in terms of their governance systems (it is worth recalling that the term 'positive' does not connote a good outcome, only a reinforcing, amplifying one). Specifically, the more public authority evolved towards a negotiated resource outside of pure state control, the fewer resources and legitimacy tended to be directed into the state, creating an effect that continuously stripped formal state institutions of a central role in governing its population.

The Mobutu era was one of the clearest cases of a positive feedback loop in a governance system. As state institutions became weaker, greater space opened for private enterprise to assume state-like roles, thus undermining formal institutions and creating even more opportunity for non-state governance. This was evident in Zaire through the 1970s and 1980s, where every state institution experienced a near total disintegration. The national army too became a decrepit force incapable of providing security or protecting the country's borders.[18] Nearly all of the country's healthcare and education were delivered by either civil society groups or religious organizations.[19] Central control of its enormous mining potential declined to the point where foreign and/or local control had become the norm.[20] As a result of the withdrawal of the state, nearly three-quarters of Zaire's state-owned land was eventually possessed by private citizens.[21] In all areas, the lack of well-developed state-led governance institutions created conditions whereby they could never expand or mature, similar to a process of natural erosion that continually strips away the root structures that would prevent more soil from being worn away. A Congolese academic in Kinshasa described it to me as a modified form of the well-known Sisyphean myth: 'Building the state in Congo has been like pushing a rock up the mountain, but each time it rolls back, it leaves the mountain a bit taller.'[22]

Here, a strong parallel with Congo emerges in southern Sudan: Khartoum's policies of perpetuating southern dependency on the North meant that formal state institutions never received adequate support, while local elites were permitted to govern largely as they saw fit. Disallowed from maintaining any budgetary surplus

[18] Stein Sundstol Eriksen, 'The Liberal Peace Is Neither: Peacebuilding, Statebuilding and the Reproduction of Conflict in the Democratic Republic of Congo', *International Peacekeeping* 16, No. 5 (2009): 652–666; see also Thomas Callaghy, *The State-Society Struggle* (New York: Columbia University Press, 1984), 294.

[19] Thomas Callaghy, *The State-Society Struggle* (New York: Columbia University Press, 1984), 294.

[20] Veit, *Intervention as Indirect Rule*, 93.

[21] Timothy Raeymaekers, *Violent Capitalism and Hybrid Identity in the Eastern Congo: Power to the Margins* (Cambridge: Cambridge University Press, 2014), 94.

[22] Interview, Kinshasa, September 2018 (translation mine).

of their own, southern leaders had no incentives to generate resources via taxation or expansion of agriculture, instead treating the state as a source of individual income via salaries.[23] The administration of southern Sudan was thus left largely in the hands of local government, distributed along ethnic lines and seen as modalities for protecting community interests. This combination of economic reliance on Khartoum and near total autonomy to govern locally meant that formal state institutions could never flourish. Lacking incentives to build independent institutions or grow their economies, southern administrators absorbed funds from Khartoum and channelled them into their respective communities. Greater funds did not increase formal state capacities or indeed the South's economic autonomy, but instead increased the growth and influence of traditional authorities. The result was that, even as late as 2003, economic dependence on Khartoum had increased steadily over time, even as the southern territory was granted greater legal autonomy to govern.[24]

Understanding both settings in terms of their respective feedback loops offers a parallel that might not be apparent merely by examining their historical trajectories: in quite different systems, centre/periphery dynamics tended to erode formal state institutions over time. As described below, it also meant that efforts to build governance capacity by directing resources at state institutions did not alter the underlying pattern but rather participated in these feedback loops, at times reinforcing tendencies towards predatory, violent forms of rule.

A strong attractor to violence

As complex social systems evolve, they self-organize through reinforcing behaviours, patterns that narrow the range of likely outcomes and stabilize the system. These reinforcing patterns are called 'attractors', the strongest of which can be said to play a central role in maintaining the system in its current state.[25] While the civil wars in Sudan and the DRC varied enormously, a common feature was the evolution of violent forms of order within both governance systems. In both, violence became a strong attractor, a way in which the respective systems stabilized themselves.

During the course of Sudan's civil war, the Southern People's Liberation Army (SPLA) superimposed itself over traditional authorities, creating a kind of superficial homogeneity to the governance landscape of southern Sudan (even while

[23] See Thomas, *A Slow Liberation*, 93 (noting that 96 per cent of expenditures in southern Sudan went on salaries).

[24] International Monetary Fund, 'Sudan: Selected Issues Paper', No 12/299, November 2012, available at https://www.imf.org/external/pubs/ft/scr/2012/cr12299.pdf.

[25] Peter Coleman et al., *Attracted to Conflict: Dynamic Foundations of Destructive Social Relations* (New York: Springer, 2013).

the rebel group continually fractured and fought within itself). SPLA commanders were deployed to their home communities to recruit young men into their ranks, levy taxes, and feed their troops from local sources.[26] And while this allowed the SPLA to overrule traditional authorities in many cases, the commanders relied upon customary rule to legitimate their presence and ensure they could rely on communities for their resources. Frequently, traditional chiefs were placed directly within the SPLA's chain of command. As such, a new symbiotic relationship developed involving the SPLA, traditional authorities, and communities, where protection by the SPLA was exchanged for food, shelter, recruits, and legitimacy. What I earlier call the SPLA's 'ethno-military' character arose from this relationship, where the governance system of southern Sudan became the product of a symbiotic relationship between the SPLA and traditional, kinship-based community leadership.[27]

The Southern People's Liberation Movement (SPLM) / SPLA's poor governance is one of the most widely accepted reasons for the many fractures that appeared within the southern communities during the civil war. While nominally deployed to protect community interests from Khartoum, the SPLA was better known for its theft of food, forced taxation, looting, and other forms of predation.[28] Offered little recourse other than via violence, communities that wished to exert their rights within the SPLA-dominated landscape of southern Sudan had to do so via armed rebellion against the SPLA itself. Dozens of defections took place, often in a recurrent manner with the same leadership demanding similar rights within the SPLA structure. Faced with a constant barrage of defections and rebellions, the SPLM leadership tended to offer integration into the SPLA as its main inducement, placing the rebelling communities on the SPLA payroll and offering it the same privileges within southern Sudan.[29]

The outcome of southern Sudan's recurrent rebellions and integrations was that its governance system evolved towards a patronage network expressed through the military chain of command and organized by violence. Frequent uprisings from communities that had been ignored or abused were dealt with by inducements to join the SPLA, further cementing violence as a primary means to express discontent, and the military as the primary vehicle for dispensing patronage. This constituted a strong attractor within southern Sudan's governance system: whenever a disruption or threat to its stability arose, the system tended to react by

[26] Clémence Pinaud, 'South Sudan: Civil War, Predation and the Making of a Military Aristocracy', *African Affairs* 113, No. 451 (2014): 192–211.

[27] See Sukanya Podder, 'Mainstreaming the Non-state in Bottom-Up State-building: Linkages between Rebel Governance and Post-conflict Legitimacy', *Conflict, Security and Development* 14, No. 2 (2014): 213–243.

[28] Anne Walraet, 'Governance, Violence and the Struggle for Economic Regulation in South Sudan: The Case of Budi County (Eastern Equatoria)', *Afrika Focus* (2008).

[29] See Matthew Le Riche, 'Conflict Governance: The SPLA, Factionalism, and Peacemaking', in Steven E. Roach, ed., *The Challenges of Governance in South Sudan* (London: Routledge 2018), 22–26.

incorporating that threat into the military. One former militia member in South Sudan described this phenomenon, 'We learned that violence was how to get attention and how to get what we needed. Without violence, we would not be heard and we could not survive.'[30] Other avenues, such as civil society discourse, institutionalized forms of governance, or even independent customary governance became attenuated and largely closed off. In an interview, a former SPLA soldier told me, 'During the war, the SPLA became everything: we were the judges, the chiefs, the police, the teachers, and the politicians. Everything was SPLA, there was no other place to go.'[31]

Even after independence in 2011, this strong attractor exerted a powerful pull within South Sudan. The newly formed government (still calling itself the SPLM much of the time), suddenly facing the prospect of more than $100 million per month in oil revenues, funnelled those resources almost exclusively into the army. Post-war military spending skyrocketed, as nearly 70 per cent of government salaries going to the military and very little remaining for other state institutions like education, justice, or infrastructure.[32] These funds were not generically distributed across the army, but were rather used as a tool to maintain unity within southern Sudan, to prevent the kinds of fractures that had occurred during the civil war.[33] 'When [President Salva] Kiir got hold of the South's oil revenues, it might have looked like he could turn around and build up South Sudan's state', a South Sudanese civil society leader told me, 'but he didn't actually have any other choice but to keep using the army because it had become the only way he could govern our people.'[34]

This is a typical function for a strong attractor in a system: while on the surface it may appear that individuals can take any range of actions, deeply embedded patterns and relationships in the system mean that action is powerfully pulled towards a much smaller scope of options. In this case, the SPLM/SPLA had become so integral to the governance system of South Sudan, so intimately bound up with the way communities considered their own protection and identity, that the chances of developing institutions independent from the military were extremely slim. Moreover, the ethno-military character of the SPLA meant it operated largely along community lines, which appear quite fixed to those living within them.

The two Congolese Wars that wracked the country from 1996 to 2002 resulted in a similar militarization of governance in many parts of the DRC, though with

[30] Interview, Juba, December 2018.

[31] Interview, December 2010 (UN Department of Peacekeeping Operations (DPKO)'s Southern Sudan Conflict Assessment, on file with author).

[32] See Luka Biong Deng Kuol, 'The Federalism-Decentralisation-Peace Nexus in South Sudan', in Luka Biong Deng Kuol and Sarah Logan, eds., *The Struggle for South Sudan: Challenges of Security and State Formation* (London: I.B. Tauris, 2019), 228.

[33] Alex De Waal, 'When Kleptocracy becomes Insolvent: Brute Causes of the Civil War in South Sudan', *African Affairs* 113, No. 452 (2014).

[34] Interview, Juba, December 2018.

some important differences to South Sudan's system. The First Congolese War was triggered by Rwanda's invasion of what was then called Zaire in 1996, provoking an influx of foreign troops from Uganda, Burundi, and Uganda to invade as well. For much of both wars, the continuing presence of the national armies of Rwanda and Uganda—along with a range of other armed groups that arose in collaboration and competition with them—resulted in networks formed to extract Congolese natural resources, artisanal mining, timber, and agricultural production. The Congolese armed groups that arose during this period became part of these networks, securing their livelihoods from the ability to control natural resource sites and market their goods internationally.

As described in Chapter 5, Congo's armed groups, however, did not merely prey upon communities, they institutionalized their roles in a number of ways and became integral to the governance structures in eastern Congo. Many community-based armed groups extracted rents in the form of local taxes, in exchange for which they offered protection from other militias in the area.[35] Some groups—such as the Rwandaphone Democratic Forces for the Liberation of Rwanda (FDLR)—built sprawling networks that serviced large communities, bringing charcoal, goods, and basic services that would in liberal Western models be the responsibility of the state.[36] In fact, in much of eastern Congo a symbiotic relationship formed between militias and the surrounding communities: villages needed armed groups to secure their exclusive access to land, protect them from the attacks of neighbouring communities, and facilitate the export of resources to international markets. In turn, communities provided basic goods to armed groups, as well as a form of legitimacy to pursue their territorial control and exclusive access to artisanal mining sites in particular.[37]

Unlike Western forms of liberal governance—in which the state exchanges protections and services for legitimacy—wartime governance in eastern Congo evolved away from the central state. Profits from the international sale of precious metals and timber flowed through militias, traditional authorities, local businesspeople, and the elites in Kinshasa, rarely feeding into formal state coffers. And lacking any meaningful role of the state in their day-to-day lives, communities of eastern Congo came to rely upon these informal modes of governance for nearly all of their goods and protections. This did not mean the state was irrelevant to the Congolese; however, it did mean that the production of governance—the

[35] Kasper Hoffmann, Koen Vlassenroot, and G. Marchais, 'Taxation, Stateness and Armed Groups: Public Authority and Resource Extraction in Eastern Congo', *Development and Change* 47, No. 6 (2016): 1434–1456.

[36] During my time as the Senior Political Adviser to MONUSCO in 2016, I proposed the creation of a Criminal Networks Taskforce, which was subsequently tasked to analyse the role of the FDLR in the charcoal trade in Goma. This internal MONUSCO analysis is the basis for my points on the FDLR's role in the charcoal trade.

[37] For a description of different forms of symbiosis in the DRC, see Day and Hunt, 'UN Stabilisation Operations and the Problem of Non-Linear Change'.

competitions over the right to provide protection, the negotiations over who maintained control over resource delivery—were not between state and citizen, but rather among a broader network of actors in which the state was but one. And importantly, this network did not feed the state per se; taxes, rents, and profits from natural resources did not flow into a state budget to be redistributed through formal institutions, but rather to individual power-brokers. The result was the feedback loop described above, a continual erosion of state institutions allowing for the flourishing of other forms of governance, guaranteed by violence.

Here, a significant difference between the wartime trajectories of the DRC and southern Sudan should be highlighted. In southern Sudan, the SPLA grew into a hegemonic force, subsuming traditional/communal forms of governance and acting as the state in many areas that would have typically been filled by police, judiciaries, land authorities, and other ministries. The militarization of governance in this context was the direct result of a blurring between the rebel fighters and the movement that eventually became the state. As a South Sudanese government official told me in 2011, 'We are a government, but people still think of us as freedom fighters. We will always be fighters. It is how we learned to rule our country.'[38] This meant that, even after independence in 2011, much of the SPLA continued to behave like a rebel army, continuing the same patterns of predation, informal taxation, and fealty along ethnic lines.

In contrast to South Sudan, the DRC never witnessed a hegemonic national army during its post-colonial history. Instead, the two Congolese Wars created conditions for a proliferation of militias, some circling closely around artisanal mining sites, others more directly linked to regional power hubs in Kigali and Kampala. If anything, the wars contributed to a fracturing and dissolution of the national military in the DRC, which then had to be rebuilt as the Armed Forces of the Democratic Republic of the Congo (FARDC) following the 2003 peace process. Even then, state security services never operated in the same dominant fashion as the SPLA. Instead, they became enmeshed in the broader network of relationships that exploited resources, participated in intercommunal rivalries, and competed over the right to govern. The result—and here note a parallel with southern Sudan—was that resources and influence never flowed into formal state institutions: the national defence budget was never fed by taxation; salaries accounted for a paltry proportion of a security official's actual income; and the state infrastructure for courts, prisons, administration, and transport never developed. If anything, the wartime governance structures that emerged in the DRC functioned as a centrifugal force, pushing influence and resources to the peripheries of the country, where armed actors provided the security guarantee for community survival.[39]

[38] Interview, former minister in government of South Sudan, Juba, January 2011.

[39] I here recognize the incongruity of using a Newtonian concept when employing the non-linear concepts of complexity theory.

This points to a crucial commonality between the wartime periods of both southern Sudan and the DRC: in both, violence became a strong attractor in the governance system. In southern Sudan, the dominant presence of the SPLA meant that governance was controlled and expressed through a military actor. Negotiations over the right to govern were achieved with force, as communities wishing to change the terms of the relationship with the SPLA had to do so via a cycle of rebellion and integration back into the SPLA's fold. Thousands of insurrections during the civil war (some small, some mobilizing entire ethnic groups) expressed attempts by communities to renegotiate the terms of their relationship with the SPLM/SPLA.[40] As a South Sudanese expert described to me in 2011, 'In the war, we learned the language of violence, and it became the only language that made sense. If I am a chief in Bor and I need something from the SPLM, my only choice is to begin fighting against them until they are ready to talk to me.'[41]

The strong attractor to violence was equally visible in the wartime governance of the DRC, where armed groups came to constitute the underlying guarantee for communities, not only in terms of physical protection, but also in terms of a broader set of services and goods. Armed groups became the vehicle for marketing the resources from artisanal mining, timber, and agriculture; they formed nodes in the delivery of key services like water, charcoal, and imported goods.[42] A Congolese expert based in Goma described the dynamic to me in 2016,

> If my community wants charcoal for cooking, we need to negotiate with the FDLR [armed group]. If we have a dispute over land with our neighbours, we need to ask for help from the FDLR. There is no court that can solve this for us. If we want to survive, we need the FDLR to help us sell our resources outside Congo.[43]

The concept of strong attractors enables useful cross-case comparison in a number of ways. First, it offers a language to describe causality at a systemic level, demonstrating how underlying rules and patterns in systems influence change. This allows for significant differences in the characteristics of the systems—as shown in the widely varying trajectories of southern Sudan and Congo described above—while still explaining why they might gravitate towards a similar strong attractor. In process tracing terms, a strong attractor acts in a similar way to a causal mechanism, providing an explanation for change over time. But by employing what Byrne and Callaghan call 'a complexity-informed version of process tracing', comparison is possible across systems rather than individual moments.

[40] See Le Riche, 'Conflict Governance', 30.

[41] Interview with UN Mission in Sudan (UNMIS) national civil affairs officer, January 2011.

[42] For example, while I was working in United Nations Organization Stabilization Mission in the Democratic Republic of Congo (MONUSCO), we discovered that large portions of Goma's charcoal was delivered via a network composed of an armed group (the FDLR), the Congolese army, and local communities in the nearby national reserve.

[43] Interview, Goma, September 2017.

The strong attractors in the Congolese and south Sudanese systems did not exclude the possibility of governing peacefully, but they did create a powerful pattern in which both systems stabilized themselves on the basis of violence.

The phase space for governance

Post-war consolidation in both South Sudan and the DRC may appear as a sort of renaissance of the state. In 2011, the formal end of the Comprehensive Peace Agreement saw South Sudan emerge an independent nation as rebel SPLM became a ruling government. Likewise, the 2003 peace agreement that ended the Second Congolese War witnessed the creation of a transitional government, quickly legitimized by the 2006 elections and the development of a set of national institutions (army, police force, legislature, judiciary). As President Kiir captured at the moment of independence, there was a feeling in both countries of *tabula rasa*: that these countries could emerge with a completely new way of governing themselves.[44] The overarching argument of this book, however, suggests that this apparent fresh start was a mirage. The governance systems that had evolved in both settings proved resilient to the kinds of change that were envisioned by the architects of a liberal state in both the DRC and South Sudan. In complex systems terms, the phase space—the range of possible outcomes at a given moment—did not include a direct, linear transition to a liberal model of governance. Instead, strong attractors in both systems acted to prevent the growth of formal state institutions, working directly against efforts to statebuild. By comparing these two settings in terms of their phase spaces, I here argue that a broader conclusion can be drawn about the kinds of settings where the UN is deployed to engage in statebuilding. The existence of parallel, shadow, and what Western interveners call 'corrupt' forms of governance are not a deviation from the norm; they reflect the realistic scope of activity for the people and institutions in these systems. This does not mean that changing such systems is impossible, only that they are very unlikely to change unless the underlying relationships enter into new constellations and forms. This may be the case even in so-called 'success' stories, such as Liberia, where vibrant forms of non-state governance continue well beyond the UN's declaration that the country had been stabilized.[45]

On its surface, South Sudan's post-war spending may appear as a concentration of resources on building up the state. For the first time fully able to control its massive oil revenues, the SPLM spent overwhelmingly on its national army, providing

[44] President Salva Kiir's Martyr's Day Speech, 30 July 2011, available at https://paanluelwel.com/2011/07/31/president-kiirs-speech-in-the-6th-martyrs-day-30-7-2011/.

[45] See Christine Cheng, *Extralegal Groups in Post-Conflict Liberia: How Trade Makes the State* (Oxford: Oxford University Press, 2018).

far more in salaries to its soldiers than did any of its neighbours.[46] Provisions were also made for the establishment of judicial and administrative authorities across the country, in which the state would have a formal relationship with traditional chiefs.[47] However, the dominant role of the SPLA led to the army disregarding and overriding these local authorities; as Marieke Schomerus has demonstrated, the SPLA was able to overrule local authorities, following the patterns established during the war in which it was the dominant entity in southern Sudan.[48] Rather than a distribution of governance responsibilities across a range of state institutions, post-war South Sudan resulted in the SPLA continuing to monopolize them. Evidence of this can be found in the role of the SPLA in administering land disputes, running cattle markets, and controlling tax collection.[49]

In fact, the large influx of oil revenues in 2011 appeared to strengthen the underlying ethno-military network dominated by the SPLM/SPLA rather than replace it with independent state institutions in areas like rule of law, justice, and provision of basic services. As argued in Chapters 3 and 4, SPLA units strongly tended to follow ethnic lines, with soldiers marrying into families within their chain of command.[50] These dynamics continued in the post-war era; indeed during my visits to South Sudan after independence, members of the national army continued to refer to themselves mainly as 'SPLA', despite their new moniker South Sudan People's Defense Forces (SSPDF). Now possessed of far greater means to secure loyalty via the military chain of command, Kiir's government continued to do so through the payroll: In places like Upper Nile State, salaries for the security forces constituted 80 per cent of the government's expenditure, while payments for administrative, judicial, and other services remained close to zero.[51] Instead of institutional growth, what Clémence Pinaud has called 'a form of solidaristic graft' emerged, in which the enormous revenues of southern Sudan's oil industry were channelled through the SPLA network and into communities, largely along ethnic lines.[52]

In complexity terms, the combination of new revenues and greater autonomy from the North did not fundamentally alter the underlying relationships

[46] Kuol, 'The Federalism-Decentralisation-Peace Nexus in South Sudan', 228.

[47] See Cherry Leonardi, *Dealing with Government in South Sudan: Histories of Chiefship, Community and State* (Oxford: James Currey Press, 2015).

[48] Marieke Schomerus and Lovise Aalen, 'Considering the State: Perspectives on South Sudan's Subdivision and Federalism Debate', Overseas Development Institute, August 2016.

[49] See World Bank, 'Southern Sudan: Enabling the State: Estimating the Non-Oil Revenue Potential of State and Local Governments', Washington, DC, 2010; Thomas, *A Slow Liberation*, 228.

[50] Pinaud, 'South Sudan: Civil War', 192–211.

[51] Wolfram Lacher, 'South Sudan: International State-Building and Its Limits', German Institute for International and Security Affairs, 2012, available at, https://www.swp-berlin.org/fileadmin/contents/products/research_papers/2012_RP04_lac.pdf

[52] Pinaud, 'South Sudan: Civil War', 211. The term 'solidaristic graft' was taken from Ernest Harsch, 'Accumulators and Democrats: Challenging State Corruption in Africa', *The Journal of Modern African Studies* 31 (1993): 31–48.

that ordered southern Sudan's governance system. In 2011, an SPLA commander explained the key relationship to me in quite straightforward terms:

> I am SPLA, so I represent the army and obey my chain of command. But I am from Kodok [a town in Upper Nile State] so I must feed and protect my community. How do I do this? I make sure it is *my* SPLA, filled with *my* sons, feeding *my* people, fighting *my* enemies.[53]

Perhaps the most important symbiotic relationship in this context is an exchange of loyalty for protection: an individual member of the SPLA maintains loyalty to the army in exchange for the right to instrumentalize the position to protect and feed their community. This relationship was not changed by the creation of a new state in South Sudan, nor was it transformed by the establishment of formal state institutions.

Rather, what Alex de Waal has called 'the hegemonic power of the SPLM-SPLA patronage-coercion nexus' left no room for other forms of governance to emerge in the post-war period.[54] In the years following the war, when southern Sudan's resources skyrocketed and donor investment in state capacities soared, state institutional capacity beyond the army never meaningfully grew. Six years after the war, half of the statutory positions within ministries of southern Sudan still had not been filled, basic infrastructure and institutional capacity had not developed, and southern Sudan remained near or at the bottom of every governance indicator worldwide.[55] This went beyond economics as well: in dozens of interviews and conversations with South Sudanese over the past decade, I found an almost uniform view that formal state institutions were not their source of protection or services, and that the SPLA was more of a community protection actor than a national army. Not to say that communities thought positively of the SPLA—an army known for its human rights abuses and predatory behaviour—but rather they saw the group more in terms of its ethnic and community affiliation rather than as a formal state actor.

Similarly, post-war Congo also appeared to transform dramatically. Following the 2002 peace accord, the FARDC was reconstituted; interim national institutions were formed to oversee legislative and executive functions; and a range of integration processes were initiated to bring the dozens of rebel groups out of the bush. Indeed, the 2006 elections, in which Joseph Kabila ascended to the presidency,

[53] Interview, Malakal, January 2011.

[54] De Waal, 'When Kleptocracy becomes Insolvent', 349.

[55] De Waal, 'When Kleptocracy becomes Insolvent', 30; Magali Mores, 'Overview of Corruption and Anti-corruption in South Sudan', Transparency International, 4 March 2013.

were widely touted as a legitimate expression of the Congolese people, setting the country on the path to liberal democracy.[56]

While the post-war transitional period did in fact produce new state institutions, beneath the surface a form of parallel governance persisted. Similar to southern Sudan, this system was based on an exchange of loyalty for protection, in which state actors like the army and the police were instrumentalized for patronage.[57] Congo's *rapportage* system, in which underpaid state actors were expected to pay up their chain of command in exchange for the privileges associated with the post, became the dominant practice across government, echoing the patterns of the Mobutu era. Congo's *parapluie*—the umbrella of the state—demanded that state actors extract from the peripheries, feeding resources upwards.

This system, however, had to adapt to a post-war landscape dominated by networks of armed groups that had come to control much of the resource production in eastern Congo. Rather than disrupt these networks and replace them with state institutions, the post-war transition witnessed a partial integration of the *rapportage* system into them. Here, a form of symbiosis emerged: militias could guarantee resources for the *rapportage* system, thus securing local state actors in their positions, while in turn militias found they could benefit from the protections offered by Kabila's *parapluie*.

Here, an example from research I conducted for the UN in 2017 illustrates an important relationship: In Beni (a town in North Kivu), an armed group called the Allied Democratic Forces (ADF) had been operating for twenty years. While it was responsible for hundreds of deaths and was widely considered one of the most vicious groups in eastern Congo, it also collaborated with some elements of the FARDC to secure the extraction and marketing of timber and other resources from areas near Beni. In return, some elements of the FARDC collaborated with the ADF, allowing it to operate with few constraints, even as it was nominally a target of military operations by the Congolese government. A Congolese civil society activist in Beni described this dynamic to me: 'You think of the ADF as this terrible group attacking civilians, but it is also part of the chain that feeds some of the big men in Kinshasa. They are under an umbrella, just like everyone.'[58] Even the ADF, the group considered so far beyond the pale that the UN had essentially no contacts with its leadership, participated in the networked set of relations that resulted in the violent, ruthless, but highly ordered governance of eastern Congo.

[56] See The Carter Center, 'International Election Observation Mission to Democratic Republic of Congo 2006: Presidential and Legislative Elections Final Report', available at https://www.cartercenter.org/resources/pdfs/news/peace_publications/election_reports/drc-2006-final-rpt.pdf

[57] Judith Verweijen, *Stable Instability: Political Settlements and Armed Groups in the Congo* (London: Rift Valley Institute, 2016).

[58] This analysis of the ADF is based on my research while serving as Senior Political Adviser to MONUSCO in 2016.

The *rapportage* system in the DRC relied upon a certain amount of instability and state dysfunction. Elites controlling the top of the patronage network were beholden to the armed groups that secured resources and protected their interests in the peripheries. Negotiations over the right to govern thus played out via violence, as armed groups fought over land, resource routes, and access to influential actors in the elite.[59] Judith Verweijen has called this 'stable instability', while Bell and Pospisil have referred to the 'political unsettlement' underlying such systems.[60] Moreover, this dynamic meant that formal state institutions never fully formed, or if they did, they formed largely in symbiosis with armed groups and businesspeople. In many settings, state institutions remained completely absent, while a combination of armed groups and private actors assumed the day-to-day tasks of governing.[61]

Even as they were apparently consolidating state authority in the post-war period, both the DRC and South Sudan continued to display similar signs that their systems had not in fact transformed. Evidence of 'parallel', 'shadow', and 'corrupt' forms of governance were not deviations from a norm, they constituted the basis for both systems. Their respective phase spaces were constrained by their underlying rules, which were not altered by new flows of money or even the creation of formal institutions. Of course, phase spaces can change over time as systems evolve, but during the periods described above, there appeared no scope for the Congolese or South Sudanese system to transition in a direct, linear way into a version of the liberal Western state. As the final sub-section will argue, the UN's efforts to prompt such a transition in many ways reinforced the underlying relationships, acting to maintain the status quo rather than prompt a shift in phase space.

Systemic resilience to statebuilding

I have here argued that both South Sudan and the DRC, while different in many respects, converged towards governance systems that shared several key characteristics of complex systems. Both systems were ordered by symbiotic relationships among state and non-state actors, and both relied upon violence as a guarantee to that relationship. As a result, a strong attractor developed, where resources and energy ostensibly directed towards formal state institutions were diverted into parallel networks. In fact, large-scale efforts at building state capacity appear to have contributed to a positive feedback loop in both systems, reinforcing existing forms of governance in the peripheries and perversely undermining the objective

[59] See Vlassenroot and Raeymaekers, 'New Political Order in the DR Congo?', 39–52.

[60] Verweijen, 'Stable Instability'; Christine Bell and Jan Pospisil, 'Navigating Inclusion in Transitions from Conflict: The Formalised Political *Un*settlement', *Journal of International Development* 29, No. 5 (2017): 576–593.

[61] See Raeymaekers, *Violent Capitalism*.

of forming a strong centralized state along the lines of the liberal model. This section explores how the UN's statebuilding efforts fell into this pattern in both countries, ultimately participating in and reinforcing the underlying system rather than transforming it.

At the heart of UN statebuilding in both the DRC and South Sudan is the concept of 'state consolidation'. In the immediate post-war period, this meant integrating hundreds of thousands of rebel forces into a newly formed national army,[62] putting in place a viable police force, developing regulatory frameworks for rule of law institutions, and establishing ministries to oversee service delivery across the country. In 2011, a senior UN official in Juba described this process in vivid terms: 'Think of the government as an empty vessel, waiting to be filled. We need to fill it with our expertise, with our resources, and with models for them to follow. It is a fundamental lack of state capacity that is preventing South Sudan from becoming a functioning country.'[63] A senior member of United Nations Organization Stabilization Mission in the Democratic Republic of Congo (MONUSCO) described a similar pathway for the DRC: 'The Congolese state has been disintegrating for decades. Our job is to integrate it, consolidate authority in a state that can then function like we do in the West.'[64]

Related to consolidation is the notion of 'extension of state authority', one of the most frequently used phrases in UN parlance in places like the DRC and South Sudan. Here, MONUSCO's 'islands of stability' is perhaps the best example, where the mission conceived of eastern Congo as a sea of ungoverned space awaiting the presence of state institutions. In South Sudan too, UNMISS placed extension of state authority as its highest priority, establishing county support bases and funnelling much of the UN's sizeable resources into building capacities in the rural peripheries of the country. In both settings, the underlying concept of how change would take place was a linear one: the UN would help the government secure areas, build state institutional capacity, and on that basis transform what had been a lawless, dangerous area into a stable, governed one. MONUSCO's 2013 Mission Concept (Figure 7.1) captures this thinking perfectly:[65]

Reality, however, was far less linear, conforming instead to the kinds of change one should expect from a complex system ordered by feedback loops and attractors. In South Sudan, for example, UNMISS deployed 900 police to help build the capacities of the rural police force, an approach that aligned with the government of South Sudan's national development plan: both were ostensibly meant to shift resources and capacities away from the SPLA into local policing and justice.[66]

[62] In South Sudan, this was less integration of rebel groups and more a re-hatting of the SPLA into a national army.

[63] Meeting with senior UNMIS official for the South Sudan conflict assessment, 10 January 2011.

[64] Notes on Senior Mission Leadership group, March 2016 (on file with author).

[65] 2013 UNMISS Mission Concept (confidential, on file with author).

[66] South Sudan Ministry of Foreign Affairs, 'Multi Annual Strategic Plan South Sudan 2012–2015', 2011, available at http://extwprlegs1.fao.org/docs/pdf/ssd148386.pdf

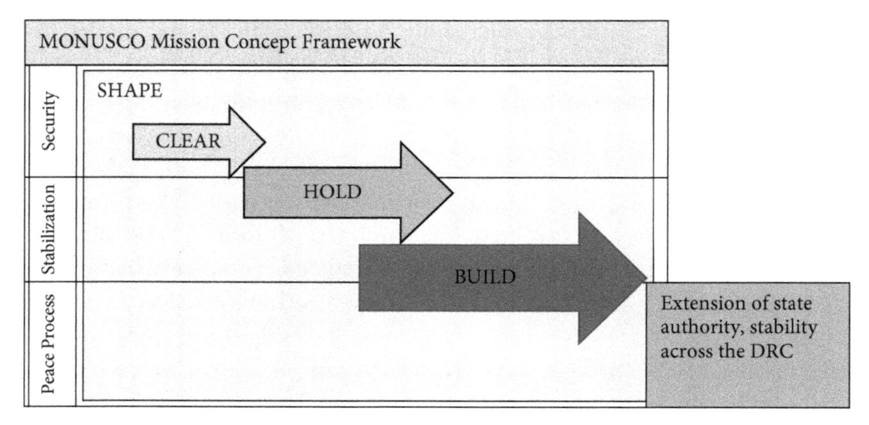

Fig. 7.1 MONUSCO Mission Concept Framework.

'We need to make South Sudan about more than the SPLA', a local politician in Malakal told me. 'And that means courts, police, local administrations, not just the SPLA controlling everything.'[67] This should have resulted in greater resources going to state institutions in the peripheries, accompanied by a gradual decline in the responsibilities of the army in several areas. However, during the immediate post-independence period, government spending on development and fiscal transfers to the states in fact dropped, while salaries for the SPLA rose.[68] To the extent institutions were built—and it should be noted that some police stations and courts were established with UNMISS' support—they functioned more as empty shells, what Wolfram Lacher has called 'patronage instruments' that funnelled resources into the same network as that largely controlled by the SPLA.[69]

UNMISS's support to the state thus appeared to play into a system that was becoming increasingly elite-dominated, tilted towards the Dinka community, and reliant on force to maintain stability. 'UNMISS put its finger on the scales, it only helped the Dinka', a South Sudanese expert described to me in 2018.[70] Had the UN's capacitybuilding support flowed directly into local institutions, these institutions would have reflected their local ethnic make-up; likewise, the formal government put in place by President Kiir (which was well balanced in ethnic terms) should have ensured that power and resources were equitably distributed to regions and ethnic groups. Neither was the case: deeply ingrained patterns in the South Sudanese ethno-military governance system meant that UNMISS' support appeared to slip through cracks in formal institutions and end up in the hands of the largely Dinka SPLA elite, which in turn fed its own community networks.

[67] Interview, Malakal, January 2011.
[68] De Waal, 'When Kleptocracy becomes Insolvent', 349.
[69] Lacher, 'South Sudan: International State-Building'.
[70] Interview, Juba, 13 December 2018.

This effect went well beyond financial resources (in fact Øystein Rolandsen has demonstrated the fairly negligible financial impact of UNMISS in South Sudan's formal economy) but also included crucial disputes over land.[71] UNMISS' efforts to strengthen state administration over land played directly into longstanding intercommunal disputes, giving power-brokers linked to the SPLM/SPLA a stronger hand. Alienation of land by the SPLM/SPLA became a flashpoint of discontent among many communities, and UNMISS' role in supporting the state appeared to strengthen patterns of rent seeking and inequitable distribution of territories.[72] In 2018, I met with a group of land advocates in Juba during which they described widespread discontent at the role of the UN in addressing land disputes. 'UNMISS doesn't understand that individuals within the SPLA are stealing land, which belongs to the people', one advocate told me. Another said, 'When UNMISS says it's here to support the government, this means the people near [President] Kiir are able to take more land. It gives them and their communities a free hand.' If the SPLA had truly represented institutions of the state, state ownership of land would have dramatically increased during this period. However, more than three years after independence, efforts to place land under state control had failed—less than 10 per cent of South Sudan's rural land was even registered by the state—while tensions among communities over land proliferated.[73]

UNMISS' efforts to extend state authority were taking place at a crucial moment in South Sudan's history where a newly formed state flush with oil revenues was flooding the system with cash, even as many communities were attempting to maintain their largely cashless lifestyle. As Cherry Leonardi has explored, many southern Sudanese populations held strong associations between money and corrupt, predatory governments dating back to the colonial periods. Particularly in cattle-owning societies, cash has been seen as an imposition of the state into their way of life, whereas land and cattle remain the principle sources of value.[74] Following the civil war, reports of land grabbing by the SPLA were commonplace as soldiers claimed to have 'bought' land with the blood spilled during the war. *De facto* control of state institutions by former SPLA networks meant that UNMISS' efforts to extend state control over land tended to legitimize this dynamic, enabling the ethno-military network to entrench itself further in land disputes. And as the oil revenues flowed more heavily through this network, local communities saw their largely cashless societies becoming unbalanced.

While I was on a research trip to Juba in 2011, an SPLA soldier turned politician explained this phenomenon in stark terms:

[71] Øystein H. Rolandsen, 'Small and Far Between: Peacekeeping Economies in South Sudan', *Journal of Intervention and Statebuilding* 9, No. 3 (2015): 353–371.
[72] For a description of inequitable distribution, see Tiernan Mennan, 'Customary Law and Land Rights in South Sudan', Norwegian Refugee Council, March 2012.
[73] See Leonardi, 'Paying "Buckets of Blood"'.
[74] Leonardi, 'Paying "Buckets of Blood"'.

> For hundreds of years, my community had a way of doing things. We had an economy that ran on cattle, food, and bridewealth.[75] But then the war happened and we all joined the SPLA. And millions of us died fighting Khartoum. Now, when I come back to my community I don't have cattle or land to get a bride, but I have money from Salva [Kiir]. And I have rights, rights to land that I earned on the battlefield. So what do I do? I plant the SPLA flag on this land and I say 'this is mine.' And who is to say it isn't? Not the government, because I am the government now.[76]

Amidst a deepening crisis over land tenure and the role of government in the post-civil war South, UNMISS' extension of state authority work was seen by many in South Sudan as enabling these kinds of land grabs. Rather than leading to effective state control over land, it strengthened a pattern in the system in which ethnically affiliated elements of the SPLA were able to manipulate land ownership in the name of the state.

The DRC's *parapluie* protection system differed significantly from that of South Sudan—principally in that it tended to draw resources upwards to the elite, rather than distribute them outwards to the periphery—but the results of the UN's extension of state authority efforts followed similar patterns. Between 2008 and 2012, MONUC/MONUSCO spent roughly $400 million on projects designed to extend state authority into areas affected by armed group activity, demobilizing tens of thousands of former combatants, rehabilitating hundreds of kilometres of road, and helping to set up new institutions.[77] According to the UN's models, stability should have improved as state security institutions replaced the armed groups and gradually built up their capacities to serve communities there. But in all six of the priority areas identified in the joint UN/government plan, armed group activity continued, increasing in some areas; on roads rehabilitated by MONUSCO illegal checkpoints proliferated, often controlled by state security agents trying to feed their upward chain of command; and newly built courts and prisons were left empty or marginalized by local authorities who had built up their own forms of rule.[78]

Similar to South Sudan, this failure to extend formal state authority can be explained by the underlying rules of the Congolese governance system. A crucial

[75] NB: 'Bridewealth' in this context refers to the number of cows given by a man's family when he married a woman.

[76] Interview, Juba, January 2011.

[77] MONUSCO, 'International Security and Stabilisation Support Strategy Quarterly Report, 2009–2012'.

[78] See earlier chapters for more detail. See also Hugo de Vries, *Going Around in Circles: The Challenges of Peacekeeping and Stabilisation in the Democratic Republic of the Congo* (The Hague: Clingendael, 2005), 50; Sarah Bailey, 'Humanitarian Action, Early Recovery and Stabilisation in the Democratic Republic of Congo', Overseas Development Institute Humanitarian Policy Working Group Paper, July 2011; Sam Dixon, 'Why Efforts to Stabilise the DR Congo Are Not Working', Oxfam Horn, East and Central Africa Blog, 4 July 2012, available at. https://www.oxfamblogs.org/eastafrica/?p=4484

set of relationships undergirding this system was an exchange of protection for resources, resulting in funds flowing from the periphery to the centre, which in turn maintained the elite power structure, simultaneously preserving the need for armed group activity in eastern Congo. The UN's approach to increase funds and other resources to state-run projects in the periphery did not alter that underlying relationship, but rather fed it. Nascent institutions in eastern Congo were not, as MONUSCO's planning assumed, used for governing their populations, but were instruments in the *trafic d'influence* that maintained the protection network intact.[79]

In fact, MONUSCO's stabilization activities contributed to an existing gravitational pull within the system: Those areas experiencing conflict were more likely to receive new injections of resources from the UN and international donors. In a system based upon resources moving from rural peripheries to elite coffers in Kinshasa, this contributed to the underlying strong attractor to violence. An international non-governmental organization (NGO) worker who had been living in the DRC for more than twenty years explained the dynamic to me in these terms:

> It is like MONUSCO is playing a game of whack-a-mole with the armed groups, but instead of a mallet, the mission has mole food. Every time a mole comes up, it may look like we strike it, but in fact we reward violent behaviour. Over time, this causes an incentive to grow, and the communities start to understand that violence pays, that the UN will come and build a road if things get bad enough.

MONUSCO was a relatively small player in this, but as I explained in Chapters 5 and 6, the broader approach of the government of the DRC too tended to reward violent behaviour, offering integration into the army as a typical response to insecurity. Broadly, MONUSCO's approach ran with the grain of Congo's system, tending to create incentives for violence even while ostensibly combating them.

At a national level, UNMISS' and MONUSCO's statebuilding efforts were founded on a hope for a fundamental transformation of the state, where reforms at the highest level would cause a dramatic change in the way both countries were governed. As described in previous chapters, these reforms largely failed to materialize in either country. In some areas, isomorphic mimicry appeared to occur: national plans and budgets took the shape of the models being offered by the UN and major donors.[80] But over time, most national institutions showed themselves to be mirages, images of a Western-style state without content. In South Sudan, donors spoke of a 'fake ministry' set up to deal with them, while the 'real ministry'

[79] Ian D. Quick, *Follies in Fragile States: How International Stabilisation Failed in the Congo* (London: Double Loop Press, 2015), 57.

[80] For more on isomorphism, see Paul DiMaggio and Walter Powell, 'The Iron Cage Revisited: Institutional Isomorphism and Collective Rationality in Organizational Fields', *American Sociological Review* 48, No. 2 (1983): 147–160.

operated behind the scenes and distributed Kiir's largesse to his loyalists.[81] In the DRC, legislation aimed at overhauling the security services and building functioning administrative institutions languished, failed to receive funding, and was often forgotten in the myriad crises that erupt constantly in Congolese politics.

The most common explanation for the flat trajectory of reform in both countries is lack of political will. International analysts consistently suggest that venal politicians, bent on self-enrichment and governed by the 'politics of the belly' have distorted the bureaucracy to their own ends, refusing to push for the kinds of reforms that would lead to better lives for the broader citizenry. While corruption and patronage offer a partial explanation for some of the ways in which resources were diverted and reforms thwarted, they do not capture the deeper systemic character of the governance systems in both countries. Even where leaders attempted to push for reform—for example, President Kiir's appointment of a multi-ethnic, fairly balanced cabinet in his first government, or President Kabila's approval of a national-level stabilization plan—strong attractors in the system soon pulled their energy elsewhere. One of the most important recognitions of complexity thinking is that human agency matters, that things can be done, but that systems only change when the underlying rules are altered. For all of the effort at reform in the DRC and South Sudan, those underlying relationships, the symbioses that had evolved over decades of war, misrule, and predation, proved highly resilient to change.

The UN's approach in both countries can be described as a failure to understand that these systems were complex, treating them instead as complicated. In a complicated system, such as an engine, a mechanic can alter the outputs by introducing new inputs, or by replacing parts of the machine. This mindset was evident in South Sudan where a senior UN official once told me, 'We just need to clear out the corrupt elements of the [interior] ministry and replace them with good, clean functioning ones.' In eastern DRC, the UN likewise envisioned a clearing out of bad elements (the armed groups) to be replaced by shiny new courts and police stations that would produce a new output: good governance.

Change in complex systems, however, cannot be determined merely by new interventions. If a doctor wishes to trigger a particular result in an immune system, she administers medicines that affect how elements within that system interact, altering the underlying relationships and dynamics. Likewise in social systems, an input will have unintended consequences unless the often invisible ordering relationships are taken into account. In the cases of South Sudan and the DRC, the interventions of the peacekeeping missions were overwhelmingly state-centric—the UN poured resources, hours, and legitimacy into setting up state institutions.

[81] Greg Larson, Peter Biar Ajak, and Lant Pritchett, 'South Sudan's Capability Trap: Building a State with Disruptive Innovation', Harvard Kennedy School, 2013.

If those countries had been merely complicated machines, the input of state support might have generated the output of stronger formal state institutions. But in the complex systems present in both countries, the UN's interventions were the wrong kind of medicine, reinforcing the relationships rather than altering them.

Complexity thus provides insights that are not fully captured by either the political economy scholarship or the more anthropological work in the DRC and South Sudan. Complexity theory supports the findings of Séverine Autesserre, Roger Mac Ginty, and others who suggest that the UN's inability to understand and connect with local realities contributes to lack of traction on the ground. Complexity also aligns with the major political economy readings of both countries, especially those of Koen Vlassenroot, Timothy Raeymaekers, Judith Verweijen, Alex de Waal, and Matthew Le Riche, which explore how public authority results from competition, negotiation, and overlapping spheres of power. But complexity also adds a set of tools that goes beyond economic readings of each setting, examining how different constellations of actors and types of symbiotic relationships generate patterns over time, displaying emergent behaviour that tends to work against the goals of statebuilding. Ultimately, complexity offers a heuristic to investigate the UN as part of a system rather than as an external actor trying to change it.

The final chapter will explore what insights the cases of South Sudan and the DRC may offer for the statebuilding agenda globally, not only in settings where the UN is deployed, but also in nationally driven efforts to consolidate state authority in places like Afghanistan, Somalia, and Iraq. It argues that complexity theory provides a dynamic and evidence-based lens through which to understand and engage in these settings. But it goes further, suggesting that international relations more generally—particularly in efforts to comprehend and shape global governance—would benefit from a complexity-driven paradigm as well.

8
Implications for a world ordered by states

This chapter moves from the specific cases of South Sudan and the Democratic Republic of Congo (DRC) to broader implications for statebuilding and global order. It argues that complex systems of governance are present in every setting where the United Nations (UN) and other actors have been tasked to consolidate and extend state authority. While the specific characteristics of each situation differ significantly, they share a common tendency to resist state-centric, top-down approaches to governance. Despite this consistent shortcoming, the UN's approach across its statebuilding work has remained remarkably consistent over time, employing nearly identical concepts of liberal statehood regardless of their recurrent inability to produce meaningful results. As such, UN statebuilding falls into a trap of considering the liberal state as a sort of 'natural' outcome of successful conflict resolution and stabilization, a socio-political equilibrium punctuated by periods of unrest or other 'unnatural' forms of ordering. UN interventions are seen as 'restoring' such an order, despite ample evidence that most systems never experienced a liberal-style model of the state, except in a distorted form during the imposition of colonial rule.

Here, complexity theory offers an empirically grounded alternative explanation for the governance systems we see from Afghanistan to Mali: these settings exhibit networks of relationships in which the right to govern is negotiated, contested, and at times violently fought over, dynamical systems in which state institutions are often fairly unimportant nodes. Seen through the lens of complexity theory, UN statebuilding is not only chronically failing to alter the relationships constituting these systems, it is often an unwitting participant in them, strengthening exactly the patterns of violence, predation, and exclusion it ostensibly wishes to replace.

Complexity theory not only offers an explanation of the failures of statebuilding, but also a sense of what might be done differently in the future. In the second section of this chapter, I provide four insights from complexity that could be considered policy implications for future statebuilders:
(1) Moments of violent conflict—typically considered opportunities to reshape failed or failing states—may in fact be the worst points at which to try to alter the underlying rules of complex systems. When systems are in flux, strong attractors often exert their most powerful influence, meaning that interventions during conflict may be least likely to alter underlying rules.

States of Disorder, Ecosystems of Governance. Adam Day, Oxford University Press.
 DOI: 10.1093/oso/9780192863898.003.0009

(2) The widely revered concept of 'the local' in peacebuilding discourse should be reimagined; rather than think of local realities as something taking place below or apart from a national or elite-driven life (a sort of idealized village in much of the scholarship), locality should be described in relational terms as the point at which actors intersect and form a node in the system. 'Local' in this context does not mean the daily routines of distant villagers but instead a focus on the relationships that constitute systems, on the quality of exchange that sustains them and how they might be gradually reconfigured.
(3) The notion of 'resilience' has become a normative construct associated with healthy and highly complex societies, despite ample evidence that conflict-prone and so-called 'fragile' contexts display extraordinary complexity and resilience against change. This requires redefining resilience to reflect the capacity for a system to withstand shocks and interventions, regardless of whether such a system is based on violent, 'corrupt' relationships. Indeed it may require some level of comfort with so-called corruption if interveners wish to enable less violent societies over the longer term.
(4) Often, when confronted with failure, the UN turns to 'lack of political will', arguing that the national leaders were simply unwilling to support the kind of transformational change required. But this merely begs the core question: How much are individual actors able to change systems of governance, what is their agency? Here, complexity theory offers a way to understand agency that goes beyond the empty notion of political will. By mapping the systems of governance in places like South Sudan and the DRC, we can see the 'strong attractors' in each system, the gravitational pulls that resist efforts to transform them. President Kabila might have been acting in self-interest when he continually stalled on security sector reform, but the broader system also demonstrated a strong resilience against a variety of efforts to implement reforms, including by Kabila himself. Likewise, the protagonists in South Sudan's civil war were driven by the ethno-military network that had sustained governance through decades of prior wars; they had what I call 'strongly influenced agency' in their own system. Complexity provides a sense of the system's landscapes, the deep valleys that tend to capture political energy and resources, and an empirically backed method for describing the ability of actors to implement change.
Finally, (5) complexity demands what John Paul Lederach calls a 'moral imagination', a willingness to embrace the mystery of socio-political systems, even those that appear dysfunctional to outsiders, rather than trying to reduce them to single, simple narratives or fit them into external (neo-colonial) models.
The concluding section considers the broader role that statebuilding plays in maintaining international order. It argues that the liberal internationalist ideology that has dominated much of international relations (IR) theory and practice for the past thirty years has relied heavily on statebuilding as an ontological activity. Statebuilding is necessary for liberal visions of world order, reaffirming the

Western model of the state, preventing the potential spread of other modalities of statehood, while increasing predictability and control within the international system. More recently, however, this order has come under pressure as major powers have retreated from the institutions and forums that have underpinned liberal institutionalism since the end of the Cold War. While this has generated anxiety among those wishing to retain what the United Kingdom (UK) and others call a rules-based international order, complexity theory offers a framework to understand how new order might emerge from within the networks that are increasingly driving global change today.

Resilient patterns in statebuilding

'What we need in Libya', a Security Council representative told me over coffee in the UN's Delegates Lounge in 2012, 'is a real state. [Former President] Ghaddafi left a vacuum when he died, and unless we get in there and fill that space with functioning state institutions, it's going to fall apart.'[1]

At the time I was a political officer leading the Libya team in the UN's Department of Political Affairs. Compared to Congo and South Sudan, the challenges facing Libya had a familiar ring to them: Ghaddafi had built a sprawling patronage network over his forty-year rule, a centralization of power in his persona that impeded the growth of functioning state institutions, marginalized the vast majority of the population, and created a near total rentier oil economy. The result was a state entirely lacking the attributes of Western liberal order, what a UN official once described to me as 'something like the Wild West, without rules, overrun with warlords and criminals'.

The Security Council, still reeling from the highly contentious decision to authorize the international intervention that led to the Ghaddafi's demise, had recently established the UN's newest peace operation, mandated to support a transitional government in Libya. Central to this operation were two familiar goals: restoring the state's monopoly of legitimate violence and extending the state's governance capacities over the huge, apparently 'ungoverned' territory of Libya.[2] While not a peacekeeping mission wielding troops or armed police, the UN operation in Libya followed a similar model to the UN in Congo and South Sudan: the solution to instability was elections, followed by the consolidation and extension of the state.

Libya's statebuilding trajectory resulted in no better outcome than in South Sudan or the Congo. After national elections in 2012 and a few years of faltering attempts to set up a viable transitional government, competing centres of

[1] Interview notes, New York, February 2011.
[2] United Nations Security Council Resolution, S/RES/2002 (2011), para. 12.

power emerged outside of the capital, Tripoli, challenging the central government's authority and, for a time, resulting in two governments claiming legitimate rule over the country.[3] In 2014, these tensions broke out into a civil war in which dozens of militias—many formed during the 2011 revolution to fight Ghaddafi—won control of huge swathes of Libya's territory. Violent extremist groups flourished and the eastern city of Benghazi quickly became known as a pre-eminent hub for international terrorist groups, including the Islamic State and Al Qaeda. Libya's enormous oil reserves fell into the hands of a dissident general, placing a chokehold on the central government and preventing large flows of cash into state institutions.[4] Armed group proliferation, fragmentation, and interlinkages with international support networks meant that Libya's state quickly became yet another example of failure in international discourse, one in which governance was openly contested among a range of actors rather than monopolized by a centralized set of institutions.

Here, scholars turned to familiar statebuilding language, referring to Libya's 'ungoverned spaces' and employing many of the same tropes seen across liberal statebuilding discourse elsewhere in the world.[5] Libya's governance failings were frequently described as a threat to the world, rendering the country a flow-through point for weapons, extremists, and illicit flows of money. Some of the more insightful scholarship did explore the ways in which non-state forms of governance emerged, often involving a variety of relationships between armed groups, traditional authorities, state actors, and transnational economic networks.[6] In the security sector, for example, experts described 'hybrid institutions' that blurred state and non-state roles,[7] while considering justice part of a regime of 'contested governance'.[8] Capturing much of this literature, Irene Costantini noted that the failure of Libya to transition into a stable, viable state could be explained by 'the problematic and contested definition of what constitutes state and non-state actors in Libya'.[9]

[3] For a more detailed description of the lead up to the civil war, see Marc. R. DeVore, 'Exploiting Anarchy: Violent Entrepreneurs and the Collapse of Libya's Post Qadhafi Settlement', *Mediterranean Politics* 19, No. 3 (2014): 463–470; Wolfram Lacher, 'The Libyan Revolution and the Rise of Competing Power Centres', *Mediterranean Politics* (2012): 167–170.

[4] Al, Jazeera, 'Commander Khalifa Haftar's Forces Choke Libya's Oil Flow', Al Jazeera online, 19 January 2020, available at, https://www.aljazeera.com/ajimpact/commander-khalifa-haftar-forces-choke-libya-oil-flow-200119162228201.html

[5] See, e.g., Noureddine Jebnoun, 'Beyond the Mayhem: Debating Key Dilemmas in Libya's Statebuilding', *The Journal of North African Studies* 20, No. 5 (2015): 832–864.

[6] Andrea Carboni and James Moody, 'Between the Cracks: Actor Fragmentation and Local Conflict Systems in the Libyan Civil War', *Small Wars & Insurgencies* 29, No. 3 (2108): 456–490.

[7] Wolfram Lacher and Peter Cole, 'Politics by Other Means: Conflicting Interests in Libya's Security Sector', Small Arms Survey (2014).

[8] Christopher K. Lamont, 'Contested Governance: Understanding Justice Interventions in Post-Qadhafi Libya', *Journal of Intervention and Statebuilding* 10, No. 3 (2016): 382–399.

[9] Irene Costantini, 'Conflict Dynamics in Post-2011 Libya: A Political Economy Perspective', *Conflict, Security & Development* 16, No. 5 (2016): 405–422.

Unfortunately, however, these insights did not prompt a more fundamental shift in the UN's approach to conflict management and resolution. Nearly ten years after the Libyan civil war exposed the weaknesses of a state-centric approach, the Security Council has maintained more or less the same mandate for the UN operation there.[10] More frequent nods to 'national ownership' and 'inclusive political processes' indicate a recognition that solutions for Libya must be found among Libyans, but not a more profound questioning of the type of political configuration that might emerge from such socio-political systems. As my Security Council colleague noted in 2012, the UN is of the view that Libya should become a 'real state', presumably a Weberian one possessed of a central government capable of monopolizing force, exercising rule of law authority across the Libyan territory, and delivering basic services. The fact that the Libyan system already has deeply engrained patterns of governance and networks of influence in which the central state is largely absent is seen as either indicative of state failure or a level of detail too microscopic for the eyes of the statebuilder, the kind of granularity that is only of interest to the scholar, not the policymaker. Forms of order by so-called warlords, traditional authorities, and illicit traders likewise are considered exclusively through the lens of corruption, patrimony, and violence, obscuring the other functions these players maintain in the Libyan system. From the intervener's perspective, Libya will not be a 'real' state until these forces are subordinated to a central government.

Libya is one example of many. In a recent study on the Popular Mobilization Forces in Iraq, my colleagues and I found that security provision was the outcome of a highly networked set of relations among militias, local leaders, international patrons, and politicians who straddled the apparent state/non-state divide.[11] In many instances, these relationships were symbiotic, constituting essential exchanges for the survival of communities, institutions, and individuals. Speaking of extension of state authority in such a context may resonate in the Security Council chamber in New York, but it means little to a resident of Mosul who sees a locally recruited militia fight off the Islamic State and then begin policing their streets in the name of the state. Similarly, in Afghanistan—where the UN has a longstanding operation to support the consolidation and extension of the Afghan state—evidence of complex, relational systems of governance is abundant, while black and white distinctions between the Taliban, the state, and a host of other actors quickly becomes a spectrum of greys (indeed, the 2021 fall of Kabul to the Taliban points to a shift in phase space for governance there).[12] In fact,

[10] United Nations Security Council Resolution, S/RES/2846 (2019).

[11] Adam Day, Vanda Felbab-Brown, and Fanar Haddad, 'Hybrid Conflict, Hybrid Peace: How Militias and Paramilitary Groups Shape Post-Conflict Transitions', United Nations University Centre for Policy Research, 14 April 2020.

[12] See, e.g., Susanne Schmeidl and Masood Karokhail, 'The Role of Non-State Actors in "Community-Based Policing"—An Exploration of the Arbakai (Tribal Police) in South-Eastern

investigations into the major areas where UN peace operations are actively supporting extension of state authority—Mali, Colombia, Central African Republic, and Somalia—demonstrate the utility of complexity thinking: all exhibit characteristics of complex, contested systems of governance, while none falls neatly into a liberal model of statehood.[13]

In this respect, the UN's approach to statebuilding appears founded upon a normatively driven misconception of the natural way in which communities (should) order themselves into states.[14] The liberal state, in which a central government has the exclusive right to provide security, justice, and services to its citizens, is equated with stability, whereas other mechanisms of ordering are referred to uncritically as unstable. When an armed group provides cooking charcoal to the population of Goma, this is seen as a retreat of the state from its rightful place governing eastern Congo, rather than perhaps an essential aspect of an existing governance system. Al Shabaab's control of several territories in Somalia, or Taliban administration of much of Afghanistan, is typically conceived through the lens of state failure, a broken machine in need of fixing. This is not to suggest that the armed groups, traditional authorities, and/or businesspeople of Congo, Somalia, or Afghanistan are effective or peaceful providers of public authority (indeed, the evidence from the cases above suggests a high degree of violence, predation, and inequality in many of these systems), but rather that they are integral to the ordering of these countries and cannot merely be cleared out of the way without severe unintended consequences.

In fact, the widely held concept of stability embodied in UN peacekeeping runs directly against the evidence across conflict zones, which demonstrates that complex socio-political systems often stabilize around strong attractors that may be violent, predatory, and unfair to much of the population; moreover, they often stabilize around relationships in which the state is but one of many actors. In eastern DRC, armed groups have become an essential part of the underlying network of relationships that secures community livelihoods, feeds the political elite, and exports natural resources to international markets. Whether or not armed groups are 'good' or 'bad' is irrelevant to the question of how they play a role in stabilizing Congo's current governance system. The evidence provided in Chapters 5 and

Afghanistan', *Contemporary Security Policy* 30, No. 2 (2009): 318–342; Dipali Mukhopadhyay, *Warlords, Strongmen Governors, and the State in Afghanistan* (New York: Cambridge University Press, 2014).

[13] See, e.g., Adam C. Day and Charles T. Hunt, 'UN Stabilisation Operations and the Problem of Non-Linear Change: A Relational Approach to Intervening in Governance Ecosystems', *Stability International Journal of Security and Development* 9, No. 1 (2020): 1–23; Jasper Bauters, 'A Taxonomy of Non-State Actors in Central African Republic', International Peace Information Service, 2012; Timothy Raeymaekers and Ken Menkhaus, 'State and Non-State Regulation in African Protracted Crises: Governance Without Government?', *Afrika Focus* 21 (2008); Romain Malejacq, 'Warlords, Intervention, and State Consolidation: A Typology of Political Orders in Weak and Failed States', *Security Studies* 25 (2016): 85–110. For more scholarship, see Chapter 1.

[14] See Francis Fukuyama, *State-building: Governance and World Order in the 21st Century* (New York: Cornell University Press, 2004).

6 aligns with Judith Verweijen's argument that Congo's system is one of 'stable instability', where armed groups are an integral aspect of an underlying set of relations ordering the Congolese governance system.[15] In fact, in the Congolese, South Sudanese, and many other systems, strong attractors to violence mean that governance is often contested with a gun rather than a ballot and a legislature. Pouring resources into state institutions is not only unlikely to change these systems, such efforts are in fact easily co-opted by them. Where the UN has invested heavily in statebuilding, a similar pattern has emerged in which systems absorb and distort international efforts, as a strong immune system might deal with a well-recognized seasonal malady.

Implications for the statebuilder

Confronted with recurrent failure and a burgeoning literature critical of the Western model of the state, UN statebuilding and peacebuilding may have already lapsed into a listless malaise, content with an endlessly retreating peace horizon. Pol Bargués-Pedreny describes this as a sort of liberal paralysis in which the need to be respectful of local realities and avoid imposing external frameworks leads peacebuilding to be principally an act of deferral, one where the goal paradoxically becomes failure itself.[16] In my experience, we in the UN seem to revel in the organization's failures, almost taking pleasure in the recurrent weaknesses and shortcomings of our work. Perhaps we suffer collectively from atychiphilia, the love of failure? Indeed, much of this book has suggested that the UN's interventions in conflict settings may have had the unintended consequences of bolstering the patterns of predatory behaviour, exclusion, and violence ostensibly the target of statebuilding efforts. The implication is fairly direct: these settings might be better off without the UN intervention, unless a serious adjustment is made. Scholarship suggesting a 'local turn' to more culturally sensitive, less neo-colonial approaches to peacebuilding may help to prevent unwarranted interventions, but it offers very little to answer the question 'What do we do now?' Here, complexity theory yields potentially more constructive lessons for future engagement in conflict-prone settings, five of which I describe here.

Timing interventions

First, complexity theory suggests that we may have misunderstood the best moment to generate change in societies. Like a thixotropic substance, societies

[15] Judith Verweijen, *Stable Instability: Political Settlements and Armed Groups in the Congo* (London: Rift Valley Institute, 2016).

[16] Pol Bargués-Pedreny, *Deferring Peace in International Statebuilding: Difference, Resilience and Critique* (London: Routledge, 2018), 8–17.

may appear to become more fluid when they are shaken by conflict, only returning to a more viscous, steady state when the conflict has been stabilized.[17] The UN implicitly has adopted this mindset, viewing periods of violent conflict and social upheaval as moments of fluidity and opportunity in which countries that have suffered dictatorships, repressive governments, or other forms of corrupt, undemocratic rule become ripe for transformation. Internal wars are called 'transitions' where the prospects for a shift towards better systems of governance are highest, in part because of the vulnerability of the ruling elite and the consolidation of oppositional forces.[18] In fact, much of the UN's diplomatic effort during conflicts over the past thirty years can be summarized as an attempt to broker an elite bargain among belligerents that will take advantage of the fluid conditions of conflict and transform a society into a liberal democratic state.[19] The hope of UN statebuilding has been that periods of flux and fluidity offer the potential to reorder societies, consolidating legitimate authority in a phalanx of effective, well-funded state institutions.

In contrast, evidence from the DRC and South Sudan suggests that periods of violent conflict may trigger strong attractors in systems to exert their most powerful undercurrents, establishing themselves even more firmly within their respective systems with repercussions long after the conflict has ended. In the DRC, for example, recurrent periods of intense conflict from 2003 until 2017 did not appear to open the possibility of a fundamental reshaping of the governance system towards a liberal model, but rather demonstrated an increasing reliance on armed groups and illicit flows of natural resources as the way in which the system ordered itself. When some viscous substances like honey or mud are heated or shaken up, they become fluid and may appear to have changed their characteristics; however, this has only briefly set their particles in motion, and over time they will again harden into their former state, one decided by their underlying atomic structure. Similarly, when societies fall into conflict, the period chaos and flux may display the appearance of potential change, while under the surface the system is quietly—but powerfully—reasserting itself. Alex de Waal hints at this in his description of 'turbulence' where systems may appear unpredictable and chaotic from one moment to the next, but still maintain a recognizable structure over the longer term.[20]

[17] I owe the concept of thixotropic substances and its application to social systems to a conversation with Stephen Jackson. I have not seen it published elsewhere.

[18] Indeed, my own published work falls into this problematic pattern. See Adam Day, Dirk Druit, and Luise Quaritsch, 'When Dictators Fall: Preventing Violent Conflict During Transitions from Authoritarian Rule', United Nations University Centre for Policy Research, May 2020.

[19] See Christine Cheng, Jonathan Goodhand, and Patrick Meehan, 'Securing and Sustaining Elite Bargains that Reduce Violent Conflict', UK Stabilisation Unit Synthesis Paper, April 2018.

[20] Alex De Waal, *The Real Politics of the Horn of Africa: Money, War and the Business of Power* (London: Polity Press, 2016), 17.

An important value of complexity theory is that it offers insight into the moments of systemic crisis, helping to identify the underlying relationships that generate recognizable structure over time, including those operating during moments of high intensity conflict. If one imagines a society as a complicated machine in need of fixing, violent conflict may appear to be an opportunity to remove the broken or unwanted pieces and replace them with good parts.[21] If, however, a society is described as a complex system exhibiting emergent properties that result from networked relations, then periods of violent conflict may present difficult or even dangerous moments to try to generate change. What appears as fluidity and potential for change may in fact be a moment when the system is relying most heavily on its most powerful relationships to stabilize itself. Rather than attempting to build a house during a seasonal hurricane, complexity oriented approaches suggest that construction might be more viable in the calm between the storms, or preferably before the inclement weather strikes. At the very least, the findings from the case studies in this book suggest that efforts to impose new forms of order and/or build alternative institutions during or immediately after conflict may suffer unintended consequences that could have been anticipated by adopting a complexity lens.

This does not mean that moments of flux should be disregarded by international interveners. Complex systems can indeed shift to new attractors when they are strongly disturbed. The removal of powerful leaders like Ghaddafi, Bashir, or Mobutu could present an opportunity for systemic change. However, it is a mistake to assume that their departure creates a vacuum that can be quickly filled with democratic, transparent institutions. In fact, the moments immediately following a leadership transition are often those in which other elements regroup and push for greater fields of influence. Consider the armed group proliferation in the wake of the 2003 transition in the DRC, or the rise of warlords in eastern Libya after Ghaddafi's fall. A stable set of institutions cannot merely be inserted into violently contested landscapes like these; instead, governance will need to emerge from among the relationships themselves.

'The local' reimagined

Second, complexity theory requires a reimagining of 'the local' in conflict settings. Peacebuilding scholarship currently gravitates strongly to the local as both a principled rejection of top-down Western approaches and a pragmatic demand that interventions be grounded in the everyday experiences of citizens. From James C. Scott's notion of 'infra-politics of resistance' to Mac Ginty and Richmond's 'local turn' in peacebuilding, there is a growing consensus—including within the

[21] Ashraf Ghani and Clare Lockhardt, *Fixing Failed States* (Oxford: Oxford University Press, 2009).

UN—that everyday citizens are the 'primary architects, owners and long-term stakeholders' of peace.[22] The most virulent critiques of the UN likewise accuse the organization of failing to connect with local realities, uncritically imposing foreign constructs that match poorly with the lived experience of citizens.[23] At best, critics point out, international interventions consider local culture as 'a route through which top-down institution peacebuilding can co-opt the local'.[24]

This scholarship juxtaposes local against national and international, creating a binary in which local activities are either below or otherwise separate from the realm of elite politicians and international actors. While the local turn has been rightly criticized by scholars as a neo-colonial glorification of local culture,[25] there is also a more pragmatic concern: 'the local' is an extraordinarily fuzzy term that offers no meaningful guideposts to understand how the broader system works.[26] Concepts of hybridity and friction—which argue that local, national, and international actors/institutions combine and interact in different ways—do little more than restate the messiness and complexity of societies.[27]

Instead of imagining the local as a series of villagers going about their everyday routines, complexity theory suggests that locality is a point of connection among actors, a node in the system. The relationship between a Southern People's Liberation Army (SPLA) commander, a traditional chief, and a state governor in South Sudan constitutes one such node; the relationship between an armed group, a business owner, and a Forces of the Democratic Republic of the Congo (FARDC) squadron in eastern Congo is another. Some nodes may be geographically located within a periphery—such as a police officer extracting rent from villagers—but the fact that the activity takes place in a village rather than a capital is not the point.[28] President Kabila's relationships with the head of his praetorian guard, state governors, and mining executives also constitute 'local' nodes in the sense that they can be identified specifically. Some nodes may be more influential across the system,

[22] James C. Scott, *Domination and the Arts of Resistance: Hidden Transcripts* (New Haven, CT: Yale University Press, 1998); Roger Mac Ginty and Oliver Richmond, 'The Local Turn in Peacebuilding: A Critical Agenda for Peace', *Third World Quarterly* 34, No. 5 (2013): 763–783; A. B. Fetherston and Carolyn Nordstrom, 'Overcoming Habitus in Conflict Management: UN Peacekeeping and War Zone Ethnography', *Peace & Change* 20, No. 1 (1995): 94–119. See also Karl Adalbert Hampel, 'The Dark(er) Side of "State Failure": State Formation and Socio-political Variation', *Third World Quarterly* 36, No. 9 (2015): 1629–1648 (The 'dark side' of statebuilding may be its ignorance of the sub-national level).

[23] See, e.g., Séverine Autesserre, *The Trouble with the Congo: Local Violence and the Failure of International Peacebuilding* (New York: Cambridge University Press, 2010).

[24] Autesserre, *The Trouble with the Congo*, 49.

[25] Meera Sabaratnam, 'Avatars of Eurocentrism in the Critique of the Liberal Peace', *Security Dialogue* 44, No. 3 (2013): 259–278.

[26] See Finn Stepputat, 'Pragmatic Peace in Emerging Governscapes', *International Affairs* 94 No. 2 (2018): 400.

[27] See Roger Mac Ginty, *International Peacebuilding and Local Resistance: Hybrid Forms of Peace* (Basingstoke: Palgrave MacMillan, 2011), 73 ('everything and everyone is a hybrid'); see also Annika Björkdahl et al., eds., *Peacebuilding and Friction: Global and Local Encounters in Post-conflict Societies* (New York: Routledge, 2016).

[28] For recent analysis focused on locality, see Volker Boege and Charles T. Hunt, 'On "Traveling Traditions": Emplaced Security in Liberia and Vanuatu', *Cooperation and Conflict* (2020): 1–21.

but this is the result of their relationships, not their status as a villager, a CEO, or a politician per se.

Here, complexity theory allows the peacebuilder to explore the empirics of Alex de Waal's insight that '[p]olitics is fractal in the sense that the same patterns of authority and bargaining are reproduced at all levels: local, provincial, national and interstate.'[29] In the DRC, for example, there is a basic relationship of protection within the security services, where a police officer will be expected to pay upwards in his/her chain of command in exchange for the protections of the job. This type of relationship exists in villages but is also replicated in urban capitals, within the highest levels of government in Kinshasa, and well beyond national boundaries. An overriding focus on local experiences as something exclusively in the sub-national or non-elite domain may miss that fractal across the system; likewise, those trying to drive an elite bargain with the country's leadership will overlook how such a deal might interact with related nodes in the system. Complexity theory allows analysis to cut through artificial local/national divides and explore the underlying patterns holding a system together; it suggests, following John Paul Lederach's metaphor, that we should avoid thinking of change as driven by a critical mass at the top, but rather as a 'critical yeast' that may transform systems via a myriad of small changes from within.[30]

Resilience revisited

The third insight from complexity theory concerns the autonomy of the societies in which statebuilding is taking place. Critics of statebuilding like Dominik Zaum and David Chandler have rightly pointed to the paradox at the heart of the practice: international intervention, ostensibly designed to restore the sovereign independence of failed or failing states, in fact tends to take over state functions, thus removing the key attribute of sovereignty itself, autonomy.[31] James Mayall and Ricardo Soares de Oliveira have likewise pointed to the deeply rooted notions of tutelage underlying international interventions, suggesting that the outcome of statebuilding tends to be a relationship of control rather than autonomy.[32] The response to this criticism within academic scholarship and the UN has been a recognition that 'peace cannot be imposed from the outside, peace needs to emerge

[29] De Waal, *The Real Politics of the Horn of Africa*, 17. See also Paul Cilliers, *Complexity and Postmodernism: Understanding Complex Systems* (New York: Routledge, 1998) (arguing that complexity is scalable at all levels of a system).

[30] John Paul Lederach, *The Moral Imagination: The Art and Soul of Building Peace* (New York: Oxford University Press, 2005), 91.

[31] David Chandler, *International Statebuilding: The Rise of Post-Liberal Governance* (London: Routledge, 2010), 34; Dominik Zaum, *The Sovereignty Paradox: The Norms and Politics of International Statebuilding* (Oxford: Oxford University Press, 2007).

[32] James Mayall and Ricardo Soares de Oliveira, eds., *The New Protectorates: International Tutelage and the Making of Liberal States* (London: Hurst, 2011).

organically from within society.'[33] The role of the intervener in this context is to enable societies to build up their own resilience, to help them develop their own capacities for self-management, thus achieving autonomy.

Drawn from complex ecosystems thinking, resilience refers to the capacity of a system to self-organize; it has a reinforcing tendency where a system learns from disturbances and adapts to altered circumstances without collapsing.[34] Building up the resilience of conflict-prone countries has become a mantra of development and statebuilding around the world and is fairly uncritically viewed as a positive step towards more culturally sensitive, locally rooted interventions.[35] As David Chandler has noted, this conceptualization of resilience understands that complex systems cannot be governed via top-down, controlling approaches, but must emerge from within societies.[36] Cedric de Coning—one of the foremost proponents of complexity thinking in peace and conflict scholarship today—has argued that peacebuilding should foster resilience, it 'should be about stimulating and facilitating the capacity of societies to self-organize, so that they can increase their ability to absorb and adapt to stress, to the degree necessary to sustain peace.'[37]

Here, state fragility is seen as the absence of resilience, a 'complexity deficit' in which the state has insufficient capacity to self-organize and develop its own ability to combat tendencies towards violent conflict.[38] In this view, the role of the intervener should be one of encouragement and enabling within an essentially internal process of self-organization, leading to increased resilience against the tendencies towards violence.[39] Autonomy is equated with a (self-organization): for states to be autonomous from external guidance and support, they must build a sort of Emersonian self-reliance.

While this book broadly aligns with viewing resilience as the ability to withstand shocks, it also suggests that resilience is not necessarily the positive outcome of self-organized systems. Contrary to de Coning's characterization of fragility as a 'complexity deficit', the cases of South Sudan and the DRC demonstrate that so-called fragile settings display high degrees of complexity, deeply interlinked systems of governance capable of resisting even the most robust and well-funded attempts to change them. In other words, societies in conflict are

[33] Gert Rosenthal et al., 'The Challenge of Sustaining Peace: Report of the Advisory Group of Experts for the Review of the 2105 Peacebuilding Architecture', United Nations, New York, 29 June 2015.

[34] Daniela Körppen et al., eds., *The Non-Linearity of Peace Processes: Theory and Practice of Systemic Conflict Transformation* (Opladen: Verlag Barbara Budrich, 2011).

[35] See, e.g., UNDP (United Nations Development Programme), 'Putting Resilience at the Heart of Development', UN Development Programme Report, 2015.

[36] David Chandler, *Resilience: The Governance of Complexity* (London: Routledge, 2014), 65–66.

[37] Cedric de Coning, 'From Peacebuilding to Sustaining Peace: Implications of Complexity for Resilience and Sustainability', *Resilience* 4, No. 3 (2016): 166–181.

[38] De Coning, 'From Peacebuilding to Sustaining Peace.

[39] Walter C. Clemens Jr., *Complexity Science and World Affairs* (Albany: State University of New York Press, 2013), 114.

no less complex than those enjoying long periods of peace. In fact, the continuous contestation over public authority in situations of endemic conflict may create more deeply enmeshed webs of relationships than in peaceful societies, rendering apparently fragile societies potentially more complex than their more peaceful counterparts (though I would caution against discussions of 'more' or 'less' complexity when speaking of societies). The fact that South Sudan and the DRC have maintained their underlying systems of governance despite decades of international efforts to transform them speaks to their extraordinary resilience, to the capacity of their systems to adapt without breaking down. The problem is not that external interventions 'interrupt the internal feedback processes' of these systems and inhibit their complexity, but rather that the systems have developed an extraordinary resilience against the intended impacts of such intervention.[40]

The experiences of South Sudan and the DRC suggest that we should jettison the normative gloss on our definition of resilience: it is not the positive outcome of a society that has developed healthy internal behaviours and high levels of complexity, but rather describes the capacity of a system to maintain its underlying rules in the face of major disturbances, even if such a system is violent, unequal, and 'corrupt'. Seen in this light, the goal of international interventions should not be an uncritical attempt to build greater resilience; indeed this might well be counterproductive if a system's resilience is founded upon violence. Instead, it should start with the question 'What are the ways in which this system stabilizes itself, and how might it respond to our proposed intervention?' In many cases, the answer may be sufficiently uncertain as to warrant no intervention at all, or at most an iterative process to test hypotheses about the system.[41] In others, the intervener may need to grapple with potentially uncomfortable questions of working within corrupt, neo-patrimonial, or even ideologically opposed systems, rather than attempting to transform them.

Agency: The dance between form and individualism

In 2016, I was sitting in the office of one of President Kabila's senior advisors who was dressed in a beautifully cut suit with a silver silk tie. I was embarrassed, having been talked out of a tie by a colleague who had assured me that the meeting would be informal. The topic was Congo's long-stalled disarmament, demobilization, and reintegration, which had increasingly become United Nations Organization Stabilization Mission in the Democratic Republic of Congo (MONUSCO)'s problem

[40] Clemens Jr., *Complexity Science and World Affairs*, 175.
[41] Such an adaptive, iterative approach is laid out in Cedric de Coning, 'Adaptive Peacebuilding', *International Affairs* 94, No. 2 (2018): 301–317.

as the government progressively underfunded and disengaged with the process. As was typical of MONUSCO, we had tended to blame the issue on 'lack of political will' at the highest levels of government. 'It's a political problem', one of the mission leaders told me. 'We can only move forward on DDR [disarmament, demobilization, and reintegration] if Kabila decides it's a priority.'

Kabila's advisor told a different story when I suggested that top-level decisions were needed to unblock DDR and increase international donor confidence. 'You think the President can just decide something and it happens', he said.

> But DDR is not like that. If DDR is going to work, we need the Rwandans to hold up their end and accept returnees, which they aren't interested in doing. We need the local communities to be ready to take on demobilized fighters, which they won't do unless they feel safe and rewarded. We need the fighters themselves to drop their chain of command, and most of them won't do that because that's their livelihood. And we need billions of dollars of international aid now to help build communities where these people can thrive. You just see the President blocking things. We Congolese understand that it's many things tied together.

Many things tied together. In other words, a complex, interdependent system in which the actions of a single individual are not necessarily fettered, but strongly influenced by the patterns and rules of the system. In fact, this entire book is about agency, the change that occurs via a combination of an individual's action and the influences of the system around them, what Jane Boulton calls a 'dance between form and individualism'.[42] But agency is where the UN's concepts become nearly hollow. In the fifteen years I have worked in and out of the UN, 'lack of political will' is by the far the most cited reason for any range of failures: from fumbled security sector reform processes to poorly run elections, to constitutionbuilding, all are excused as lack of political will by the countries' leaders. In the UN's results-based budgets, 'political will' is listed as an external factor, something that will either enable or inhibit implementation of mandates. In the UN's reporting to the Security Council, the secretary-general frequently demands that conflict parties demonstrate the 'political will' to de-escalate and move into a peace process.

But these calls for greater political will (and indeed this dumping of the UN's failures on the lack of will) do little more than beg the question of what influences the agency of conflict actors. Yes, President Kiir and Vice-President Machar had a great deal of influence over the decisions that led towards the 2013 civil war, but to claim that the war could have been prevented by their political will alone grossly underestimates the broader forces in the South Sudanese system. As laid out in Chapters 3 and 4, South Sudan's governance system had extraordinarily strong

[42] Jean G. Boulton et al., eds., *Embracing Complexity: Strategic Perspectives for an Age of Turbulence* (Oxford: Oxford University Press, 2015), 32.

attractors to the ethno-military network that had sustained the region through twenty years of conflict with Khartoum, with gravitational pulls that made any efforts to build independent, fair, equitable state institutions extremely difficult. The fact that President Kiir initially appointed an ethnically well-balanced cabinet when South Sudan became independent may have indicated that he had at least some political will to enable national reforms. President Kabila also took many steps that seemed to indicate he was willing to instigate serious changes to the way the Congo was governed.

Here, complexity theory offers a way to understand agency that goes beyond the empty notion of political will. By mapping the systems of governance in places like South Sudan and the DRC, we can see the 'strong attractors' in each system, the gravitational pulls that resist efforts to transform them. This kind of mapping moves political will from an external factor in the UN's budgeting documents to the central point of inquiry. The question 'How can we generate political will?' necessarily requires us to understand the contours of that governance landscape, the steep ravines that will capture energy and resources, the deeply entrenched patterns that will work (almost) inexorably against efforts to change. But complexity thinking also gives us the tools to see how change takes place in these systems. Like an archaeologist who can see the movement of glaciers and mountains in rock formations, the complexity thinker can trace change over time, understanding the moments and processes that shifted the landscape in the past and helping to identify similar moments in the future.

Listening

Finally, complexity demands that scholars and practitioners be creative, embracing the many mysteries that longstanding conflicts present rather than trying to simplify and overwrite them. It evokes John Paul Lederach's call for a moral imagination in which we see ourselves in a web of relationships that includes our enemies, willing to enter the unknown despite the risks, humbled by the knowledge that we might never know (or indeed change) the full story.[43] While working in southern Sudan in 2010, I had tea with a prominent Nuer politician and activist in Malakal, a northern town with a long and conflictual history involving Nuer, Dinka, and Shilluk communities. I was co-authoring a conflict assessment that would eventually be used as a basis for planning the UN's new statebuilding mission in South Sudan. After about an hour of discussion in which I asked about local land disputes, interethnic tensions, cattle raiding, and the political fault lines in the South Sudanese Government, she stopped me and said,

[43] Lederach, *The Moral Imagination.*

> You see our country like a single story, starting in one place and ending in another. You want to say that it all fits together. You want to say, 'Now I understand how cattle works in South Sudan' so you can fit it into your story. But there will always be another story that you need to hear. Listen. One hundred years ago, our prophet told a story about a left-handed Nuer with a gap in his front teeth who would lead South Sudan into independence. Today, when we see Riek Machar [a left-handed Nuer with a prominent gap in his teeth who assumed the vice-presidency upon independence] we see the chance to fulfil our prophecy. That is one of our stories, that is something pushing us as a Nuer community, even if you aren't able to put it into your report because you think it's witchcraft. But it is real to us, and without that story you will never understand why things are the way they are in South Sudan.[44]

The Nuer prophecy is part of South Sudan's system, invisibly playing into strong attractors that guide day-to-day decisions of the South Sudanese and combining with hundreds of other narratives that shape how their society evolves. When the civil war broke out in 2013, I recalled this prophecy in a conversation with UN colleagues. 'You see', I said, feeling very locally sensitive and superior, 'the whole war can be explained by the prophecy. The Nuer believe they are entitled to the presidency because of a hundred year-old prophecy that points to Riek Machar and they are willing to fight to the death over it.' But, of course, I had missed the point. In complex systems, there is never one story, never a single narrative that can capture or explain how a society evolves. We will never become sufficiently local to understand the lived experience of the communities in which we work. Complexity demands that we resign ourselves to at best a very partial knowledge of society. But it also equips us with a lens to begin to see patterns at work and encourages us to accept every story—even hundred year-old prophecies—as part of the system. The first step, as my South Sudanese activist friend suggested, is to listen.

Statebuilding within the complex global system

This section returns to the initial point of global order that began the book, briefly exploring how complexity thinking might help us understand the ways in which statebuilding operates within the broader global system of IR. It argues that the project of building strong, functioning states is central to liberal concepts of world order, one in which so-called failed states represent a direct threat. Mainstream IR theories—whether embodying Hobbesian notions of hierarchical power or more

[44] Author's interview notes, Malakal, December 2010.

neo-Kantian visions of soft power and cooperation—converge around the necessity of sovereign states as essential to global governance. As such, intervention in failed states can be understood as a necessary aspect of the liberal vision of world order, both a reaffirmation of the ideology of the Westphalian state as the principal unit within the global system and also a pragmatic act to prevent its erosion and/or collapse. Today, however, many proponents of liberal internationalism see the system fraying, perhaps nearing its demise, leading to an anarchical world in disarray.[45] Resuscitating liberal internationalism and bolstering it against the forces of disorder has become a major preoccupation of scholars across disciplines, though few ideas have emerged beyond general handwringing and a hope that liberal order will somehow reassert itself.[46] Here, complexity theory offers insights into how new orders might form amidst today's apparent chaos, and indeed how multilateral institutions could participate in that emergent order.

A useful starting point for a discussion of global governance is Hedley Bull's famous statement, 'Order among states cannot be, for international society is an anarchical society, a society without government.'[47] For Bull, order emerges among states via a sense of common interest, expressed as a set of rules and patterns sustained by institutions. This notion of common interests and the need for cooperation is the bedrock of the English School of IR but also resonates with liberal theories of IR, most famously espoused by Keohane and Nye, whose work underscores the centrality of international institutions to preserving world order.[48] Faced with the same conundrum of an anarchical global system, Kenneth Waltz put forward a power-based, realist approach, arguing that states acting in self-interest will maximize their own power, eventually reaching some form of equilibrium (though certainly not equality) over time.[49] These two schools of thought—liberalism and realism—are typically contrasted as two ends of a spectrum of IR thinking.[50] However, both liberalism and realism converge around two points: (1) that world order can be achieved without a hegemonic governing body, through competition and/or cooperation; and (2) that such order rests upon relationships among sovereign states (though each school sees those relationships differently). As John Bew has pointed out, the Western vision of international order has easily traversed the divide between realists and idealists, offering a sort of

[45] Richard Haas, *A World in Disarray: American Foreign Policy and the Crisis of the Old Order* (New York: Penguin, 2018).

[46] See, e.g., G. John Ikenberry, 'The End of the Liberal International Order?', *International Affairs* 94, No. 1 (2018): 7–23.

[47] Hedley Bull, *The Anarchical Society: A Study of Order in World Politics*, 2nd edition (New York: Columbia University Press, 1977), 57.

[48] Robert O. Keohane and Joseph S. Nye Jr., 'Power and Interdependence', *Survival* 15, No. 4 (1973): 158–165

[49] Kenneth N. Waltz, *A Theory of International Politics* (New York: McGraw-Hill, 1979).

[50] See, e.g., David A. Baldwin, ed., *Neoliberalism and Neorealism: The Contemporary Debate* (New York: Columbia University Press, 1993).

common 'noble pursuit'.[51] Failed states thus represent a threat within both schools of thought, a security risk to realist defenders of national interest, an inhibition on the spread of free markets to proponents of the liberal institutional ideal.[52] Both broadly agree that global order depends upon a concerted project of intervention in the domestic spheres of those countries falling short of the key attributes of Weberian statehood (though realists would do so in a more limited number of settings where the national interest was clearly at stake).[53]

It is my final contention that complexity theory offers a framework for understanding the role of statebuilding in world politics, capturing the motivations of both realism and liberalism and offering insights into how the international system might be reimagined. Systems thinking is, of course, not new to IR; the opening chapter of this book describes the range of literature in which systemic analysis has been applied to public policy, IR, and even aspects of statebuilding.[54] Recently, three pieces of scholarship have directly approached the question of how complexity theory itself might be applied to the question of global governance.[55] Seyle and Spivak argue that the aggregate actions of institutions and systems operating in global affairs can generate coordinated action despite the lack of an overarching authority; what matters in this context is 'repeated interactions with each other over time'.[56] They argue that global governance therefore should focus on generating as much interface—as many interactions among actors—as possible to increase complexity and drive collective action.[57] Amandine Orsine et al. similarly argue that the global system should be viewed as complex and self-organizing in non-linear ways that defy easy prediction or any kind of orchestral role for governing bodies. Advocating a network approach, they suggest a refocusing on interactions and interconnections in IR, rather than the identity or strength of

[51] John Bew, 'World Order: Many-Headed Monster or Noble Pursuit?' *Texas National Security Review*, December 2017.

[52] See, e.g., G. John Ikenberry, Inderjeet Parmar, and Doug Stokes, 'Ordering the World? Liberal Internationalism in Theory and Practice', *International Affairs* 94, No. 1 (2018): 1–5.

[53] See Chandler, *International Statebuilding*, 44.

[54] Robert Jervis, *System Effects: Complexity in Political and Social Life* (Princeton, NJ: Princeton University Press, 1997), 243–245. See Chapter 1 of this book for a full list of scholarship in this field. See also, Morton Kaplan, *System and Process in International Relations* (New York: Wiley, 1957); Oran R. Young, *A Systemic Approach to International Politics* (Princeton, NJ: Center of International Studies Woodrow Wilson School of Public and International Affairs, 1968).

[55] I highlight three here because they are focused on global governance in general. Several other publications have approached the issue of global governance of the specific issue of climate change. See, e.g., Norichika Kanie, 'Governance with Multilateral Environmental Agreements: A Healthy or Ill-equipped Fragmentation?', in Lydia Swart and Estelle Perry, eds., *Global Environmental Governance: Perspectives on the Current Debate* (New York: Center for UN Reform Education, 2007), 67–86; Victor Galaz et al., 'Polycentric Systems and Interacting Planetary Boundaries: Emerging Governance of Climate Change–Ocean Acidification–Marine Biodiversity', *Ecological Economics* 81 (2012): 21–32.

[56] Conor Seyle and Roberta Spivak, 'Complexity Theory and Global Governance: Is More Different?' *Global Governance* 24 (2018): 491–495.

[57] It is worth pointing out here that most complexity scholars would reject this kind of scalar approach: systems are either complex or they are not. But the underlying point—that interdependence is the foundation for complexity—is useful.

specific actors.[58] Walter Clemens too makes a direct call for the application of complexity science to world affairs, suggesting that the notion of evolutionary fitness accurately describes the extent to which states self-organize and participate in the global system.[59] In defence of liberalism, Clemens argues that high levels of fitness are unlikely to be found at either the pole of rigid hierarchy or outright anarchy, but rather in the realm of freedom afforded by liberal democracy. Liberal institutions offer the most promise to Clemens, as they 'buffer the ravages of free markets and curb the excesses of wilful governments', thus permitting the highest levels of self-organization.[60]

While this scholarship on complexity and world affairs has yielded some important insights into the interrelated nature of the global system, none has yet directly addressed the potential implications of state failure and statebuilding. Indeed, as I argue below, my case study findings appear to work against Clemens' argument in favour of liberal institutions as necessarily the most expedient path to fitness. Adopting the same relational approach used in the case studies in Chapters 3 through 6, I here suggest that international order can be broadly characterized by three types of relationship: (1) the 'ordinary' relationship between sovereign equals, defined by well-understood laws and customs such as *pacta sunt servanda* and respect for the territorial integrity of states; (2) the relationship between global superpowers and other states, in which the superpowers may feel they can occasionally disregard some of the basic rules of the system, but nonetheless rely heavily on the broader system to respect the ordering rules more generally (examples include the United States (US) invasion of Iraq in 2003; North Atlantic Treaty Organization (NATO) countries intervening in Kosovo; and China's stance on many human rights); and (3) so-called failed or failing states which are in one way or another unable to fully participate in the global system, relating to other states either in a donor/recipient relation or as the subject of some form of intervention.

While some scholars have suggested that the willingness of superpowers to flout international law points to the absence of meaningful ordering mechanisms in the global system,[61] the most direct risk to the liberal world order for mainstream IR scholarship is the third category: failed states. As David Chandler points out, 'the problem of failed states is precisely that they are autonomous, that they control themselves'.[62] By 'falling short' of full Weberian statehood, failed states present a risk to the broader international system. Seen as home to international terrorist

[58] Amandine Orsini et al., 'Complex Systems and International Governance', *International Studies Review* (2019): 1–30. For a network approach to international affairs, see also Rakhyune E. Kim, 'Is Global Governance Fragmented, Polycentric, or Complex? The State of the Art of the Network Approach', *International Studies Review* (2019): 1–29.

[59] Clemens Jr., *Complexity Science and World Affairs*.

[60] Clemens Jr., *Complexity Science and World Affairs*, 115.

[61] See, e.g., Michael Glennon, *Limits of Law, Prerogatives of Power: Interventionism after Kosovo* (New York: Palgrave, 2001).

[62] Chandler, *International Statebuilding*, 45.

groups with global agendas, often led by dictators who see little value in pandering to the West, and offering potential alternative models of statehood to their neighbours, the autonomy of failed states comes at a direct cost to the rest of the system. They constitute what Stewart Patrick calls 'weak links' that threaten to break the entire chain unless they are strengthened and brought within the ambit of international order.[63] Proponents of international order must fix failed states as a bulwark against entropy.

This means statebuilding is an activity of reciprocal exchange between the intervener and intervened, a form of symbiosis. On one side, the fragile state sacrifices a certain amount of sovereignty to the statebuilder in exchange for the prospect of large flows of development aid, commitments to restore its standing in the international community, and the promise that stability will lead to improved conditions for its citizens. But the intervener stands to gain as well, often well beyond the immediate benefit of establishing a preferential relationship with the recipient country. For example, Mark Duffield has argued that a principal purpose of statebuilding is to guarantee a stable recipient of donor aid, increasing the dependence of the recipient country on donors, and allowing them to be controlled for future benefit to the donor.[64] Failed states, unable to enter into such a stable relationship, are beyond the reach of such controlling mechanisms.

Susan Woodward's very different critique of statebuilding suggests that its principal purpose is to justify the continued build-up of statebuilding capacities on the part of interveners, even while ostensibly supporting a country in need.[65] In her view, statebuilding has very little to do with improving the lot of fragile countries and everything to do with domestic capacitybuilding in the West, demonstrated by the continued practice of statebuilding in the face of recurrent failure (here, the phrase 'statebuilding industrial complex' may be apt).

Dominik Zaum suggests a broader benefit to the West from statebuilding: intervention recognizes and amplifies the importance of sovereignty in the international system. While 'forcing states to be sovereign' may seem paradoxical, it also reinforces the state-centric order and avoids a descent into disorder.[66] Statebuilding thus acts to prevent the spread of other models of statehood, adding predictability to global governance, rendering unstable regions 'more like us and less like Russians or Chinese'.[67]

[63] Stewart Patrick, *Weak Links: Fragile States, Global Threats and International Security* (Oxford: Oxford University Press, 2011).

[64] Mark Duffield, 'Fragile States and the Return of Native Administration', International Congress on Human Development, 2006.

[65] Susan Woodward, *The Ideology of Failed States: Why Intervention Fails* (Cambridge: Cambridge University Press, 2017), 9–11.

[66] Zaum, *The Sovereignty Paradox.*

[67] Nils Gilman, *Mandarins of The Future: Modernization Theory in Cold War America* (Baltimore: Johns Hopkins University Press, 2003), 3; see also Nejal Bhuta, 'Against Statebuilding', *Constellations* 15, No. 4 (2008): 517–542.

Regardless of the benefit gained (and it could be a combination of all of the above), it is clear that liberal international order is highly dependent upon statebuilding as a necessary practice to constitute and defend the liberal model. It is identity-affirming, prevents the growth of alternative modes of statehood, and allows interveners to directly confront some of the perceived security threats growing in the 'ungoverned voids' of failed states. This points to the validity of Roland Paris' statement that peacebuilding is more than a tool of conflict management but rather '[a] new phase in the ongoing and evolving relationship between the core and the periphery of the international system, with the core continuing to define the standards of acceptable behaviour, and international peacebuilding agencies serving as "transmission belts" that convey these standards to the periphery.'[68] The notion of symbiosis suggests that this transmission is also constitutive for the centre: the liberal model of global governance depends upon interventions into failed states for its continued existence. Statebuilding is an ontological activity for liberal internationalism.

As such, today's dominant ideology of international order rests upon the ability and willingness of major powers to intervene in failed states, to prevent what Walter Clemens has called the 'self-organized criticality' that might occur if too many ungoverned spaces caused a collapse in the system.[69] In the immediate post-Cold War period, this willingness was amply demonstrated by the UN Security Council which established fifteen new peacekeeping missions in fragile states and issued over 200 resolutions concerning international peace and security.[70] Buoyed by the hegemonic role of the US on the international stage, liberal internationalism spread rapidly in the 1990s, bolstered by democratic transitions in Europe and Latin America and consolidated by the expansion of NATO and the establishment of the World Trade Organization (WTO) and the Group of Twenty (G20).[71] This period produced an extraordinary confidence in the liberal democratic order, captured by Francis Fukuyama's declaration that humanity was witnessing 'the end of history as such: That is, the end-point of mankind's ideological evolution and the universalization of Western liberal democracy as the final form of human government.'[72]

However, soon after the high watermark of international unity that followed the terrorist attacks of 11 September 2001 (9/11), the liberal internationalist vision of the world has rapidly fallen apart. Rifts among major powers following

[68] Roland Paris, 'International Peacebuilding and the "Mission Civilisatrice"', *Review of International Studies* 28 (2002): 637–656.

[69] Clemens Jr., *Complexity Science and World Affairs*.

[70] Mats Berdal, 'The Security Council and Peacekeeping', in Vaughan Lowe et al., eds., *The United Nations Security Council and War: The Evolution of Thought and Practice since 1945* (Oxford: Oxford University Press, 2008), 176.

[71] Ikenberry, 'The End of the Liberal International Order?', 7–23.

[72] Francis Fukuyama, 'The End of History?', *The National Interest* 16 (1989): 3–18.

the 2003 US invasion of Iraq have continued to deepen over time, driven by polarizing events like the 2011 intervention in Libya and growing great power tensions among the US, Russia, and China. These divisions have coincided with a retreat of the hegemonic vision of liberal institutionalism and multilateralism, evidenced by the UK's decision to leave the European Union (EU), Donald Trump's election in the US, and the rise of nationalist/populist/xenophobic leaders in Hungary, Poland, Turkey, and the Philippines.[73] Facing an unravelling of the tenets of international cooperation and liberal order that had maintained the global system for half a century, and increasingly unable to grapple with new transnational crises around climate change and cybersecurity without some sort of multilateral action, Richard Haas has predicted, 'the twenty-first century will prove extremely difficult to manage'.[74] If anything, the COVID-19 pandemic has counterintuitively accelerated these trends, driving narratives of isolation, nationalism, and competition, even as it demonstrates the extent to which we are all interconnected.

Western preoccupation with the risks of disarray at a global level is driven by fears of an increasingly multipolar system, one where no single hegemon or group of major powers can dictate predictable outcomes. Rather than neatly ordered hierarchies of power, today's global system appears more like a 'spaghetti bowl' of overlapping lines of authority,[75] an impossible maze lacking a guide,[76] or worse still, a void into which non-Western models of governance may insert themselves.[77] This is the realm of complexity, which understands that interdependent systems do not need guides, or leaders, or rule books to create order. In fact, as Walter Clemens points out, self-organization is most productive 'on the edge of chaos', in situations where no single actor is dictating from above.[78] The question complexity theory asks is not whether world order is in disarray, facing failure, or becoming unstable, but how today's global system will self-organize in response to these changes.

Responding to this question, complexity offers two insights into the future of global governance. First, the trends over the past several years have demonstrated a retreat from some of the institutions that have kept major powers interrelated and mutually dependent for decades. Today's UN Security Council—the forum to which major powers have turned to address most major peace and security issues for the past thirty years—is increasingly fissiparous and dysfunctional, no longer

[73] Ikenberry, 'The End of the Liberal International Order?', 7–23.

[74] Haas, *A World in Disarray*.

[75] Peter Sutherland et al., *The Future of the WTO: Addressing Institutional Challenges in the New Millennium*. Geneva: World Trade Organization, 2015.

[76] UNEP (United Nations Environment Programme), *21 Issues for the 21st Century: Results of the UNEP Foresight Process on Emerging Environmental Issues*, Nairobi: United Nations Environment Programme, 2012.

[77] Ikenberry, 'The End of the Liberal International Order?', 7–23 (suggesting that the receding line of US hegemony might allow the non-West to rise).

[78] Clemens Jr., *Complexity Science and World Affairs*.

a meaningful clearing house for great power tensions, and better thought of as a much diminished node in the international system.[79] The WTO—the principal institution for building international commerce and interdependence among states—also faces a dramatic loss of influence as a growing US-China dispute has sent ripples around the globe.[80] The UK's withdrawal from the EU, along with US withdrawal from the Paris Climate Treaty, the Iran nuclear deal, and the World Health Organisation appear to presage an era of greater isolation and diminished cooperation among states that until now played crucial nodal roles in the global system. The multilateral system composed of interstate relations is becoming less interdependent, or at least less dependent upon relations between states.

Second, this retreat from interstate cooperation has been paralleled by a dramatic expansion of non-state actors, which are more interconnected and powerful than ever before. Global corporations like Amazon, Google, and Apple now form webs that connect billions of people across hundreds of countries, crisscrossing national boundaries and allowing for rapid information flows among societies and individuals without much state regulation. Social media giants have created highly networked societies that can wield enormous political influence, from the Arab Spring, to the mass protests Hong Kong, to the Black Lives Matter movement. Illicit flows of money, goods, and people now stretch around the world, at times funding violent groups that challenge state authority, but also providing livelihoods for hundreds of thousands of people. Artificial intelligence, already driving much of today's technology, is poised to accelerate many of these trends with implications for our public health, security, jobs, and survival.[81]

The retreat from multilateral cooperation and the concurrent rise of global non-state modes of connectivity offers an interesting parallel to the failed state discourse considered in this book. In both, the liberal model of international order appears increasingly out of touch with reality, unable to describe the forces that drive change in a system. In both, order can be better understood as an emergent outcome of the self-organization of the system, rather than as a product of a top-down management structure. And while states still play a dominant role in the web of relationships that forms the global system, they are far from the only nodes organizing it. In fact, it is the autonomy of non-state entities that may present the greatest risk to Western visions of world order: international corporations, social networks, and black-market flows are all extraordinarily resistant to regulation and control. They exhibit what I have earlier called 'thick relationality' within the global system: the importance of their role in the system is determined by the quality and

[79] See Richard Gowan, 'Minimum Order: The Role of the Security Council in an Era of Great Power Competition', United Nations Centre for Policy Research, December 2018.

[80] See Rachel Brewster, 'The Trump Administration and the Future of the WTO', *The Yale Journal of International Law* 44 (2018).

[81] See Eleonore Pauwels, 'The New Geopolitics of Converging Risks: the UN and Prevention in the Era of AI', United Nations University Centre for Policy Research, May 2019.

extent of their relationships, not their identity per se.[82] Facebook, by connecting 2.6 billion people globally, can be considered a significant node in the global system, despite having no seat in the General Assembly and no capacity to enter into international treaties. The US, by withdrawing from major multilateral treaties and scuppering its relationships with a range of countries and institutions, is likely losing influence within the global system and may presage a dramatic loss of influence over the country's stated priority of upholding rules-based international order.[83] In complexity terms, their position within the system may be becoming less influential as they become more disconnected from other nodes in the network.[84] For proponents of liberal international order, the retreat of major powers from the international stage deprives world order of the very thing that has held it together thus far: the ability to relate to each other as states.[85]

A similar dynamic holds true of the UN. Established seventy-five years ago to rebuild a world order than had been shattered by two world wars, the UN has played an essential role in connecting states, building institutions of multilateral cooperation, and consolidating the ideals of liberal statehood. In this, the organization can be understood as a vehicle for proponents of liberal internationalism to execute and amplify their vision for world order. And while the UN ostensibly includes the full panoply of worldviews via its 194-member General Assembly, its approach to issues of state fragility and world order have remained overwhelmingly aligned with liberal internationalism to date. Indeed, this book has explored in detail the ways in which UN statebuilding can be understood as an uncritical extension of liberal ideals of statehood and world order.

As with many septuagenarians, the UN today appears increasingly deaf and out of touch with the changes that are taking place on the world stage.[86] The ornate chambers of the General Assembly and Security Council, with an exclusive membership of states, are largely ignored when it comes to the most important challenges facing the globe today. Sidelined in the wars that have ravaged Syria and Yemen, ignored as major powers flout nuclear proliferation obligations, chronically underfunded by its biggest donors, and a bystander as decades of human rights advances are rolled back by nationalist regimes around the world, the UN is facing an existential crisis. As Secretary-General António Guterres has stated, 'the global political and economic systems are not delivering on critical global public

[82] See Morgan Brigg, 'Relational Peacebuilding: Promise beyond Crisis', in Tobias Debiel et al., eds., *Peacebuilding in Crisis: Rethinking Paradigms and Practices of Transnational Cooperation* (London: Routledge, 2016), 58.

[83] See Her Majesty's Government (HM Govt.), *National Security Strategy and Strategic Defence and Security Review 2015: A Secure and Prosperous United Kingdom* (London: HM Govt., 2015).

[84] See Kim, 'Is Global Governance Fragmented, Polycentric, or Complex?, 1–29.

[85] Vali Nasr, *The Dispensable Nation: American Foreign Policy in Retreat* (Doubleday: New York, 2013).

[86] See David M. Malone and Adam Day, 'The UN at 75: How Today's Challenges Will Shape the Next 25 Years', *Global Governance* 26, No. 2 (2020).

goods: public health, climate action, sustainable development, peace.'[87] Unsaid in this statement is the fact that the UN is largely unable to influence this trajectory as it has become disconnected from the processes that matter in the global system, the 'Untied' Nations detached from the ineluctable unravelling of world order.

Parts of complex systems can wither and die out, losing the interdependence and multiplicity that allow them to self-organize, or shifting to new constellations of relationships that mean some nodes are no longer necessary. This loss of complexity may be occurring within parts of the multilateral system, as the key state-to-state relationships underlying global order shift away from states and into non-state forums and institutions. As a result, complexity may be moving elsewhere, into the dynamic relationships created by social media giants, multinational corporations, and influential individuals. Seen in this light, the withdrawal of major powers from multilateralism risks the UN becoming 'locked in' to set patterns by a complexity deficit, lacking the diversity and multiplicity of interactions needed to evolve to changing circumstances.[88] When Guterres calls for a 'new model for global governance', based on more inclusive participation in global institutions, he seems to be implicitly pointing to the need to reconnect the UN to parts of the system that matter, or else risk irrelevance.[89]

The question facing the UN today is whether that new model will be a refurbished version of the liberal institutionalism that dominated from the end of the Cold War until quite recently, or whether a system based on new rules and relationships is needed. Proponents of liberalism have argued that world order may be in crisis, but that some version of liberal institutionalism remains the best hope for future global governance.[90] This book may point in a different direction, indicated by Donella Meadows' argument, 'The only way to fix a system that is laid out poorly is to rebuild it, if you can.'[91] Lacking the means to rebuild global governance, the UN can at best probably attempt to rebuild and reposition itself within it. Perhaps it is time to imagine the thirty-eight-story UN Secretariat building lying on its side, less of a hierarchical reflection of a system ordered by states and more of a spider in a web, reaching horizontally across networks to connect with people and non-state institutions, along with states. Such a drastic change will meet with resistance from a system that has built extraordinarily strong attractors around the

[87] United Nations Secretary-General António Guterres' Nelson Mandela Annual Lecture 2020 speech, 'Tackling the Inequality Pandemic: A New Social Contract for a New Era', available at https://www.nelsonmandela.org/news/entry/annual-lecture-2020-secretary-general-guterress-full-speech

[88] Boulton, *Embracing Complexity*, 24.

[89] Indeed, António Guterres regularly speaks of Jürgen Habermas, whose theories of communicative rationality appear well-suited for a discussion of networked complexity.

[90] See, e.g., Ikenberry, 'The End of the Liberal International Order?', 7–23; Haas, *A World in Disarray*; Clemens Jr., *Complexity Science and World Affairs*; John. G. Mearsheimer, *The Great Delusion: Liberal Dreams and International Realities* (New Haven CT: Yale University Press, 2018).

[91] Donella Meadows, *Thinking in Systems: A Primer* (White River Junction, VT: Chelsea Green Publishing, 2008), 150.

nation-state since the Peace of Westphalia in 1648, but it may be the UN's best hope of avoiding the worst fate within a complex system: isolation.

Conclusion: No such thing as disorder

This book has asserted the claim that complexity theory can make a unique contribution to the problematic practice of UN statebuilding. Complexity's contribution is not an isolated one, but rather it builds on the important insights of other systemic approaches to conflict, most notably that of political economy. Unlike political economy, however, complexity avoids the tendency to reduce systems to economic marketplaces and financially motivated transactions. As the case studies have shown, the economics of governance in conflict settings matters a great deal, but it is not the defining characteristic of some of the most important nodes in socio-political systems. Instead, complexity theory demands that we view governance in relational terms, examining the types of relationships that sustain the system and allow it to adapt to new inputs. The relational approach adopted in this book has generated three central insights into how public authority is created in settings like the DRC and South Sudan, and how systems of governance react to the UN's attempts to build and extend state authority in them.

First, I have shown that the systems of governance in the DRC and South Sudan self-organize via feedback loops that tend to strip state institutions of authority and distribute influence to other nodes in the system. In the DRC, a network of armed groups, business leaders, traditional chiefs, and politicians operate symbiotically together to extract natural resources and market them beyond Congo's borders. Over time, this network has continually stripped the state of both its authority and the resources needed to build its institutional capacities, a kind of constant erosion that prevents the root structure of the state from taking hold. Similarly, in South Sudan, efforts to extend state authority into the undeveloped hinterlands of the country have been co-opted by what I have called an ethno-military network, partially embedded within the national army, but deeply reliant upon non-state systems of traditional authority and kinship.

Second, a comparison of the DRC and South Sudan reveals that two very different systems of governance may nonetheless be organized by similar strong attractors to violence. In the DRC, the complete absence of state institutions in the peripheries of the country allowed for the proliferation of armed groups during the two civil wars, rendering violence an inseparable aspect of governing the communities of eastern Congo. In South Sudan, the hegemonic role of the SPLA during and beyond the civil war subordinated other forms of public authority to the military chain of command, creating strong incentives towards violence as a means of political communication with the centre. Both settings therefore evolved on the basis of strong attractors to violence, deeply entrenched social and political patterns that proved impossible to 'correct' via the liberal peacebuilding project to date.

Taken together, the concepts of feedback loops and strong attractors led to the third insight: that UN statebuilding not only failed to transform the governance systems of the DRC and South Sudan, but it may well have reinforced their underlying tendencies towards predation and violence. Complex systems defy any notion of inside and outside—they are open to and evolve with new stimuli. UN statebuilding missions were not external actors attempting to alter the ways in which these countries were run (though this is precisely how they saw themselves); rather, the UN entered into the relationships that formed the system itself. Here, the UN's efforts to give greater legitimacy, resources, and expertise to state-run institutions fell into the feedback loops of the underlying system and were drawn ineluctably towards its strong attractors. My findings offer a worrying conclusion that some of the most dangerous tendencies of violence, exclusion, and predatory behaviour may well have been exacerbated by well-meaning statebuilders.

But complexity theory also offers the prospect of improving future engagements in conflict-prone settings, a way out of the malaise of today's liberal peacebuilding critique. Contrary to prevailing concepts of conflict management—which view violent upheaval as an opportunity for transformational change—this book has demonstrated that moments of intense flux may involve the strongest pull of a system's attractors. An attempt to overhaul the South Sudanese rule of law and service delivery systems in the fragile aftermath of a twenty-year civil war could run against the current of the system, which might be most powerfully relying on its underlying relationships to maintain order. This does not mean that systems cannot be transformed during or immediately after moments of violent upheaval, but it does send a note of caution to those who attempt statebuilding in the midst of instability.

A complexity-driven approach also demands that the notion of locality be revisited. Whereas the dominant understanding of the local in liberal peacebuilding discourse envisions a community-level existence as opposed to national or international actors, complexity sees systems as composed of highly interrelated nodes, each of which can be considered local regardless of its level or geography. What matters is the character of a relationship, not whether it takes place in a village, a national capital, or the Security Council chamber in New York. President Kabila's relationship with the head of his praetorian guard is a localized node that connects with other points in the system. An SPLA commander's relationship with a traditional chief and an international non-governmental organization (INGO) delivering goods to a needy community is another such localized node that forms part of the governance system in South Sudan. These findings suggest that the bright lines between local, national, and international should be ignored in favour of a relational understanding of governance.

Similarly, this book has made a case for redefining the notion of resilience in peacebuilding. Typically thought of in normatively positive terms, building local resilience is one of the most prevalent goals of UN interventions in conflict-prone states. Societies that fall into violent conflict are similarly thought of as lacking resilience, unable to manage the shocks of repeated atrocities and social unrest. But as the case studies above describe, even the most conflict-ridden societies develop highly resilient forms of governance that withstand enormous external efforts to change them. The persistence of both the Congolese and South Sudanese systems despite decades of Western-driven efforts at reform, billions of dollars of aid aimed at democratic transformation, and countless capacitybuilding programmes all point to their extraordinary resilience.

The implications for the statebuilder may seem distasteful to those who think of these systems as corrupt or deviant from the apotheosis of the state: the liberal Weberian model. But here complexity theory helpfully offers a value-free description of the way things are, not necessarily the way they should be, and a sense of how a system might change over time. If the goal of an intervention is to reduce violence and help build stronger peaceful ties across riven societies, complexity theory may demand that interveners work with the grain rather than against it, gradually transforming the underlying relations instead of trying to impose external models. It might require a much higher level of comfort working with so-called corruption than today's missions have shown. And it will certainly demand a much longer time-frame than a typical peace operation is mandated to implement.

Finally, this book has used complexity thinking to position statebuilding within the broader liberal international effort towards global governance. Here, I would like to end this book with a final anecdote to illustrate the implications of such an approach. In early 2021, I was asked to provide some thinking into what is now called the UN's 'Common Agenda', a process led by the secretary-general to revitalize the multilateral system and position it to solve the major risks facing the world today: global pandemics, climate change, massive inequality, demographic changes, the rise of new technologies, and growing levels of violence in many parts of the world.[92] From the outset, these challenges were almost uniformly described as needing 'global governance', more effective rules, and agreed ways of doing business to ensure that risks did not spiral out of control. On climate change, we spoke of the need to add 'teeth' to the Paris Treaty; on the risks of cyber attacks we spoke of the need for a common code of conduct to direct behaviour. We lamented the lack of an outer space treaty and considered what role a binding commitment to fund pandemic preparedness might play in stopping the next COVID catastrophe. This was how the UN had done its work for seventy-five years, establishing rules,

[92] Our Common Agenda – Report of the Secretary General, United Nations, 2021, available at: https://www.un.org/en/content/common-agenda-report/assets/pdf/Common_Agenda_Report_English.pdf

locking them into treaties, encouraging everyone to follow the rules, expressing grave concern when the rules weren't followed, occasionally expressing *very* grave concern when we thought that might add a bit more leverage to the situation.

But over a course of several weeks, one idea kept coming back to the surface: this isn't how the world works. New writers like Jeremy Heimans had pointed out that the UN was mired in 'old power' approaches of institutions and rules, whereas 'new power' operated in networks and interdependence.[93] Anne-Marie Slaughter had written that the UN needed to think of itself as a hub connecting spokes rather than as a hierarchical building, a change that would allow it to participate in the highly interdependent, networked way that change takes place in the twenty-first century.[94] And most tellingly for me, when I trotted out my usual lines on complexity thinking and interdependent systems, no one (visibly) rolled their eyes or suggested that the topic was 'way too complex for us to do anything with', as my former colleagues in the UN had done years before. Instead, they nodded as though this were a given. Complexity thinking had arrived, subtly, under the surface, and I could sense that it had become part of the way many people in the UN had begun to think about global governance. As one of the main drafters of the Common Agenda report said to me at one point, 'Of course we can't actually *do* global governance, all we can do is gradually help the multilateral system evolve around new ways of managing risks'.

This is complexity thinking at its best. It recognizes that there is no disorder anywhere on Earth; life is constantly ordering itself. And if the UN wishes to exert influence in the global system, it should do so by being a connector within it, a node with myriad relationships, rather than an isolated institution that solely relates at the state level or only responds to the demands of superpowers. The UN will never play the role of a brain ordering the global body to act, but it can be the world's heart, receiving and pumping blood in an exchange that feeds its most distant limbs.

[93] Jeremy Heimans and Henry Timms, *New Power: How Anyone Can Persuade, Mobilize, and Succeed in Our Chaotic, Connected Age* (New York, Anchor Books, 2019).

[94] Anne-Marie Slaughter and Gordon LaForge, 'Opening Up the Order: A More Inclusive International System', *Foreign Affairs*, March/April 2021.

Bibliography

Adiebo, Kimo et al., 'Public Expenditures in South Sudan: Are They Delivering?', World Bank Economic Brief, Issue 2, February 2013.

Aimé, Elsa González, 'Fragile States and Neoliberalism in Sub-Saharan Africa', African Studies Group University of Madrid, 2008.

Al Jazeera, 'Commander Khalifa Haftar's Forces Choke Libya's Oil Flow', Al Jazeera online, 19 January 2020. https://www.aljazeera.com/ajimpact/commander-khalifa-haftar-forces-choke-libya-oil-flow-200119162228201.html

Albrecht, Peter and Helene-Maria Kyed, 'Introduction: Non-State and Customary Actors in Development Programs', *Perspectives on Involving Non-State and Customary Actors in Justice and Security Reform*, Rome: International Development Law Organization, 2011: 3–23.

Aleu, Philip, 'South Sudan Ministers Invited to Answer Questions on $2 Billion Missing Grain Scandal', *Sudan Tribune*, 16 June 2011.

Aoi, Chiyuki et al., eds., *The Unintended Consequences of Peacekeeping*, Tokyo: United Nations University Press, 2007.

Arjona, Ana, *Rebelocracy*, Cambridge: Cambridge University Press, 2017.

Autesserre, Séverine, *The Trouble with the Congo: Local Violence and the Failure of International Peacebuilding*, New York: Cambridge University Press, 2010.

Autesserre, Séverine, *Peaceland: Conflict Resolution and the Everyday Politics of International Intervention*, Cambridge: Cambridge University Press, 2014.

Autesserre, Séverine, *The Frontlines of Peace: An Insider's Guide to Changing the World*, Oxford: Oxford University Press, 2021.

Ayoub, Mohamed, 'State Making, State Breaking, and State Failure: Explaining the Roots of 'Third World' Insecurity', in *Between Development and Destruction: An Enquiry into the Causes of Conflict in Post-Colonial States*, ed. Luc van de Goor, Kumar Rupesinghe, and Paul Sciarone, The Hague: Clingendael, 1996: 67–91.

Baaz, Maria Eriksson and Ola Olsson, 'Feeding the Horse: Unofficial Economic Activities within the Police Force in the Democratic Republic of the Congo', *African Security* 4 (2011): 223–241.

Baaz, Maria Eriksson and Maria Stern, 'Being Reformed: Subjectification and Security Sector Reform in the Congolese Armed Services', *Journal of Intervention and Statebuilding* 11(2) (2017): 207–224.

Baaz, Maria Eriksson and Judith Verweijen, 'Between Integration and Disintegration: The Erratic Trajectory of the Congolese Army', Social Science Research Council, Conflict Prevention and Peace Forum, 2013.

Baaz, Maria Eriksson and Judith Verweijen, 'The Volatility of a Half-cooked Bouillabaisse: Rebel-Military Integration and Conflict Dynamics in the Eastern DRC', *African Affairs* 112(449) (2013): 563–582.

Badiey, Nasseem, *The State of Post-conflict Reconstruction: Land, Urban Development and State-building in Juba Southern Sudan*, Oxford: James Currey, 2014.

Bailey, Sarah, 'Humanitarian Action, Early Recovery and Stabilisation in the Democratic Republic of Congo', Overseas Development Institute Humanitarian Policy Working Group Paper, July 2011.

Baker, Bruce and Eric Scheye, 'Access to Justice in a Post-Conflict State: Donor-Supported Multidimensional Peacekeeping in Southern Sudan', *International Peacekeeping* 16(2) (2009): 171–185.
Bakonyi, Jutta and Kirsi Stuvoy, 'Violence and Social Order Beyond the State: Somalia and Angola', *Review of African Political Economy* 32(104) (2005): 359–382.
Baldwin, David A., ed., *Neoliberalism and Neorealism: The Contemporary Debate*, New York: Columbia University Press, 1993.
Bargués-Pedreny, Pol, *Deferring Peace in International Statebuilding: Difference, Resilience and Critique*, London: Routledge, 2018.
Barnett, Michael and Christopher Zürcher, 'The Peacebuilder's Contract: How External State-building Reinforces Weak Statehood', in *The Dilemmas of Statebuilding: Confronting the Contradictions of Postwar Peace Operations*, ed. Roland Paris and Timothy Sisk, London: Routledge Press, 2009: 23–53.
Barrera, Alberto, 'The Congo Trap: Islands of Stability in a Sea of Instability', *Stability: International Journal of Security and Development* 4(1) (2015): 1–16.
Bauters, Jasper, 'A Taxonomy of Non-State Actors in Central African Republic', International Peace Information Service, 2012.
Bayart, Jean-François, *The State in Africa: the Politics of the Belly*, London: Longman Press, 1993.
Bayart, Jean-François, Stephen Ellis, and Beatrice Hibou, *Criminalization of the State in Africa*, 2nd ed., Bloomington, IN: Indiana University Press, 2009.
Beach, Derek and Rasmus Brun Pedersen, *Process Tracing Methods: Foundations and Guidelines*, Ann Arbor, MI: University of Michigan Press, 2016.
Bell, Christine and Jan Pospisil, 'Navigating Inclusion in Transitions from Conflict: The Formalised Political *Un*settlement', *Journal of International Development* 29(5) (2017): 576–593.
Bennett, Andrew and Jeffrey T. Checkel, *Process Tracing: From Metaphor to Analytic Tool*, Cambridge: Cambridge University Press, 2015.
Berdal, Mats, 'The Security Council and Peacekeeping', in *The United Nations Security Council and War: The Evolution of Thought and Practice since 1945*, ed. Vaughan Lowe et al., Oxford: Oxford University Press, 2008: 175–204.
Berdal, Mats and Dominik Zaum, eds., *Political Economy of Statebuilding: Power after Peace*, London: Routledge Press, 2013.
Bew, John, 'World Order: Many-Headed Monster or Noble Pursuit?', *Texas National Security Review*, December 2017.
Bhuta, Nejal, 'Against Statebuilding', *Constellations* 15(4) (2008): 517–542.
Bierschenk, Thomas and Jean-Pierre Olivier de Sardan, 'Local Powers and a Distant State in Rural Central African Republic', *The Journal of Modern African Studies* 35(3) (1997): 441–468.
Björkdahl, Annika et al., eds., *Peacebuilding and Friction: Global and Local Encounters in Post-conflict Societies*, New York: Routledge, 2016.
Blackham, Jonathan, 'Situation Report: SSR and DDR in the Sudans', Security Sector Reform Resource Centre, Centre for Security Governance, 11 December 2013.
Boege, Volker and Charles T. Hunt, 'On "Traveling Traditions": Emplaced Security in Liberia and Vanuatu', *Cooperation and Conflict* Vol. 55(4) (2020): 1–21.
Boege, Volker, Anne M. Brown, and Louise Moe, 'Addressing Legitimacy Issues in Fragile Post-conflict Situations to Advance Conflict Transformation and Peacebuilding', Berghof Collection, 2012.

Boege, Volker et al., 'On Hybrid Political Orders and Fragile States: State Formation in the Context of Fragility', Berghof Research Center, October 2008.

Boege, Volker M. et al., 'States Emerging from Hybrid Political Orders—Pacific Experiences', The Australian Centre for Peace and Conflict Studies, Occasional Paper Series, 2008.

Boege, Volker et al., 'On Hybrid Political Orders and Emerging States: What is Failing—States in the Global South or Research and Politics in the West', *Berghof Handbook for Conflict Transformation Dialogue Series* 8 (2009): 15–35.

Bonner, John Tyler, *The Evolution of Complexity by Means of Natural Selection*, Princeton, NJ: Princeton University Press, 1988.

Boone, Catherine, *Political Topographies of the African State: Territorial Authority and Institutional Choice*, Cambridge: Cambridge University Press, 2003.

Boshoff, Henri, Dylan Hendrickson, Sylvie More et al., *Supporting SSR in the DRC: Between a Rock and a Hard Place*, The Hague: Netherlands Institute of International Relations, 2010.

Boulding, Kenneth, *Evolutionary Economics*, London: Sage, 1981.

Boulton, Jane, 'Why Is Economics Not an Evolutionary Science?' *Emergence, Complexity and Organisation* 12(2) (2010): 41–69.

Boulton, Jean G. et al., eds., *Embracing Complexity: Strategic Perspectives for an Age of Turbulence*, Oxford: Oxford University Press, 2015.

Bousquet, Antoine and Simon Curtis, 'Beyond Models and Metaphors: Complexity Theory, Systems Thinking and International Relations', *Cambridge Review of International Affairs* 24(01) (2011): 43–62.

Branch, Adam and Zachariah Cherian Mampilly, 'Winning the War, but Losing the Peace? The Dilemma of SPLM / A Civil Administration and the Tasks Ahead', *Journal of Modern African Studies* 43(1) (2005): 1–20

Brast, Benjamin, 'The Regional Dimension of Statebuilding Interventions', *International Peacekeeping* 22(1) (2015) 81–99.

Braumoeller, Bear F. and Gary Goetz, 'The Methodology of Necessary Conditions', *American Journal of Political Science* 44 (2000): 844–858.

Brewster, Rachel, 'The Trump Administration and the Future of the WTO', *The Yale Journal of International Law* 44 (2018).

Brigg, Morgan, 'Relational Peacebuilding: Promise beyond Crisis', *Peacebuilding in Crisis: Rethinking Paradigms and Practices of Transnational Cooperation*, ed. Tobias Debiel et al., London: Routledge, 2016: 56–70.

Brinkerhoff, Derick, 'State Fragility and Governance: Conflict Mitigation and Subnational Perspectives', *Development Policy Review* 29(2) (2011): 131–153.

Brusset, Emery, Cedric de Coning, and Bryn Hughes, eds., *Complexity Thinking for Peacebuilding Practice and Evaluation*, London: Palgrave Macmillan, 2017.

Bull, Hedley, *The Anarchical Society: A Study of Order in World Politics*, 2nd edition, New York: Columbia University Press, 1977.

Byrne, David, *Complexity Theory and the Social Sciences, An Introduction*, New York: Routledge Press, 1998.

Byrne, David and Gill Callaghan, *Complexity Theory and the Social Sciences: The State of the Art*, London: Routledge, 2014.

Call, Charles T., 'The Fallacy of the "Failed State"', *Third World Quarterly* 29(8) (2008): 1491–1507.

Call, Charles T., 'Knowing Peace When You See It: Setting Standards for Peacebuilding Success', *Civil Wars* 10(2) (2008): 173–194.

Callaghy, Thomas, *The State-Society Struggle*, New York: Columbia University Press, 1984.

Campbell, Susanna, 'Routine Learning? How Peacebuilding Organisations Prevent Liberal Peace', in *A Liberal Peace? The Problems and Practices of Peacebuilding*, ed. Susanna Campbell, David Chandler, and Meera Sabaratnam, London: Zed Books, 2011: 89–105.

Carayannis, Tatiana, José Bazonzi, and Aaron Pangburn, 'Configurations of Authority in Kongo Central Province: Governance, Access to Justice and Security in the Territory of Muanda', Social Science Research Council, JSRP Working Paper No. 31, 2017.

Carayannis, Tatiana, Koen Vlassenroot, Kasper Hoffmann, and Aaron Pangburn, 'Competing Networks and Political Order in the Democratic Republic of Congo: A Literature Review on the Logics of Public Authority and International Intervention', Conflict Research Programme, London School of Economics, 2018.

Carboni, Andrea and James Moody, 'Between the Cracks: Actor Fragmentation and Local Conflict Systems in the Libyan Civil War', *Small Wars & Insurgencies* 29(3) (2108): 456–490.

Carothers, Thomas, *Promoting the Rule of Law Abroad: In Search of Knowledge*, Washington, DC: Carnegie Endowment for International Peace, 2006.

The Carter Center, 'International Election Observation Mission to Democratic Republic of Congo 2006: Presidential and Legislative Elections Final Report', https://www.cartercenter.org/resources/pdfs/news/peace_publications/election_reports/drc-2006-final-rpt.pdf

Chabal, Patrick and Jean-Paul Daloz, *Africa Works: Disorder as Political Instrument*, Oxford: James Currey Press, 1999.

Chandler, David, *Empire in Denial: The Politics of Statebuilding*, London: Pluto Press, 2006.

Chandler, David, *International Statebuilding: The Rise of Post-Liberal Governance*, London: Routledge, 2010.

Chandler, David, *Resilience: The Governance of Complexity*, New York: Routledge, 2014.

Chandler, David, 'Intervention and Statebuilding Beyond the Human: From the "Black Box" to the "Great Outdoors"', *Journal of Intervention and Statebuilding* 12(1) (2018): 80–97.

Chandler, David, 'Complex Systems and International Governance', *International Studies Review*, 2019.

Checchi, Franceso et al., 'South Sudan: Estimates of Crisis-Attributable Mortality', London School of Hygiene and Tropical Medicine, September 2018.

Cheng, Christine, *Extralegal Groups in Post-Conflict Liberia: How Trade Makes the State*, Oxford: Oxford University Press, 2018.

Cheng, Christine, Jonathan Goodhand, and Patrick Meehan, 'Securing and Sustaining Elite Bargains that Reduce Violent Conflict', UK Stabilisation Unit Synthesis Paper, April 2018.

Chirayath, Leila, Caroline Sage, and Michael Woolcock, 'Customary Law and Policy Reform: Engaging with the Plurality of Justice Systems', Background Paper for the World Development Report, 2006.

Cilliers, Paul, *Complexity and Postmodernism: Understanding Complex Systems*, New York: Routledge, 1998.

Clapham, Christopher, *Africa and the International System: The Politics of State Survival*, Cambridge: Cambridge University Press, 1996.

Clemens Jr., Walter C., *Complexity Science and World Affairs*, Albany, NY: State University of New York Press, 2013.

Cliffe, Lionel and Robin Luckham, 'Complex Political Emergencies and the State: Failure and the Fate of the State', *Third World Quarterly* 20(1) (1999): 27–50.

Clunan, Anne L. and Harold A. Trinkunas, eds., *Ungoverned Spaces: Alternatives to State Authority in an Era of Softened Sovereignty*, Stanford, CA: Stanford University Press, 2010.

Coleman, Peter et al., 'Intractable Conflict as an Attractor: A Dynamical Systems Approach to Conflict Escalation and Intractability', *American Behavioral Scientist* 50(11) (2007): 1454–1475.

Coleman, Peter et al., 'Navigating the Landscape of Conflict: Applications of Dynamical Systems Theory to Addressing Protracted Conflict', in *The Non-Linearity of Peace Processes: Theory and Practice of Systemic Conflict Transformation*, ed. Daniela Körppen et al., Opladen: Verlag Barbara Budrich, 2011: 39–56.

Coleman, Peter et al., *Attracted to Conflict: Dynamic Foundations of Destructive Social Relations*, New York: Springer, 2013.

Coleman, Peter T. et al., 'Attracted to Peace: Modeling the Core Dynamics of Sustainably Peaceful Societies' (unpublished, on file with author).

Collier, David and Henry E. Brady, *Rethinking Social Inquiry: Diverse Tools, Shared Standards*, Lanham, MD: Rowman & Littlefield, 2004.

Collier, Paul and Anke Hoeffler, 'On the Economic Consequences of War', *Oxford Economic Papers* 50 (1998): 563–573.

Combes, Claude, *The Art of Being a Parasite*, Chicago, IL: University of Chicago Press, 2005.

Cooper, Hannah, 'More Harm than Good? UN's Islands of Stability in DRC', Oxfam Policy and Practice Blog, 8 May 2014. https://views-voices.oxfam.org.uk/2014/05/islands-of-stability-in-drc/

Costantini, Irene, 'Conflict Dynamics in Post-2011 Libya: A Political Economy Perspective', *Conflict, Security & Development* 16(5) (2016): 405–422.

Cramer, Christopher, 'Trajectories of Accumulation through War and Peace', in *The Dilemmas of Statebuilding: Confronting the Contradictions of Postwar Peace Operations*, ed. Roland Paris and Timothy Sisk, London: Routledge, 2009: 129–148.

Cummins, Deborah, 'A State of Hybridity: Lessons in Institutionalism from a Local Perspective', *The Fletcher Forum on World Affairs* 37(1) (2013): 143–160.

Curran, David and Charles T. Hunt, 'Stabilization at the Expense of Peacebuilding in UN Peacekeeping Operations: More than Just a Phase?' *Global Governance: A Review of Multilateralism and International Organizations* 26(1) (2020): 1–23.

Da Costa, Diana Felix and Cedric de Coning, 'United Nations Mission in the Republic of South Sudan (UNMISS)', in *The Oxford Handbook of United Nations Peacekeeping Operations*, ed. Joachim Koops et al., Oxford: Oxford University Press, 2015, 831–840.

Davidson, Donald, 'What Metaphors Mean', in *On Metaphor*, ed. Sheldon Sacks, Chicago, IL: Chicago University Press, 1978.

Day, Adam C. and Charles T. Hunt, 'UN Stabilisation Operations and the Problem of Non-Linear Change: A Relational Approach to Intervening in Governance Ecosystems', *Stability International Journal of Security and Development* 9(1) (2020): 1–23.

Day, Adam, Dirk Druit, and Luise Quaritsch, 'When Dictators Fall: Preventing Violent Conflict During Transitions from Authoritarian Rule', United Nations University Centre for Policy Research, May 2020.

Day, Adam et al., 'Assessing the Effectiveness of the UN Mission in South Sudan', Norwegian Institute of International Affairs, March 2019. https://effectivepeaceops.net/unmiss/

Day, Adam, Vanda Felbab-Brown, and Fanar Haddad, 'Hybrid Conflict, Hybrid Peace: How Militias and Paramilitary Groups Shape Post-Conflict Transitions', United Nations University Centre for Policy Research, 14 April 2020.

Day, Adam, Sarah Von Billerbeck, Oisín Tansey, and Ayham Al Ahsan, 'Peacebuilding and Authoritarianism: The Unintended Consequences of UN Intervention in Post-Conflict Settings', United Nations University, 2021

De Coning Cedric, 'Understanding Peacebuilding as Essentially Local', *Stability* 2(1) (2013): 1–6.

De Coning, Cedric, 'From Peacebuilding to Sustaining Peace: Implications of Complexity for Resilience and Sustainability', *Resilience* 4(3) (2016): 166–181.

De Coning, Cedric, 'Adaptive Peacebuilding', *International Affairs* 94(2) (2018): 301–317.

De Herdt, Tom and Claudine Tshimanga, 'War and the Political Economy of Kinshasa', in *The Political Economy of the Great Lakes Region in Africa*, ed. Stefaan Marysse and Filip Reyntjens, New York: Springer Press, 2005: 223–243.

De Vries, Hugo, 'The Ebb and Flow of Stabilisation in the Congo', Political Settlements Research Programme Briefing Papers No. 8, Political Settlements Research Programme, 2014.

De Vries, Hugo, *Going Around in Circles: The Challenges of Peacekeeping and Stabilisation in the Democratic Republic of the Congo*, The Hague: Clingendael, 2015.

De Waal, Alex, 'When Kleptocracy becomes Insolvent: Brute Causes of the Civil War in South Sudan', *African Affairs* 113(452) (2014): 347–369.

De Waal, Alex, *The Real Politics of the Horn of Africa: Money, War and the Business of Power*, London: Polity Press, 2016.

De Waal, Alex, 'Inclusion in Peacemaking: From Moral Claim to Political Fact', in *The Fabric of Peace in Africa: Looking Beyond the State*, ed. Pamela Aall and Chester A. Crocker, Ontario: Center for International Governance Innovation, 2017, 176–177.

De Waal, Alex, 'Peace and the Security Sector in Sudan, 2002–11', *African Security Review* 26(2) (2017): 180–198.

De Waal, Alex and Naomi Pendle, 'Decentralisation and the Logic of the Political Marketplace in South Sudan', in *Struggle for South Sudan: Challenges of Security and State Formation*, ed. Luka Biong Deng Kuol and Sarah Logan, London: I.B. Tauris, 2019, 172–194.

Debiel, Tobias and Daniel Lambach, 'How State-building Strategies Miss Local Realities', *Peace Review* 21 (2009): 22–28.

Development International, 'Resource Flows to Sudan: Aid to South Sudan', Global Humanitarian Assistance Report, July 2011. http://devinit.org/wp-content/uploads/2011/07/gha-Sudan-aid-factsheet-2011-South-Sudan-focus.pdf

Devey, Muriel, 'Moïse Katumbi: Je gère le Katanga comme un entreprise', *Jeune Afrique*, 24 May 2011.

DeVore, Marc. R., 'Exploiting Anarchy: Violent Entrepreneurs and the Collapse of Libya's Post Qadhafi Settlement', *Mediterranean Politics* 19(3) (2014): 463–470.

DFID (Department for International Development), 'Written Evidence Submitted by the Department for International Development (DFID) to the International Development Committee', UK Parliament, 2011. https://www.publications.parliament.uk/pa/cm201012/cmselect/cmintdev/1570/1570we08.htm

DFID (Department for International Development), 'Annual Review Security Sector Development & Defence Transformation', Report No. 200329, Development Tracker, 16–27 July 2012. http://iati.dfid.gov.uk/iati_documents/3644468.odt

DFID (Department for International Development), 'Project Completion Review (PCR)', Development Tracker, 2012. http://iati.dfid.gov.uk/iati_documents/4511971.odt

DFID (Department for International Development), 'Governance and Accountability Tracker: Democratic Republic of the Congo', n.d. https://devtracker.dfid.gov.uk/projects/GB-COH-1110949-GB-COH-1110949-351911

DigitalCongo, 'Rétrocession de 40% des recettes aux provinces: Gouverneurs et deputés provinciaux prêts à traduire le gouvernement devant la justice', 17 June 2009.

DiMaggio, Paul and Walter Powell, 'The Iron Cage Revisited: Institutional Isomorphism and Collective Rationality in Organizational Fields', *American Sociological Review* 48(2) (1983): 147–160.

Dion, Douglas, 'Evidence and Inference in the Comparative Case Study', *Comparative Politics* 30 (1998): 127–145.

Dixon, Sam, 'Why Efforts to Stabilise the DR Congo Are Not Working', Oxfam Horn, East and Central Africa Blog, 4 July 2012. https://www.oxfamblogs.org/eastafrica/?p=4484

Dowden, Richard, 'South Sudan's Leaders Have Learnt Nothing from 50 Years of Independence in Africa', *African Arguments*, 22 January 2014.

Downs, George and Stephen John Stedman, 'Evaluation Issues in Peace Implementation', in *Ending Civil Wars: The Implementation of Peace Agreements*, ed. Stephen John Stedman, Donald Rothchild, and Elisabeth M. Cousens, Boulder, CO: Lynne Rienner, 2002: 43–70.

Doyle, Michael and Nicholas Sambanis, *Making War, Building Peace*, Princeton, NJ: Princeton University Press, 2006.

Duffield, Mark, 'Post-Modern Conflict: Warlords, Post-Adjustment States and Private Protection' *Civil Wars* 1 (1998): 5–102.

Duffield, Mark, 'Fragile States and the Return of Native Administration', International Congress on Human Development, 2006.

Duffield, Mark, *Development, Security, and the Unending War*, London: Polity Press, 2007.

Edelstein, David, 'Foreign Militaries, Sustainable Institutions, and Postwar Statebuilding', in *The Dilemmas of Statebuilding: Confronting the Contradictions of Postwar Peace Operations*, ed. Roland Paris and Timothy Sisk, New York: Routledge, 2009: 81–103.

Einsiedel, Sebastian, James Cockyane, Cale Salih, and Wilfred Wan, 'Civil War Trends and the Changing Nature of Armed Conflict', United Nations University Centre for Policy Research, 2017.

El-Batahani, Atta, Ibrahim A. Elbadawi, and Ali Abdel Gadir Ali, 'Sudan's Civil War. Why Has It Prevailed for So Long?', in *Understanding Civil War. Evidence and analysis*, Vol. 1: *Africa*, ed. Nicholas Sambanis and Paul Collier, Washington, DC: World Bank, 2005: 193–220.

Elias, Norbert, 'The Retreat of Sociologists into the Present', *Theory Culture Society* 4(2) (1987): 223–47.

Englebert, Pierre, 'Décentralisation, incertitude, et despotism de proximité en République Démocratique du Congo', Papier Préparé pour le Projet RDC—Provinces-Décentralisation du Musée Royal de Tervuren, Belgique, 2011.

Englebert, Pierre, 'Congo Blues: Scoring Kabila's Rule', Atlantic Council, Africa Center, Issue Brief, May 2016.

Englebert, Pierre and Emmanuel Kasongo Mungongo, 'Misguided and Misdiagnosed: The Failure of Decentralization Reforms in the DR Congo', *African Studies Review* 59(1) (2016): 5–32.

Eriksen, Stein Sundstol, 'The Liberal Peace Is Neither: Peacebuilding, Statebuilding and the Reproduction of Conflict in the Democratic Republic of Congo', *International Peacekeeping* 16(5) (2009): 652–666.

Evans-Pritchard, Edward, *The Nuer: A Description of the Modes of Livelihood and Political Institutions of a Nilotic People*, Oxford: Oxford University Press, 1940.

Evans-Pritchard, Edward, 'The Ethnic Composition of the Azande of Central Africa', *Anthropological Quarterly* 31(4) (1958): 95–119.

Exenberger, Andreas and Simon Hartmann, 'Extractive Institutions in the Congo: Checks and Balances in the Longue Durée', in *Colonial Exploitation and Economic Development:*

The Belgian Congo and the Netherlands Indies compared, ed. Ewout Frankema and Frans Buelens, London and New York: Routledge, 2013: 1–24.
Fearon, James and David Laitlin, 'Ethnicity, Insurgency and Civil War', *American Political Science Review* 97(1) (2003): 75–90.
Fearon, James and David Laitlin, 'Neotrusteeship and the Problem of Weak States', *International Security* 28(4) (2004): 5–43.
Feldman, Noah, *What We Owe Iraq: War and the Ethics of Nation Building*, Princeton, NJ: Princeton University Press, 2004.
Fetherston, A. B. and Carolyn Nordstrom, 'Overcoming Habitus in Conflict Management: UN Peacekeeping and War Zone Ethnography', *Peace & Change* 20(1) (1995): 94–119.
Fortna, Page, *Does Peacekeeping Work? Shaping Belligerents' Choices after Civil War*, Princeton, NJ: Princeton University Press, 2004.
Foucault, Michel, *The Archeology of Knowledge*, New York, Pantheon Books, 1972.
Foucault, Michel, *The History of Sexuality: An Introduction*, New York: Vintage Books, 1990.
Fukuyama, Francis, 'The End of History?' *The National Interest* 16 (1989): 3–18.
Fukuyama, Francis, *The End of History and the Last Man*, New York: Avon Books, 1992.
Fukuyama, Francis, *State-building: Governance and World Order in the 21st Century*, New York: Cornell University Press, 2004.
Galaz, Victor et al., 'Polycentric Systems and Interacting Planetary Boundaries: Emerging Governance of Climate Change–Ocean Acidification–Marine Biodiversity', *Ecological Economics* 81 (2012): 21–32.
Garang, James Alic, 'The Question of Big Government and Financial Viability: The Case of South Sudan', Sudd Institute, 1 February 2013.
George, Alexander L. and Andrew Bennett, 'Case Studies and Theory Development in the Social Sciences', *BCSIA Studies in International Security* (2004).
George, Alexander and Andrew Bennett, *Case Studies and the Theory of Development in the Social Sciences*, Cambridge MA: MIT Press, 2005.
Gerring, John, *Case Study Research: Principles and Practice*, Cambridge: Cambridge University Press, 2007.
Geyer, Robert and Samir Rihani, *Complexity and Public Policy: A New Approach to 21st Century Politics, Policy and Society*, New York: Routledge, 2010.
Ghani, Ashraf and Clare Lockhardt, *Fixing Failed States*, Oxford: Oxford University Press, 2009.
Gilman, Nils, *Mandarins of The Future: Modernization Theory in Cold War America*, Baltimore: Johns Hopkins University Press, 2003.
Gisselquist, Rachel M., 'Paired Comparison and Theory Development: Considerations for Case Selection', *PS: Political Science & Politics* 47(2) (2014): 477–484.
Giustozzi, Antonio, 'War and Peace Economies of Afghanistan's Strongmen', *International Peacekeeping* 14(1) (2007): 75–89.
Glennon, Michael, *Limits of Law, Prerogatives of Power: Interventionism after Kosovo*, New York: Palgrave, 2001.
Government of the Republic of South Sudan, 'South Sudan Development Plan (2011–2013): Realising Freedom, Justice, Equality, Prosperity and Peace for All', August 2011.
Gowan, Richard, 'Minimum Order: The Role of the Security Council in an Era of Great Power Competition', United Nations Centre for Policy Research, December 2018.
Graeber, David, 'The Divine Kingship of the Shilluk: On Violence, Utopia, and the Human Condition', in *On Kings*, ed. David Graeber and Marshal Sahlins, Chicago, IL: Hau Books, 2017, 65–139.
Green, Duncan, *From Poverty to Power*, Oxfam e-books. https://oxfamblogs.org/fp2p/

Guyer, Jane, *Marginal Gains: Monetary Transactions in Atlantic Africa*, Chicago, IL: University of Chicago Press, 2004.

Gyorgy, Anna, 'Guerillas in the Mist: The Congolese Experience of the FDLR War in Eastern Congo and the Role of the International Community', Pole Institute, February 2010.

Haas, Richard, *A World in Disarray: American Foreign Policy and the Crisis of the Old Order*, New York: Penguin, 2018.

Haas, Richard, 'How a World Order Ends and What Comes in Its Wake', *Foreign Affairs*, February 2019.

Hagmann, Tobias and Markus Hoehne, 'Failures of the State Failure Debate: Evidence from the Somali Territories', *Journal of International Development* 21 (2012): 42–57.

Hagmann, Tobias and Didier Péclard, 'Negotiating Statehood: Dynamics of Power and Domination in Africa', *Development and Change* 41(4) (2010): 539–562.

Haldrup, Søren Vester and Frederik Rosén, 'Developing Resilience: A Retreat from Grand Planning', *Resilience* 1(2) (2013): 130–145.

Hall, Rodney B. and Thomas J Bierstecker, eds., *The Emergence of Private Authority in Global Governance*, Cambridge: Cambridge University Press, 2009.

Hameiri, Shahar and Lee Jones, 'Against Hybridity in the Study of Peacebuilding and Statebuilding', in *Hybridity on the Ground in Peacebuilding and Development*, ed. Joanne Wallis et al., New South Wales: Australian National University Press, 2018: 99–112.

Hammer, Jort and Nick Grinstead, 'When Peace Is the Exception: Shifting the Donor Narrative in South Sudan', Clingendael Policy Brief, June 2015.

Hampel, Karl Adalbert, 'The Dark(er) Side of "State Failure": State Formation and Socio-political Variation', *Third World Quarterly* 36(9) (2015): 1629–1648.

Harragin, Simon, 'Waiting for Pay-day: Anthropological Research on Local-level Governance Structures in South Sudan', Save the Children Report, 2007. http://southsudanhumanitarianproject.com/wp-content/uploads/sites/21/formidable/Harragin-2007-Waiting-for-pay-day-Anthropological-Research-on-Local-level-Governance-Structures-in-South-Sudan2-annotated.pdf

Harsch, Ernest, 'Accumulators and Democrats: Challenging State Corruption in Africa', *The Journal of Modern African Studies* 31 (1993): 31–48.

Harvey, Martin, 'Grotius and Hobbes', *British Journal for the History of Philosophy*, vol. 14 (2006): 27–50.

Hegre, Håvard, Lisa Hultman, and Håvard Mokleiv Nygård, 'Evaluating the Conflict-Reducing Effect of UN Peacekeeping Operations', *The Journal of Politics* 81(1) (2019): 215–232.

Heimans, Jeremy and Henry Timms, *New Power: How Anyone Can Persuade, Mobilize, and Succeed in Our Chaotic, Connected Age*, New York: Anchor Books, 2019.

Helland, Leonardo Figueroa and Stefan Borg, 'The Lure of State Failure: A Critique of State Failure Discourse in World Politics', *Interventions* 16(6) (2014): 877–897.

Helme, Gretchen and Steven Levitsky, 'Informal Institutions and Comparative Politics: A Research Agenda', *Perspectives on Politics* 2(4) (2004): 725–740.

Henderson, Kenneth D., *Sudan Republic*, London: Benn Press, 1965.

Herbst, Jeffrey, *States and Power in Africa*, Princeton, NJ: Princeton University Press, 2000.

Herbst, Jeffrey, 'Let Them Fail: State Failure in Theory and Practice: Implications for Policy', in *When States Fail: Causes and Consequences*, ed. Robert Rotberg et al., Princeton, NJ: Princeton University Press, 2004: 302–318.

Her Majesty's Government (HM Govt.), *National Security Strategy and Strategic Defence and Security Review 2015: A Secure and Prosperous United Kingdom*, London: HM Govt., 2015.

Hill, Jonathan, 'Beyond the Other? A Postcolonial Critique of the Failed State Thesis', *African Identities* 3(2) (2005): 139–154.
Hobbes, Thomas, *Leviathan, or The Matter, Form and Power of a Commonwealth Ecclesiasticall and Civil*, Oxford: Oxford University Press, 1996 [1651].
Hochschild, Fabrizio and Adam Day, 'Southern Sudan Assessment', UN Department of Peacekeeping Operations, January 2010 (on file with author).
Hoffman, Kasper and Tom Kirk, 'Public Authority and the Provision of Public Goods in Conflict-Affected and Transitioning Regions', Conflict Research Group, 2013. https://core.ac.uk/download/pdf/20050777.pdf
Hoffmann, Kasper and Koen Vlassenroot, 'Armed Groups and the Exercise of Public Authority: The Cases of the Mayi-Mayi and Raya Mutomboki in Kalehe, South Kivu', *Peacebuilding* 2(2) (2014): 202–220.
Hoffmann, Kasper, Koen Vlassenroot, and Gauthier Marchais, 'Taxation, Stateness and Armed Groups: Public Authority and Resource Extraction in Eastern Congo', *Development and Change* 47(6) (2006): 1434–1456.
Howard, Lise Morjé, *Power in Peacekeeping*, Washington DC: Georgetown University Press, 2019.
Human Rights Watch, 'Democracy on Hold: Human Rights Violations in the April 2010 Sudan Elections', 30 June 2010.
Hunt, Charles T., *UN Peace Operations and International Policing: Negotiating Complexity, Assessing Impact and Learning to Learn*, London: Routledge, 2015.
Hunt, Charles T., 'All Necessary Means to What Ends? The Unintended Consequences of the 'Robust Turn' in UN Peace Operations', *International Peacekeeping* 24(1) (1 January 2017): 108–131.
Hunt, Charles T., 'Beyond the Binaries: Towards a Relational Approach to Peacebuilding', *Global Change, Peace and Security* 29(3) (2017): 209–227.
Hunt, Charles T., 'Complexity Theory' in *United Nations Peace Operations and International Relations Theory*, ed. K. Oksamytna and J.Karlsrud, Manchester: Manchester University Press, 2020: 195–216.
Ignatieff, Michael, 'Human Rights, Power and the State', in *Making States Work: State Failure and the Crisis of Governance*, ed. Simon Chesterman, Michael Ignatieff, and Ramesh Thakur, New York: United Nations University Press, 2005: 59–76.
Ikenberry, G. John, 'The End of the Liberal International Order?' *International Affairs* 94(1) (2018): 7–23.
Ikenberry, G. John, 'Inderjeet Parmar and Doug Stokes, "Ordering the World?" Liberal Internationalism in Theory and Practice', *International Affairs* 94(1) (2018): 1–5.
International Crisis Group, 'Congo: Quatre priorités pour un paix durable en Ituri', Nairobi, 2008.
International Crisis Group 'Congo: A Stalled Democratic Agenda', Africa Briefing 73, 2010.
International Crisis Group, 'Eastern Congo: Why Stabilisation Failed', Briefing 91, 4 October 2012.
International Development Association and International Finance Corporation, 'South Sudan—Interim Strategy Note for FY2013–2014', Report No: 74767-SS, World Bank, 30 January 2013, 5.
International Development Committee, 'Written Evidence of UK International Development Committee', 11 April 2012. https://www.publications.parliament.uk/pa/cm201012/cmselect/cmintdev/1570/1570we08.htm
International Monetary Fund, 'Sudan: Selected Issues Paper', No 12/299, November 2012. https://www.imf.org/external/pubs/ft/scr/2012/cr12299.pdf

Jackson, Paul, 'Warlords as Alternative Forms of Governance', *Small Wars and Insurgencies* 14 (2003): 131–150.

Jackson, Robert H., *Quasi-States, Sovereignty, International Relations, and the Third World*, Cambridge: Cambridge University Press, 1990.

Jackson, Stephen, 'The State Didn't Even Exist: Non-Governmentality in Kivu, Eastern DR Congo', in *Between a Rock and a Hard Place: African NGOs, Donors and the State*, ed. Tim Kelsall and Jim Igoe, Durham, NC: Carolina Academic Press, 2004: 165–194.

Jackson, Stephen, 'Borderlands and the Transformation of War Economies: Lessons from the DR Congo', *Conflict, Security & Development* 6(3) (2006): 425–447.

Jebnoun, Noureddine, 'Beyond the Mayhem: Debating Key Dilemmas in Libya's Statebuilding', *The Journal of North African Studies* 20(5) (2015): 832–864.

Jervis, Robert, *System Effects: Complexity in Political and Social Life*, Princeton, NJ: Princeton University Press, 1997.

Johnson, Douglas H., *The Root Causes of Sudan's Civil Wars*, Oxford: James Currey Press, 2003.

Johnson, Douglas H., 'Federalism in the History of South Sudanese Political Thought', in *Struggle for South Sudan: Challenges of Security and State Formation*, ed. Luka Biong Deng Kuol and Sarah Logan, London: I.B. Tauris, 2019, 103–123.

Johnson, Hilde, 'In South Sudan, Old Feuds Test a New State', *Sudan Tribune*, 1 February 2012.

Johnson, Hilde F., *South Sudan: The Untold Story from Independence to Civil War*, London: L.B. Tauris, 2016.

Johnstone, Ian, 'Managing Consent in Contemporary Peacekeeping Operations', *International Peacekeeping* 18(2) (2011): 168–182.

Jones, Branwyn Gruffydd, '"Good Governance" and "State Failure": Genealogies of Imperial Discourse', *Cambridge Review of International Affairs* 26(1) (2013): 49–70.

Joseph, Jonathan, 'Resilience as Embedded Neoliberalism: A Governmentality Approach', *Resilience* 1(1) (2013): 38–52.

Jourdan, Luca, 'New Forms of Political Order in North Kivu: The Case of the Governor Eugene Serufuli', Paper presented at the conference 'Beside the State: New Forms of Political Power in Post-1990's Africa', Milan, December 2005.

Jütersonke, Oliver and Moncef Kartas, 'Resilience: Conceptual Reflections', Centre on Conflict Development and Peacebuilding, Brief No. 6, 2012.

Kaldor, Mary, *New and Old Wars*, 2nd edition, Stanford, CA: Stanford University Press, 2007.

Kanie, Norichika, 'Governance with Multilateral Environmental Agreements: A Healthy or Ill-equipped Fragmentation?' In *Global Environmental Governance: Perspectives on the Current Debate*, ed. Lydia Swart and Estelle Perry, New York: Center for UN Reform Education, 2007, 67–86.

Kaplan, Morton, *System and Process in International Relations*, New York: Wiley, 1957.

Kavalski, Emilian, *World Politics at the Edge of Chaos: Reflections on Complexity and Global Life*, Albany, NY: State University of New York, 2015.

Keohane, Robert O. and Joseph S. Nye Jr., 'Power and Interdependence', *Survival* 15(4) (1973): 158–165.

Kets, Evert and Hugo de Vries, 'Limits to Supporting Security Sector Interventions in the DRC', Institute for Security Studies Paper No. 257, July 2014.

Kim, Rakhyune E., 'Is Global Governance Fragmented, Polycentric, or Complex? The State of the Art of the Network Approach', *International Studies Review* 22(4) (2019): 1–29.

Kleinfeld, Rachel, 'Improving Development Aid Design and Implementation: Plan for Sailboats Not Traintracks', Carnegie Endowment for International Peace, 2015.

Kopling, Peter, 'Peaceful Coexistence: How the Equatorians Got It Right!', South Sudan Nation. www.southsudannation.com/peaceful-coexistence-how-the-equatorians-got-it-right/

Körppen, Daniela, 'Space Beyond the Liberal Peacebuilding Consensus—A Systemic Perspective', in *The Non-Linearity of Peace Processes: Theory and Practice of Systemic Conflict Transformation*, ed. Daniela Körppen et al., Opladen: Verlag Barbara Budrich, 2011: 77–96.

Körppen, Daniela et al., eds., *The Non-Linearity of Peace Processes: Theory and Practice of Systemic Conflict Transformation*, Opladen: Verlag Barbara Budrich, 2011.

Krasner, Stephen, *Sovereignty: Organised Hypocrisy*, Princeton, NJ: Princeton University Press, 1999.

Krasniqi, Valon and Yibur Aliu, 'The Role of the International Administration in the Process of the State-building in Kosovo, *Academic Journal of Interdisciplinary Studies* 4(3) (2015): 409–416.

Kraushaar, Maren and Daniel Lambasch, 'Hybrid Political Orders: The Added Value of a New Concept', *Australian Center for Peace and Conflict Studies: Occasional Papers Series* 14 (2009): 1–20.

Kuol, Luka Biong Deng, 'The Federalism-Decentralisation-Peace Nexus in South Sudan', in *The Struggle for South Sudan: Challenges of Security and State Formation*, ed. Luka Biong Deng Kuol and Sarah Logan, London: I.B. Tauris, 2019: 82–102.

Kuol, Luka Biong Deng and Sarah Logan, eds., *The Struggle for South Sudan: Challenges of Security and State Formation*, London: I.B. Tauris, 2019.

Lacher, Wolfram, 'The Libyan Revolution and the Rise of Competing Power Centres', *Mediterranean Politics* (2012): 167–170.

Lacher, Wolfram, 'South Sudan: International State-Building and Its Limits', German Institute for International and Security Affairs, 2012. https://www.swp-berlin.org/fileadmin/contents/products/research_papers/2012_RP04_lac.pdf

Lacher, Wolfram and Peter Cole, 'Politics by Other Means: Conflicting Interests in Libya's Security Sector', Small Arms Survey, 2014.

Lamont, Christopher K., 'Contested Governance: Understanding Justice Interventions in Post-Qadhafi Libya', *Journal of Intervention and Statebuilding* 10(3) (2016): 382–399.

Larson, Greg, Peter Biar Ajak, and Lant Pritchett, 'South Sudan's Capability Trap: Building a State with Disruptive Innovation', Harvard Kennedy School, 2013.

Latour, Bruno, *Reassembling the Social: An Introduction to Actor-Network Theory*, Oxford: Oxford University Press, 2005.

Le Billon, Philippe, 'Diamond Wars? Conflict Diamonds and Geographies of Resource Wars', *Annals of the Association of American Geographers* 98 (2008): 345–372.

Le Riche, Matthew, 'Conflict Governance: The SPLA, Factionalism, and Peacemaking', in *The Challenges of Governance in South Sudan*, ed. Steven E. Roach, London: Routledge 2018: 17–49.

Lederach, Jean Paul, *Building Peace: Sustainable Reconciliation in Divided Societies*, Washington, DC: United States Institute of Peace, 1997.

Lederach, John Paul, *Preparing for Peace: Conflict Transformation Across Cultures*, Syracuse, NY: Syracuse University Press, 1995.

Lederach, John Paul, *The Moral Imagination: The Art and Soul of Building Peace*, New York: Oxford University Press, 2005.

Lemarchand, René, 'The Democratic Republic of Congo: From Collapse to Potential Reconstruction', in *State Failure and State Weakness in a Time of Terror*, ed. Robert Rotberg, Washington, DC: Brookings Institution Press, 2003: 29–70.

Lemarchand, René, *The Dynamics of Violence in Central Africa*, Philadelphia, PA: University of Pennsylvania Press, 2009.

Leonardi, Cherry, 'Paying "Buckets of Blood" for the Land: Moral Debates over the Economy, War and State in Southern Sudan', *Journal of Modern African Studies* 49(2) (2011): 215–240.

Leonardi, Cherry, *Dealing with Government in South Sudan: Histories of Chiefship, Community and State*, Oxford: James Currey Press, 2015.

Leonardsson, Hanna and Gustav Rudd, 'The "Local Turn" in Peacebuilding: A Literature Review of Effective and Emancipatory Local Peacebuilding', *Third World Quarterly* 36(5) (2015): 825–839.

Lino, Edward, 'There Was No Coup in Juba', 9 February 2014. https://paanluelwel.com/2014/02/09/edward-lino-there-was-no-coup-in-juba/

Lund, Christian, 'Twilight Institutions: An Introduction', *Development and Change* 37(4) (2006): 673–678.

Lund, Christian and Michael Eilenberg, *Rule and Rupture: State Formation through the Production of Property and Citizenship*, Sussex: Wiley Blackwell, 2017.

Luttwak, Edward, 'Give War a Chance', *Foreign Affairs* 78(4) (1999).

Lyotard, Jean-François, *The Postmodern Condition: A Report on the Knowledge (Theory and History) of Literature*, Minneapolis, MN: University of Minnesota Press, 1984.

Mac Ginty, Roger, 'Indigenous Peace-making versus the Liberal Peace', *Journal of Cooperation and Conflict* 43(2) (2008): 139–163.

Mac Ginty, Roger, 'Hybrid Peace: The Interaction between Top-Down and Bottom-Up Peace', *Security Dialogue* 41(4) (2010): 391–412.

Mac Ginty, Roger, *International Peacebuilding and Local Resistance: Hybrid Forms of Peace*, Basingstoke: Palgrave MacMillan, 2011.

Mac Ginty, Roger and Oliver Richmond, 'The Local Turn in Peacebuilding: A Critical Agenda for Peace', *Third World Quarterly* 34(5) (2013): 763–783.

Mahoney, James and Gary Goetz, 'A Tale of Two Cultures: Contrasting Quantitative and Qualitative Research', *Political Analysis* 14(3) (2006): 227–49.

Malan, Mark and Charles T. Hunt. 'Between a Rock and a Hard Place: The UN and the Protection of Civilians in South Sudan', International Strategic Studies Paper 275 (2014).

Malejacq, Romain, 'Warlords, Intervention, and State Consolidation: A Typology of Political Orders in Weak and Failed States', *Security Studies* 25 (2016): 85–110.

Mallett, Richard, 'Beyond Failed States and Ungoverned Spaces: Hybrid Political Orders in the Post-Conflict Landscape', *eSharp* 15 (2010): 65–91.

Malone, David M. and Adam Day, 'The UN at 75: How Today's Challenges Will Shape the Next 25 Years', *Global Governance* 26(2) (2020): 236–250.

Mampilly, Zachariah, 'Rebels with a Cause: The History of Rebel Governance, From the U.S. Civil War to Libya', *Foreign Affairs*, 13 April 2011.

Mampilly, Zachariah Cherian, *Rebel Rulers: Insurgent Governance and Civilian Life during War*, Ithaca, NY: Cornell University Press, 2011.

Management Systems International (MSI). 'Government of Southern Sudan: Functional Capacity Prioritization Study', USAID, December 3, 2009.

Manjikian, Mary, 'Diagnosis, Intervention, and Cure: The Illness Narrative in the Discourse of the Failed State', *Alternatives* 33(3) (2008): 335–357.

Mayall, James and Ricardo Soares de Oliveira, eds., *The New Protectorates: International Tutelage and the Making of Liberal States*, London: Hurst, 2011.

Meadows, Donella, *Thinking in Systems: A Primer*, White River Junction, VT: Chelsea Green Publishing, 2008.

Meadows, Donella, 'Leverage Points: Places to Intervene in a System'. http://donellameadows.org/archives/leverage-points-places-to-intervene-in-a-system/

Meagher, Kate, 'Non-state Security Forces and Hybrid Governance in Africa', *Development and Change* 43(5) (2012): 1073–1101.

Mearsheimer, John. G., *The Great Delusion: Liberal Dreams and International Realities*, New Haven, CT: Yale University Press, 2018.

Mehler, Andreas and Denis Tull, 'The Hidden Costs of Power-sharing: Reproducing Insurgent Violence in Africa', *African Affairs* 104(416) (2006): 375–398;

Mehta, Uday Singh, *Liberalism and Empire: A Study in Nineteenth Century Liberal Thought*, Chicago, IL: Chicago University Press, 1999.

Melmot, Sébastien, 'Candide au Congo: L'échec annoncé de la réforme du secteur de sécurité', Focus Stratégique 9, Institut Français des Relations Internationales, 2009.

Menkhaus, Ken, 'Governance without Government in Somalia: Spoilers, State Building, and the Politics of Coping', *International Security* 31(3) (Winter 2006/7): 74–106.

Mennan, Tiernan, 'Customary Law and Land Rights in South Sudan', Norwegian Refugee Council, March 2012.

Migdal, Joel, *Strong Societies, Weak States: State-Society Relations and State Capabilities in the Third World*, Princeton, NJ: Princeton University Press, 1988.

Millar, Gearoid, 'Respecting Complexity: Compound Friction and Unpredictability in Peacebuilding', in *Peacebuilding and Friction: Global and Local Encounters in Post-conflict Societies*, ed. Annika Bjökdahl et al., New York: Routledge, 2017: 32–47.

Mitchell, Melanie, *Complexity: A Guided Tour*, Oxford: Oxford University Press, 2009.

Mobekk, Eirin, 'Security Sector Reform and the UN Mission in the Democratic Republic of the Congo: Protecting Civilians in the East', *International Peacekeeping* 16(2) (2009): 273–286.

Moe, Louise Wiuff and Markus-Michael Müller, *Reconfiguring Intervention: Complexity, Resilience and the 'Local Turn' in Counterinsurgent Warfare*, London: Palgrave MacMillan, 2017.

Moe, Louise Wiuff and Finn Stepputat, 'Peacebuilding in an Era of Pragmatism', *International Affairs* 94(2) (2018): 293–299.

MONUSCO (United Nations Organization Stabilization Mission in the Democratic Republic of Congo), 'International Security and Stabilisation Support Strategy', Quarterly Report, 2009–12.

MONUSCO (United Nations Organization Stabilization Mission in the Democratic Republic of Congo), 'International Security and Stabilisation Support Strategy', Situation Assessment, 2011.

MONUSCO (United Nations Organization Stabilization Mission in the Democratic Republic of Congo), 'International Security and Stabilisation Support Strategy', Quarterly Report, January to March 2012.

MONUSCO (United Nations Organization Stabilization Mission in the Democratic Republic of Congo), 'International Security and Stabilisation Support Strategy', 2013–17 (on file with author).

MONUSCO (United Nations Organization Stabilization Mission in the Democratic Republic of Congo), 'International Security and Stabilization Support Strategy', Annual

Report, 2016. https://monusco.unmissions.org/sites/default/files/issss_annual_report_2016_english.pdf
Morçöl, Göktug, *A Complexity Theory for Public Policy*, New York: Routledge, 2012.
Mores, Magali, 'Overview of Corruption and Anti-corruption in South Sudan', Transparency International, 4 March 2013.
Morland, Anthony, 'The State of State-building in Somalia', *IRIN News*, 21 October 2014. http://www.irinnews.org/report/100745/analysis-state-state-building-somalia
Mukhopadhyay, Dipali, *Warlords, Strongmen Governors, and the State in Afghanistan*, New York: Cambridge University Press, 2014.
Munive, Jairo, 'Invisible Labour: The Political Economy of Reintegration in South Sudan', *Journal of Intervention and Statebuilding* 8(4) (2014): 224–356.
Nam, Illan, *Democratizing Health Care: Welfare State Building in Korea and Thailand*, London: Palgrave Macmillan, 2015.
Nasr, Vali, *The Dispensable Nation: American Foreign Policy in Retreat*, Doubleday: New York, 2013.
Nell, Karl E., 'A Doctrine of Contingent Sovereignty', *Science Direct* 62(2) (March 2018): 313–334.
Nest, Michael, François Grignon and Emizet F. Kisangani, *The Democratic Republic of Congo: Economic Dimensions of War and Peace*, Boulder, CO: Lynne Rienner Press, 2006: 136-138.
Nyaba, Peter Adwok, *Politics of Liberation in South Sudan: An Insider's View*, Kampala: Fountain Publishers, 1997.
Office of the Secretary-General, 'Special Report of the Secretary-General on the Sudan', S/2011/314, United Nations Security Council, UNMIS, 17 May 2011.
Onana, Renner and Hannah Taylor, 'MONUC and SSR in the Democratic Republic of the Congo', *International Peacekeeping* 15(4) (2008): 501–516.
Organisation for Economic Cooperation and Development (OECD), 'Principles for Good International Engagement in Fragile States and Situations', 2007.
Organisation for Economic Co-operation and Development (OECD), 'Conflict and Fragility: The State's Legitimacy in Fragile Situations, Unpacking Complexity', 2010.
Organisation for Economic Cooperation and Development (OECD), 'Supporting State-building in Situations of Conflict and Fragility', 2011.
Organisation for Economic Cooperation and Development (OECD), 'Building Blocks to Prosperity: the Peacebuilding and State-building Goals', 2012. http://www.oecd.org/dac/HLM%20one%20pager%20PSGs.pdf
Orsini, Amandine et al., 'Complex Systems and International Governance', *International Studies Review* (2019): 1–30.
Ostrom, Elinor, 'Beyond Markets and States: Polycentric Governance of Complex Economic Systems', *American Economic Review* 100(3) (2010): 641–672.
Overseas Development Institute Briefing Paper, 'Planning and Budgeting in South Sudan: Starting from Scratch', October 2010. https://www.odi.org/sites/odi.org.uk/files/odi-assets/publications-opinion-files/6093.pdf
Oxfam, '"For Me, but Without Me, Is Against Me": Why Efforts to Stabilize the Democratic Republic of the Congo Are Not Working', Oxfam Lobby Briefing, 2012.
Oxfam America, 'No Will, No Way: US-Funded Security Sector Reform in the Democratic Republic of the Congo', 2010.
Paddon, Emily and Guillaume Lacaille, 'Stabilising the Congo: Forced Migration', Policy Briefing 8, Refugee Studies Centre, Oxford Department of International Development (2011).

Paris, Roland, 'International Peacebuilding and the "Mission Civilisatrice"', *Review of International Studies* 28 (2002): 637–656.

Paris, Roland, *At War's End: Building Peace after Civil Conflict*, Cambridge: Cambridge University Press, 2004.

Paris, Roland, 'Saving Liberal Peacebuilding', *Review of International Studies* 36(2) (2010): 337–365.

Paris, Roland, 'Critiques of Liberal Peace', in *A Liberal Peace? The Problems and Practices of Peacebuilding*, ed. Susanna Campbell, David Chandler, and Meera Sabaratnam, London: Zed Books, 2011: 31–54.

Paris, Roland and Timothy Sisk, eds., *The Dilemmas of Statebuilding: Confronting the Contradictions of Postwar Peace Operations*, London: Routledge Press, 2009.

Patey, Luke, 'Crude Days Ahead? Oil and the Resource Curse in Sudan', *African Affairs* 109(437) (2010): 617–636.

Patrick, Stewart, *Weak Links: Fragile States, Global Threats and International Security*, Oxford: Oxford University Press, 2011.

Pauwels, Eleonore, 'The New Geopolitics of Converging Risks: the UN and Prevention in the Era of AI', United Nations University Centre for Policy Research, May 2019.

Pendle, Naomi and Chirrilo Madut Anei, 'Wartime Trade and the Reshaping of Power in South Sudan', South Sudan Customary Authorities Project, Rift Valley Institute, 2018. https://riftvalley.net/download/file/fid/4966

Peters, Krijn, *War and the Crisis of Youth in Sierra Leone*, Cambridge: Cambridge University Press, 2011.

Pinaud, Clémence, 'South Sudan: Civil War, Predation and the Making of a Military Aristocracy', *African Affairs* 113(451) (2014): 192–211.

Podder, Sukanya, 'Mainstreaming the Non-state in Bottom-Up State-building: Linkages between Rebel Governance and Post-conflict Legitimacy', *Conflict, Security and Development* 14(2) (2014): 213–243.

Pospisil, Jan, *Peace in Political Unsettlement: Beyond Solving Conflict*, Cham: Springer Nature Press, 2019.

Pospisil, Jan and Florian Kühn, 'The Resilient State: New Regulatory Modes in International Approaches to State Building', *Third World Quarterly* 37(1) (2016): 1–16.

President Salva Kiir's Martyr's Day Speech, 30 July 2011. https://paanluelwel.com/2011/07/31/president-kiirs-speech-in-the-6th-martyrs-day-30-7-2011/

Prigonine, Ilya, 'Time, Structure and Fluctuations', *Science* 201(4358) (1978): 777–785.

Prigonine, Ilya et al., 'Long Term Trends and the Evolution of Complexity', in *Goals in a Global Community*, Vol. 1: *Studies on the Conceptual Foundations*, ed. E. Lazlo and J. Bierman, New York: Pergamon Press, 1977: 1–4.

Pugh, Michael, 'The Political Economy of Peacebuilding: A Critical Theory Perspective', *International Journal of Peace Studies* 10(2) (2005): 23–42.

Quick, Ian D., *Follies in Fragile States: How International Stabilisation Failed in the Congo*, London: Double Loop Press, 2015.

Radio Okapi, 'DRC Security Sector Reform: Alan Doss Recommends Coherency in the Implementation of the Programme', 27 February 2008.

Raeymaekers, Timothy, 'Post-war Conflict and the Market for Protection: The Challenges to Congo's Hybrid Peace', *International Peacekeeping* 20(5) (2013): 600–617.

Raeymaekers, Timothy, *Violent Capitalism and Hybrid Identity in the Eastern Congo: Power to the Margins*, Cambridge: Cambridge University Press, 2014.

Raeymaekers, Timothy and Ken Menkhaus, 'State and Non-State Regulation in African Protracted Crises: Governance without Government?' *Afrika Focus* 21 (2008): 1–20.

Raeymaekers, Timothy and Koen Vlassenroot, 'Reshaping Congolese Statehood in the Midst of Crisis and Transition', in *Respacing Africa*, ed. Ulf Engel and Paul Nugent, New York: Brill, 2010: 139–168.

Ramalingam, Ben, *Aid on the Edge of Chaos: Rethinking International Cooperation in a Complex World*, Oxford: Oxford University Press, 2013.

Ramalingham, Ben and Harry Jones, 'Exploring the Science of Complexity: Ideas and Implications for Development and Humanitarian Efforts', Overseas Development Institute, Working Paper No. 285, 2008.

Randles, William Graham Lister, *L'ancien royaume du Congo des origins à la fin du XIXe siècle*, Paris: Éditions de l'École des hautes études en sciences sociales, 2002.

Rands, Richard, 'In Need of Review: SPLA Transformation in 2006–10 and Beyond', Small Arms Survey, Working Paper No. 23, November 2012.

Ratner, Steven R., 'Saving Failed States', *Foreign Policy* 89(3) (Winter 1992–3).

Reno, William, *Warlord Politics and African States*, Boulder, CO: Lynne Rienner Publishers, 1998.

Reno, William, 'Congo: From State Collapse to "Absolutism", to State Failure', *Third World Quarterly* 27(1) (2006): 43–56;

Rhodes, Mary Lee et al., *Public Management and Complexity Theory: Richer Decision-making in Public Services*, New York: Routledge, 2011.

Richardson, Kurt A., 'Complex Systems Thinking and Its Implications for Policy Analysis', in *Handbook on Decisionmaking*, ed. Göktug Morçöl, University Park, PA: Penn State University Press, 2006, 189–221.

Richardson, Kurt, Graham Mathieso, and Paul Cilliers, 'Complexity Thinking and Military Operational Analysis', in *Knots, Lace and Tartan: Making Sense of Complex Human Systems in Military Operations Research*, ed. Kurt Richardson, Litchfield Park, AZ: ISE Publishing, 2009: 72–98.

Richmond, Oliver, 'De-romanticising the Local, De-mystifying the International: Hybridity in Timor Leste and the Solomon Islands', *The Pacific Review* 24(1) (2011): 115–136.

Richmond, Oliver, *A Post-Liberal Peace*, New York: Routledge, 2011.

Richmond, Oliver P. and Jason Franks, *Liberal Peace Transitions: Between Statebuilding and Peacebuilding*, Edinburgh: Edinburgh University Press, 2009.

Riehl, Volker, *Who is Ruling in South Sudan? The Role of NGOs in Rebuilding the Socio-Political Order*, Uppsala: Nordic Africa Institute, 2001.

Rios, Luis et al., 'On the Rationale for Hysteresis in Economic Decisions', *Journal of Physics*, Conference Series, 811 (2015).

Risse, Thomas, *Governance without a State: Policies and Politics in Areas of Limited Statehood*, New York: Columbia University Press, 2013.

Rolandsen, Øystein, *Guerrilla Government: Political Changes in Southern Sudan during the 1990s*, Uppsala: Nordic Africa Institute, 2005.

Rolandsen, Øystein H., 'Small and Far Between: Peacekeeping Economies in South Sudan', *Journal of Intervention and Statebuilding* 9(3) (2015): 353–371.

Room, Graham, *Complexity, Institutions and Public Policy: Agile Decision-making in a Turbulent World*, Cheltenham: Edward Elgar, 2010.

Rosenau, James N. and Ernst-Otto Czempiel, *Governance without Government: Order and Change in World Politics*, Cambridge: Cambridge University Press, 2010.

Rosenthal, Gert et al., 'The Challenge of Sustaining Peace: Report of the Advisory Group of Experts for the Review of the 2105 Peacebuilding Architecture', United Nations, New York, 29 June 2015.

Rotberg, Robert I., 'The New Nature of Nation-State Failure', *Washington Quarterly* 25(3) (2002): 85–96.

Rotberg, Robert I., *When States Fail: Causes and Consequences*, Princeton, NJ: Princeton University Press, 2004.

Sabaratnam, Meera, 'Avatars of Eurocentrism in the Critique of the Liberal Peace', *Security Dialogue* 44(3) (2013): 259–278.

Schatzberg, Michael, *The Dialectics of Oppression in Zaire*, Bloomington, IN: Indiana University Press, 1988.

Scheye, Eric and Andrew McLean, 'Enhancing the Delivery of Justice and Security in Fragile States', Organisation for Economic Cooperation and Development—Development Assistance Committee, Paris, 2006.

Schmeidl, Susanne and Masood Karokhail, 'The Role of Non-State Actors in "Community-Based Policing"—An Exploration of the Arbakai (Tribal Police) in South-Eastern Afghanistan', *Contemporary Security Policy* 30(2) (2009): 318–342.

Schomerus, Marieke, and Lovise Aalen, 'Considering the State: Perspectives on South Sudan's Subdivision and Federalism Debate', Overseas Development Institute, August 2016.

Schrodt, Philip A., 'Beyond the Linear Frequentist Orthodoxy', *Political Analysis* 14(3) (2006): 337.

Scott, James C., *Weapons of the Weak: Everyday Peasant Resistance*, New Haven, CT: Yale University Press, 1985.

Scott, James C., *Domination and the Arts of Resistance: Hidden Transcripts*, New Haven, CT: Yale University Press, 1998.

Sending, Ole Jacob, 'The Effects of Peacebuilding: Sovereignty, Patronage and Power', in *A Liberal Peace? The Problems and Practices of Peacebuilding*, ed. Susanna Campbell, David Chandler, and Meera Sabaratnam, London: Zed Books, 2011: 55–68.

Seyle, Conor and Roberta Spivak, 'Complexity Theory and Global Governance: Is More Different?' *Global Governance* 24 (2018): 491–495.

Shankleman, Jill, 'Oil and State-building in South Sudan', United States Institute of Peace, July 2011.

Skocpol, Theda, *States and Social Revolutions*, Cambridge: Cambridge University Press, 1979.

Slater, Dan and Daniel Ziblatt, 'The Enduring Indispensability of the Controlled Comparison', *Comparative Political Studies* 46(10) (2013): 1301–1327.

Slaughter, Anne-Marie and Gordon LaForge, 'Opening Up the Order: A More Inclusive International System', *Foreign Affairs*, March/April 2021.

Small Arms Survey, 'Failures and Opportunities, Rethinking DDR in South Sudan', Issue Brief, Geneva, 2011.

Smith, David, 'South Sudan President Accuses Officials of Stealing $4 Bn of Public Money', *The Guardian*, 5 June 2012.

Snowden, John A., 'Work in Progress: Security Force Development in South Sudan through February 2012', Small Arm Survey, 2012.

Sohhjell, Randi and Madel Rosland, 'New Strategies for Old Conflicts? Lessons in Stabilisation from the Democratic Republic of the Congo', Norwegian Centre for Human Rights, Thematic Paper Series, June 2016.

Solhjell, Randi and Madel Rosland, 'Stabilisation in the Congo: Opportunities and Challenges', *Stability: International Journal of Security & Development* 6(1) (2017): 1–13.

Sørensen, Georg, 'War and State Making—Why Doesn't It Work in the Third World?' *Security Dialogue* 32(3) (2001): 341–354.

South Sudan Ministry of Foreign Affairs, 'Multi Annual Strategic Plan South Sudan 2012–2015', 2011. http://extwprlegs1.fao.org/docs/pdf/ssd148386.pdf

South Sudan NGO Forum. http://southsudanngoforum.org/ngos-in-southern-sudan

Splinter, Dirk and Ljubjana Wustehube, 'Discovering Hidden Dynamics: Applying Systemic Constellation Work to Ethnopolitical Conflict', in *The Non-Linearity of Peace Processes: Theory and Practice of Systemic Conflict Transformation*, ed. Daniela Korppen et al., Opladen: Verlag Barbara Budrich, 2011: 111–126.

Staniland, Paul, 'States, Insurgents, and Wartime Political Orders', *Perspectives on Politics* 10(2) (2012): 243–264.

Statement of President Barack Obama Recognition of the Republic of South Sudan, 9 July 2011. https://obamawhitehouse.archives.gov/the-press-office/2011/07/09/statement-president-barack-obama-recognition-republic-south-sudan

Statement of UN Secretary-General Ban Ki-Moon on the Independence of the Republic of South Sudan, 9 July 2011. https://news.un.org/en/story/2011/07/381102

Stearns, Jason, *Dancing in the Glory of Monsters: The Collapse of the Congo and the Great War of Africa*, New York: Perseus Books, 2011.

Stearns, Jason K., 'The Democratic Republic of the Congo: An Elusive Peace', in *War and Peace in Africa's Great Lakes Region*, ed. Gilbert Khadiagala, London: Palgrave MacMillan, 2017: 33–48.

Stein, Danielle and Craig Valters, 'Understanding Theory of Change in International Development', Justice and Security Research Programme, London School of Economics, 2012.

Stepputat, Finn, 'Pragmatic Peace in Emerging Governscapes', *International Affairs* 94(2) (2018): 399–416.

Stepputat, Finn and Lars Engberg-Petersen, 'Fragile States: Definitions, Measurements and Processes', Fragile Situations: Background Papers, Danish Institute for International Studies, 2008.

Stern, Elliott et al., 'Broadening the Range of Designs and Methods for Impact Evaluations', Department for International Development, Working Paper No. 38, 2012.

Stewart, Patrick, *Weak Links: Fragile States, Global Threats and International Security*, Oxford: Oxford University Press, 2011.

Sudan Comprehensive Peace Agreement. http://www.usip.org/publications/peace-agreements-sudan

Sudan Tribune, 'Kiir Forms First Cabinet of the Independent South Sudan', *Sudan Tribune*, 27 August 2011.

Sudan Tribune, 'Paulino Matip Nhial Nyaak, General', August 2012. http://www.sudantribune.com/spip.php?mot1948

Sutherland, Peter et al., *The Future of the WTO: Addressing Institutional Challenges in the New Millennium*. Geneva: World Trade Organization, 2015.

Suykens, Bert, 'Diffuse Authority in the Beedi Commodity Chain: Naxalite and State Governance in Tribal Telangana, India', *Development and Change* 41(1) (2010): 153–178.

Szeftel, Morris, 'Political Graft and the Spoils System in Zambia—The State as a Resource in Itself', *Review of African Political Economy* 9(24) (1982): 4–21.

Szeftel, Morris, 'Between Governance and Underdevelopment: Accumulation and Africa's "Catastrophic Corruption"', *Review of African Political Economy* 27(84) (2000): 287–306.

Tansey, Oisín, 'Evaluating the Legacies of State-building: Success, Failure, and the Role of Responsibility', *International Studies Quarterly* (2013): 1–41.

Tarrow, Sidney, 'The Strategy of Paired Comparison: Toward a Theory of Practice', *Comparative Political Studies* 43(2) (2010): 230–259.

Thelen, Tatjana et al., *Stategraphy: Toward a Relational Anthropology of the State*, New York: Berghahn Press, 2018.

Thies, Cameron G., 'State Building, Interstate and Intrastate Rivalry: A Study of Post-Colonial Developing Country Extractive Efforts, 1975–2000', *International Studies Quarterly* 48(1) (2004): 53–72.

Thomas, Edward, *South Sudan: A Slow Liberation*, London: Zed Books, 2015.

Thornton, John K., *The Kingdom of Congo: Civil War and Transition, 1641–1718*, Madison, WI: University of Wisconsin Press, 1983.

Tilly, Charles, 'War-making and State-making as Organised Crime', in *Bringing the State Back In*, ed. Peter Evans, Dietrich Rueschemeyer and Theda Skocpol, Cambridge: Cambridge University Press, 1985: 169–91.

Tilly, Charles, *Contention and Democracy in Europe, 1650–2000*, New York and Cambridge: Cambridge University Press, 2004.

Transparency International, 'Corruption Perceptions Index: The Democratic Republic of the Congo', n.d. https://www.transparency.org/country/COD

Transparency International, 'Global Corruption Barometer', 2011. https://www.transparency.org/gcb201011

Trefon, Theodore, *Reinventing Order in the Congo: How People Respond to State Failure in Kinshasa*, London: Zed Books, 2005.

Trefon, Theodore, 'Public Service Provision in a Failed State: Looking Beyond Predation in the Democratic Republic of Congo', *Review of African Political Economy*, 36(119) (2009): 9–21;

True, James L., Bryan D. Jones, and Frank R. Baumgartner, 'Punctuated-Equilibrium Theory: Explaining Stability and Change in Public Policymaking', in *Theories of the Political Process*, ed. Paul A. Sabatier, Cambridge MA: Westview Press, 2017: 97–115.

Tsing, Anne Lowenhaubt, *Friction: An Ethnography of Global Connections*, Princeton, NJ: Princeton University Press, 2005.

Tull, Denis M., 'The Reconfiguration of Political Order in Africa: A Case Study of North Kivu (DR Congo)', Hamburg: Institut für Afrika-Kunde, 2005.

Tull, Denis M., 'The Limits and Unintended Consequences of UN Peace Enforcement: The Force Intervention Brigade in Congo', *International Peacekeeping* 25(2) (2018): 167–190.

Turner, Thomas, *The Congo Wars: Conflict, Myth and Reality*, London: Zed Books, 2006.

Tvedt, Terje, 'The Collapse of the State in Southern Sudan after the Addis Ababa Agreement: A Study of Internal Causes and the Role of the NGOs', in *Short Cut to Decay: The case of Sudan'*, ed. Sharif Harir and Terje Tvedt, Uppsala: Nordiska Africkainstitut, 1994: 69–104.

UNDP, 'Empowering Lives Building Resilience', Development Stories from Europe and Central Asia, 2011.

UNDP, 'Governance for peace: securing the social contract', New York, 2012.

UNDP (United Nations Development Programme), 'Putting Resilience at the Heart of Development', UN Development Programme Report, 2015.

UNEP (United Nations Environment Programme), '21 Issues for the 21st Century: Results of the UNEP Foresight Process on Emerging Environmental Issues' United Nations Environment Programme, Nairobi, 2012.

United Nations, 'An Agenda for Peace: Preventive Diplomacy, Peacekeeping and Peace Making', Report of the Secretary-General, A/47/277, 17 June 1992.

United Nations, 'Report of the United Nations Secretary-General on Timor-Leste Pursuant to Security Council Resolution 1690 (2006)', S/2006/628, 2006.

United Nations, 'Budget for the United Nations Organization Mission in the Democratic Republic of the Congo for the Period from 1 July 2008 to 30 June 2009', UN Doc A/62/755, 18 December 2009.

United Nations, 'Performance Report on the Budget of the United Nations Organization Mission in the Democratic Republic of the Congo for the Period from 1 July 2008 to 30 June 2009', UN Doc A/64/583, 18 December 2009.

United Nations, 'Report of the United Nations Secretary General on the Situation in the Democratic Republic of the Congo', S/2009/623, 28 December 2009.

United Nations, 'Thirty-first Report of the Secretary-General on MONUC', UN Doc S/2010/164, 30 March 2010.

United Nations, 'Budget for the United Nations Mission in South Sudan for the Period from 1 July 2011 to 30 June 2012: Report of the Secretary-General', A/66/532, 2011.

United Nations, 'Report of the United Nations Secretary-General on South Sudan', S/2011/678, 2011.

United Nations, 'Country Programme Action Plan Between the Government of the Republic of South Sudan and the UN Development Programme, 2012–2013'. http://www.ss.undp.org/content/dam/southsudan/library/Reports/southsudanotherdocuments/UNDP%20South%20Sudan_CPAP%202012-2013%20Fin%20%20Signed.pdf

United Nations, 'Report of the United Nations Secretary-General on the Situation in South Sudan', S/2012/140, 7 March 2012.

United Nations, 'Report of the Secretary General on the Situation the Democratic Republic of the Congo', UN Doc S/2012/355, 23 May 2012.

United Nations, 'Report of the United Nations Secretary-General on the Situation in South Sudan', S/2012/486 (2012), 26 June 2012.

United Nations, 'Report of the United Nations Secretary-General on the Situation in South Sudan', S/2012/746, 8 October 2012, para 5.

United Nations, 'Report of the United Nations Secretary-General on the situation in South Sudan', S/2013/140, 8 May 2013.

United Nations, 'Report of the Secretary-General on the United Nations Organization Stabilization Mission in the Democratic Republic of the Congo', S/2013/757, 2013.

United Nations, 'Report of the Secretary-General on the United Nations Organization Stabilization Mission in the Democratic Republic of the Congo', S/2014/157, 2014.

United Nations, 'Report of the Secretary-General on the United Nations Organization Stabilization Mission in the Democratic Republic of the Congo', S/2014/698, 2014.

United Nations, 'Secretary-General's Remarks at Security Council Open Debate on Trends in United Nations Peacekeeping', 11 June 2014.

United Nations, *The Challenge of Sustaining Peace: Report of the Advisory Group of Experts for the 2015 Review of the United Nations Peacebuilding Architecture*, New York: United Nations, 2015.

United Nations, 'Report of the United Nations Secretary General on the Situation in Eastern Congo', S/2016/1130, 28 December 2016.

United Nations Mission in South Sudan (UNMISS), 'Rule of Law and Security Institutions Support', 1 July 2014. http://unmiss.unmissions.org/Default.aspx?tabid=4056

United Nations Mission in South Sudan (UNMISS), 'Disarmament Demobilization and Reintegration', 17 July 2014. http://unmiss.unmissions.org/Default.aspx?tabid=4055&language=en-US

United Nations Mission in South Sudan (UNMISS), 'ROLSISO—What We Do', 17 July 2014.

United Nations Panel of Experts on South Sudan, Letter dated 20 November 2017 addressed to the President of the Security Council, S/2017/979, 2017.

United Nations Secretary-General, 'A More Secure World: Our Shared Responsibility', United Nations High-Level Panel on Threats, Challenges and Change, 2004.
United Nations Secretary-General, 'Tackling the Inequality Pandemic: A New Social Contract for a New Era', António Guterres' Nelson Mandela Annual Lecture 2020 Speech. https://www.nelsonmandela.org/news/entry/annual-lecture-2020-secretary-general-guterress-full-speech
United Nations Security Council, 'Report of the Secretary-General on the United Nations Organization Stabilization Mission in the Democratic Republic of the Congo', S/2016/233, 9 March 2016. https://undocs.org/pdf?symbol=en/S/2016/233
United Nations Security Council Resolution, SC/RES/1279, 1999.
United Nations Security Council Resolution, SC/RES/1313, 2000.
United Nations Security Council Resolution, S/Res/1484, 2003.
United Nations Security Council Resolution, SC/Res/1493, 2003.
United Nations Security Council Resolution, SC/RES/1509, 2003.
United Nations Security Council Resolution, S/RES/1565, 2004.
United Nations Security Council Resolution, SC/RES/1542, 2004.
United Nations Security Council Resolution, S/RES/1827, 2008.
United Nations Security Council Resolution, SC/RES/1925, 2010.
United Nations Security Council Resolution, S/RES/2002, 2011.
United Nations Security Council Resolution, S/RES/2098, 2013.
United Nations Security Council Resolution, S/RES/2155, 2014.
United Nations Security Council Resolution, S/RES/2429, 2019.
United Nations Security Council Resolution, S/RES/2846, 2019.
United Nations Security Council Resolution on South Sudan, S/RES/1996, 8 July 2011.
Van Damme, S. and Judith Verweijen, 'In Search of an Army: How the FARDC Can Improve Civilians' Safety', Oxfam International Policy Brief, 2012.
Van der Ploeg, Frederick and Anthony J. Venables, 'Harnessing Windfall Revenues: Optimal Policies for Resource Rich Developing Economies', Oxcarre Research Paper No. 9, Oxford University, 2008.
Veblen, Thorstein, 'Why is Economics not an Evolutionary Science', *The Quarterly Journal of Economics* 12(4) (July 1898): 373–397.
Veit, Alex, *Intervention as Indirect Rule: Civil War and Statebuilding in the Democratic Republic of Congo*, New York: Campus Verlag, 2011.
Verweijen, Judith, *Stable Instability: Political Settlements and Armed Groups in the Congo*, London: Rift Valley Institute, 2016.
Verweijen, Judith and Claude Iguma Wakenge, 'Understanding Armed Group Proliferation in Eastern Congo', Rift Valley Institute PSRP Briefing Paper 7, December 2015.
Vimalarajah, Luxshi, 'Thinking Peace: Revising Analysis and Intervention in Sri Lanka', in *The Non-Linearity of Peace Processes: Theory and Practice of Systemic Conflict Transformation*, ed. Daniela Korppen et al., Opladen: Verlag Barbara Budrich, 2011: 129–146.
Vinck, Patrick and Phuong Pham, 'Living with Fear: A Population-based Survey on Attitudes about Peace, Justice, and Social Reconstruction in Eastern Democratic Republic of the Congo', Berkeley-Tulane Initiative on Vulnerable Populations, 2008.
Vinck, Patrick and Phuong Pham, 'Searching for Lasting Peace: Population-Based Survey on Perceptions and Attitudes about Peace, Security and Justice in Eastern Democratic Republic of the Congo', Harvard Humanitarian Initiative, UN Development Programme, July 2014.

Vlassenroot, Koen, 'Reading the Congolese Crisis', in *Conflict and Social Transformation in Eastern DR Congo*, ed. Koen Vlassenroot and Timothy Raeymaekers, Ghent: Conflict Research Group and Academia Press, 2004: 39–60.

Vlassenroot, Koen and Timothy Raeymaekers, *Conflict and Social Transformation in Eastern DR Congo*, Gent: Academia Press Scientific Publishers, 2004.

Vlassenroot, Koen and Timothy Raeymaekers, 'New Political Order in the DR Congo? The Transformation of Regulation', *Africa Focus* 21(2) (2008): 39–52.

Vogel, Christopher, 'Islands of Stability or Swamps of Insecurity? MONUSCO's Intervention Brigade and the Danger of Emerging Security Voids in Eastern Congo', Africa Policy Brief, February 2014.

Von Billerbeck, Sarah, *Whose Peace? Local Ownership and United Nations Peacebuilding*, Oxford: Oxford Scholarship Online, 2017.

Von Billerbeck, Sarah and Oisín Tansey, 'Enabling Autocracy? Peacebuilding and Post-conflict Authoritarianism in the Democratic Republic of Congo', *European Journal of International Relations* 25(3) (2019): 1–29.

Waldner, David, 'What Makes Process Tracing Good? Causal Mechanisms, Causal Inference, and the Completeness Standard in Comparative Politics', in *Process Tracing: From Metaphor to Analytic Tool*, ed. Andrew Bennett and Jeffrey T. Checkel, Cambridge: Cambridge University Press, 2015, 126–153.

Walraet, Anne, 'Governance, Violence and the Struggle for Economic Regulation in South Sudan: The Case of Budi County (Eastern Equatoria) ', *Afrika Focus* (2008).

Waltz, Kenneth N., *A Theory of International Politics*, New York: McGraw-Hill, 1979.

Weber, Annette, 'Transformation Backlog in South Sudan: Security Sector Reforms Stall in the Face of Growing Autocracy', German Institute for International and Security Affairs, SWP Comments 20, July 2013.

Weber, Max, *Economy and Society: An Outline of Interpretive Sociology*, Vol. 1, ed. Guenther and Claus Wittich, Berkeley, CA: University of California Press, 1978.

Weinstein, Jeremy, 'Autonomous Recovery and International Interventions in Comparative Perspective', Working Paper No. 57, Center for Global Development, Washington, DC, 2005.

Williamson, Tim, 'Coordinating Post-conflict Aid in Southern Sudan', Overseas Development Institute, September 2011.

Woodward, Susan, *The Ideology of Failed States: Why Intervention Fails*, Cambridge: Cambridge University Press, 2017.

Woolcock, Michael, 'Towards a Plurality of Methods in Project Evaluation: A Contextalised Approach to Understanding Impact Trajectories and Efficacy', *Journal of Development Effectiveness* 1(1) (2009): 1–14.

World Bank, 'Southern Sudan: Enabling the State: Estimating the Non-oil Revenue Potential of State and Local Governments', Washington, DC, 2010.

World Bank, 'Report to the Southern Sudan Multi-Donor Trust Fund', Second Quarter Report, 1 April–30 June 2010.

World Bank, 'World Development Report: Conflict, Security and Development', Washington, DC, 2011.

World Bank, 'South Sudan Overview', Washington, DC, 2013. www.worldbank.org/en/country/southsudan/overview

World Bank, 'Land Governance in South Sudan: Policies for Peace and Development', Report 86958, Washington, DC, 14 May 2014.

World Bank, 'South Sudan Governance Analysis (P156685): Building Sustainable Public Sector Capacity in a Challenging Context', World Bank Report, Washington, DC, January 2017.

Young, Crawford and Thomas Turner, *The Rise and Decline of the Zairian State*, Madison, WI: University of Wisconsin Press, 1985.

Young, Oran R., *A Systemic Approach to International Politics*, Princeton, NJ: Center of International Studies Woodrow Wilson School of Public and International Affairs, 1968.

Zartman, William, *Collapsed States: The Disintegration and Restoration of Legitimate Authority*, Boulder, CO: Lynne Rienner Press, 1995.

Zaum, Dominik, *The Sovereignty Paradox: The Norms and Politics of International State-building*, Oxford: Oxford University Press, 2007.

Zaum, Dominik, 'Beyond the Liberal Peace', *Global Governance* 18 (2012): 121–132.

Zürcher, Christoph, 'Is More Better? Evaluating External-Led State Building After 1989', Stanford Center on Democracy, Development and Rule of Law, Working Paper No. 54, 2006.

Zürcher, Christoph, 'The Liberal Peace: A Tough Sell?', in *A Liberal Peace? The Problems and Practices of Peacebuilding*, ed. Susanna Campbell, David Chandler, and Meera Sabaratnam, London: Zed Books, 2011: 69–88.

Index